PAYTON

AND BREES

PAYTON
AND BREES

THE **MEN WHO BUILT**
THE **GREATEST OFFENSE**
IN **NFL HISTORY**

JEFF DUNCAN

TRIUMPH®
BOOKS

This book is available in quantity at special discounts for your group or organization. For further information, contact:

Triumph Books LLC
814 North Franklin Street
Chicago, Illinois 60610
www.triumphbooks.com

Printed in U.S.A.

ISBN: 978-1-62937-769-8

Design by Sue Knopf
Page production by Preston Pisellini
Photos courtesy of AP Images unless otherwise indicated

This book is dedicated to Saints fans and the people of the great city of New Orleans, who deserve leaders like Drew Brees and Sean Payton.

Contents

Foreword

I met Sean Payton and Drew Brees 14 years ago, in 2006. At the time, the Saints and the city of New Orleans were just in the initial stages following the agonizing destruction of Hurricane Katrina. I played on the team for the previous six seasons and had fallen in love with the unique culture of this community—not to mention a daughter of the community I found uniquely loveable. While I was confident the people of New Orleans would recover resiliently, I was not so sure about the Saints organization. I had more pressing personal concerns. The family of my future wife, Michel Varisco, had their home completely destroyed. Even more personally, when Coach Payton first set eyes on me in the Saints cafeteria, he assumed I was just a long-haired team equipment manager.

Along with Michel's family and the city of New Orleans, I was working to find a return to success after a really difficult year following Hurricane Katrina. Ultimately, Drew Brees and Sean Payton would be the catalysts of that return—our collective rebirth.

From a personal perspective 14 years later, I consider Coach Payton and Drew Brees my brothers. Yeah, I convinced Payton that I was more than an equipment manager during 2006 training camp. But three years after I retired from the NFL, I was diagnosed with ALS, a hurricane of a disease. Painful and agonizing. Brees and Payton have been immensely supportive of me both publicly and privately. I am so grateful for their friendship. I love them.

At some point during the Saints team and organization's transition, the phrase "We will walk together forever" emerged. I have remained in New Orleans and I am raising a family with Michel. Coaches and players have come and gone, as we all do, but for the past 14 years, I have gotten to see Drew and Coach at the facility, or the Dome, or Mardi Gras, or a fundraiser, or even at the house. Both of these guys ushered in a change of plans, a change of mindset, and a change of heart, not only with the Saints organization, but the entire New Orleans region. In a completely unprecedented way, since the 2006 season, the people of this city, region, and state can all proudly say, "We will walk together forever."

I played all eight years of my NFL career with the New Orleans Saints. I made the team after a free-agent tryout midway through the 2000 season. It was your standard workout: 40-yard dash, bench press, standing long jump, agility drills. Afterward, the scouts took me and the other tryout players for a meal before our flights back home. I was surprised at their choice of dining establishment: a grungy restaurant with bars on the windows in a neglected neighborhood that served cold fried chicken from a buffet. To say the least, it was not the kind of experience a first-class organization would project. It was a little thing. But it said a lot. I got a call a week later to join the team, and two weeks after that I was on the field with the Saints playing against John Elway and the Denver Broncos.

Payton and Brees joined the team six years later in the wake of Hurricane Katrina. Before they arrived in town, the Saints teams

I played on were talented but inconsistent. On any given Sunday, we could beat the best team in the league or lose to the worst. My rookie year, maybe 10 weeks after eating a buffet lunch behind barred windows, we won our first playoff game in franchise history. But we lacked the discipline and consistency necessary to be great.

When Coach Payton took over the team in 2006, he knew he needed to change things in the organization. He knew the perception and results would not change until the culture did.

First, he had to determine what kind of culture the organization had enabled and fostered for the previous 38 years. This required him to create a sense of urgency, not only among the players, but also the existing Saints staff, management, and ownership. In an organization that seemed pretty content with mediocrity, this was a monumentally enormous task from my perspective.

I think Coach Payton knew that this would require bold action early in his tenure. For existing staff and front-office personnel, Payton ensured he and his coaches were treated in first-class fashion. He pushed for his staff members to have more favorable car lease agreements and disallowed business operations staffers to enter and interrupt coaches' meetings. Coach Payton wanted his coaches to be treated like company executives.

For the players, Coach Payton wanted to push the level of urgency. To set the tone, he hung signs around the training facility. The first sign I saw read: SAINTS PLAYERS WILL BE SMART, TOUGH, DISCIPLINED, AND WELL-CONDITIONED. It made me laugh. In an industry where players are coveted for their size, speed, and strength, I had doubts that this message was sincere. Messages like this became the theme. The coaches and management were continuously thinking about what these signs should say, underscoring their importance. They regularly changed and replaced them, sending the message that these principles were not simply collecting dust on the wall. It struck me as smart, a good first impression.

Early in the spring he made another strong impression. He told the team there was a three-year timeframe for drafted players. In Year One, players were given the benefit of the doubt as they were rookies or new to the team system. In Year Two, a transition to production would need to be observed. In Year Three, players would be at a crossroads with the team and should probably "update their résumé" if they weren't being productive. He was creating a sense of urgency with every player on the roster.

Additionally, he promised that high-level decisions that turned out to be incorrect would not be supported simply to satisfy egos or balance the books. Marques Colston exemplified this philosophy. Colston was a seventh-round draft pick out of Hofstra who clearly outperformed former first-round pick Donté Stallworth during training camp. The Saints traded Stallworth midway through training camp and elevated Colston to the starting lineup. Message sent. No player's roster spot was guaranteed—regardless of the amount of money invested in the individual player. As a former undrafted free agent who was trying to make an impression on the new coach, I already felt plenty of urgency. But I was reassured by Payton's actions. He meant what he said about the best players making the team. I felt I had a chance to be one of those players. Coach Payton's ability to persuade management to make the correct "team" decisions was refreshing.

Coach Payton also instituted a disciplinary system that consistently fined players for small transgressions like missing meetings or being overweight. These fines were reported every morning at the team meeting and no further oration was implemented. Players were not given exemption, and the fines were generally preceded by a simple statement like, "These rules had been developed and agreed upon by the team." This may not seem like a large factor in successful change, but as a player I saw it as vital. Not surprisingly, the discipline statistics in our games (penalties, mental errors, etc.) were greatly reduced as this change took place. The night before our first preseason game in 2006, Coach Payton made another strong impression. We were bused to a hotel in Jackson, Mississippi. When I was given my key, I went to my room and noticed the place smelled of mothballs and there was a hole in the sheetrock. This was early in the change effort, and I had my doubts there would be any real change with the new coach. This hotel solidified my doubts. We assembled a couple hours later for a team meeting and I anticipated Coach Payton's reaction, if any, to the hotel quality. Impressively, he stood in front of the team and not only apologized for the hotel but promised with confidence and sincerity that we would never stay in a hotel like this while he was the head coach.

For the first time in my NFL career, a coach showed us he cared enough for the players to confront the organization and create change. I thought to myself, *Maybe things are changing for the better after all.* Coach Payton's vision was starting to come into focus.

It helped that the team's quarterback was helping Coach Payton communicate the plan. It's impossible to understate how important the signing of Brees was to the franchise. While Drew's talent was impressive, I think Coach Payton wanted him just as much for his leadership skills. At the player level, Drew helped communicate Coach Payton's message and emphasized what was important in the organization. Drew's passion for football was contagious to the rest of the organization. He took great risks by vocally demanding excellence from teammates but also by encouraging the team to develop an investment in each other.

Before Drew arrived, Aaron Brooks was the quarterback. Aaron was a nice guy and a supremely talented player. Unfortunately, he lacked the leadership skills necessary to quarterback a first-class team. When Drew arrived in New Orleans, he was a successful quarterback but not a perennial All-Pro, and he was coming off a potentially career-ending injury. He had his doubters in the media and even among the players.

Toward the end of training camp, Coach Payton asked Drew to address the team. At the time, I'm not sure that was something Drew was completely comfortable with. But he knew he had to find a way to be comfortable being uncomfortable if he was going to actually lead the team and help us achieve our lofty goals.

It was a risk for Coach Payton to identify Drew as the leader of a team he had joined just six months earlier. And it was a risk for Drew to expose himself as vulnerable to the potential scorn of other players. I remember being nervous for him. Remember, this was not the guy who holds several all-time NFL records, nor did he wear a Super Bowl ring—yet. It was in this moment, when Drew chose to address the team, I realized that anything was possible for Drew Brees. I saw greatness, through courage and genuine transparency.

It seems Drew was bolstered by the confidence Coach Payton instilled in him as he stood in front of the team and presented us with goals for the upcoming season. He also talked about the characteristics he thought were necessary to accomplish these goals. He communicated them clearly and confidently. It was a great speech. After that day, every Saints player knew No. 9 was our leader.

Drew continued to set the tone for the rest of the team with his work ethic. His car was regularly the first one in the parking lot in the mornings before practice and the last one to leave that night after practice. He had an almost unreasonable belief that the team could win even under the bleakest of conditions. This passion, dedication, and sacrifice are key leadership qualities beyond being smart, tough, disciplined, and well-conditioned. Brees served as the perfect conduit to communicate Coach Payton's vision.

And as great as Payton and Brees are, none of this would have happened if ownership and management had not empowered them. By relinquishing some of his authority, Saints general manager Mickey Loomis instilled confidence in Payton and Brees to become the faces of the franchise. Payton clearly defined the kind of players he wanted in his program—smart, tough, disciplined, high character—and Loomis and the personnel department went out and found them. In turn, Payton empowered Brees to lead the team—on and off the field. This sharing and transferring of power resonated throughout the team. Everyone bought in.

After a preseason in 2006 that generated zero wins, the team went to Cleveland for the season opener. The Browns scored a touchdown on a 74-yard pass on the first play from scrimmage. I don't believe the winning culture had been entrenched in our team by that time, and I could see players thinking, *Here we go again.* The play was called back because of a holding penalty. We proceeded to win the game thanks to four field goals by John Carney. The next week we went to Green Bay and beat the Packers 34–27, avenging a 52–3 loss from the previous season. In Week 3, the NFL scheduled a Monday night game against our division rival, the Atlanta Falcons. The Falcons were 2–0 and three-point favorites. But this was a homecoming for the team and the city after Hurricane Katrina, and the Falcons never had a chance. Final score: Saints 23–3.

The 3–0 start helped validate the front-office decision to hire Coach Payton as well as Payton's choice to elevate Drew Brees as the team leader. We went on to finish 10–6, win the NFC South, and make the franchise's first-ever appearance in the NFC Championship Game. The season had reestablished the team into the city of New Orleans and its culture. The team did not win the Super Bowl that year, and some fine-tuning would be needed before we reached that level, but this allowed the organization to silence some critics and instill the belief that this was an emerging first-class operation. Thanks to Drew and Coach Payton, a winning culture had been established. The days of eating at ramshackle chicken buffets were over for the New Orleans Saints.

Steve Gleason played most of his career with the New Orleans Saints. In 2019, he was awarded the Congressional Gold Medal for his contributions to ALS awareness.

Prologue

The Superdome was melting down.

Deshaun Watson and the Houston Texans had just stunned the New Orleans Saints with a go-ahead touchdown with 37 seconds left in their game on September 29, 2019. On consecutive plays, DeAndre Hopkins and Kenny Stills somehow got behind the Saints secondary for catches of 38 and 37 yards, respectively, the latter resulting in the touchdown.

Only seconds earlier, the Dome was celebrating kicker Wil Lutz's 47-yard field goal with 50 seconds left. With the Texans out of timeouts and nearly out of time, the Saints looked assured of winning their first season opener in five years. Then everything came unraveled. In the span of 13 head-spinning seconds, the Saints' 27–21 lead had flipped into a 28–27 deficit.

Saints fans, who had suffered through heart-breaking, last-second playoff losses to the Minnesota Vikings and Los Angeles Rams each of the previous two seasons, were beside themselves.

That it was Stills, a former Saints draft pick, who caught the go-ahead score made the situation even more disgusting.

How could this happen?!

Not again!

Incredulous fans stirred and fidgeted as Drew Brees and the Saints offense took the field after the touchback on the ensuing kickoff. The Saints had 37 seconds and one timeout to work with. They needed to gain about 35 yards to reach Lutz's range for a potential game-winning field goal attempt. The situation was bleak. The Saints' win probability was 27 percent. But with Brees pulling the trigger, Saints fans had long ago learned that anything was possible.

Entering the 2019 season, Brees had orchestrated 36 fourth-quarter comebacks in his 19-year NFL career, more than any quarterback in NFL history except Peyton Manning and Tom Brady. And during his 14-year tenure with the Saints and head coach Sean Payton, he had become a master of the two-minute offense. During the final two minutes of games, his Total Quarterback Rating, a statistical metric used to measure a quarterback's overall passing efficiency, was the best in the NFL from 2017 to 2019, according to ESPN.

To watch Payton and Brees operate in the two-minute drill is to watch true football genius at work. This is where all of their practice, preparation, and planning materialize and coalesce. They know these chaotic, pressure-packed seconds are often what separate great teams from good ones and Hall of Fame quarterbacks and coaches from average ones.

Given the inherent parity of the NFL, an inordinate number of games go down to the wire. During the first 14 weeks of the 2019 NFL season alone, 140 of 208 games (67.3 percent) were within one score during the fourth quarter, and 112 of those (53.8 percent) were decided by eight or fewer points.

For Brees, the intensity and pressure of the two-minute drill is the ultimate test of a quarterback. Over the course of his career, he has grown to embrace the challenge and thrive in the moment.

For Payton, the two-minute offense is the validation or condemnation of a head coach's offseason preparation and weekly game plan. A former record-setting quarterback at Eastern Illinois, Payton has a unique understanding of the two-minute offense and its impact on winning and losing games. Payton sees the two-minute drill as the ultimate pop quiz for an offense. To prepare his team for the moment, he puts his players through countless two-minute scenarios during offseason practices. Every training camp practice ends with some form of two-minute drill between the offense and defense. The variables—score, timeouts available, time remaining, yards to go— always change to ratchet up the challenge of the situation.

One minute, three seconds to go, trailing by five points, two timeouts, ball on your own 41.

Forty-eight seconds left, no timeouts, ball at your own 29, you need a field goal.

The two-minute planning carries over to the regular season. During the weekly game-planning, Payton and the offensive staff install plays they feel will be successful against the upcoming opponent based on their defensive tendencies in previous games. On the night before each game, Payton and Brees meet to go over the game plan and categorize Brees' favorite plays. The two-minute drill is always a key part of the meeting. No one leaves the room until they feel comfortable with the two-minute plan going into the game.

Now, in the final minute of the fourth quarter of the Saints' 2019 season opener, all of the preparation and planning were about to come into play.

Thirty-seven seconds was enough time for Brees to work his magic. But with only one timeout at his disposal, there was no margin for error. He would need to be perfect to march the Saints into field-goal range.

On the sideline, Saints players and coaches consoled C.J. Gardner-Johnson, who was disconsolate on the bench. The rookie defensive back had drawn a roughing the kicker penalty moments earlier that negated Texans kicker Ka'imi Fairbairn's missed go-ahead extra-point attempt. The infraction gave Fairbairn a second try and he converted to give the Texans a one-point lead.

On the Houston sideline, Watson shared a laugh with teammates. The Texans were seconds away from one of the biggest road wins in franchise history. The electrifying comeback on a prime-time stage would be a milestone moment in Watson's nascent career.

As the Saints expected, Texans defensive coordinator Romeo Crennel employed a conservative defensive coverage scheme designed to prevent long pass plays. Cornerbacks Bradley Roby, Aaron Colvin, Keion Crossen, and Jonathan Joseph aligned in loose man-to-man coverage about five yards off the line of scrimmage. Behind them, safeties Tashaun Gipson and Justin Reid were positioned 15 yards downfield just outside the hash marks, and safety Jahleel Addae stood another 10 yards back on the fleur-de-lis logo at midfield. To reach Texans territory against this defense, Brees would have to move the ball in bites, not chunks.

Since they would be running a no-huddle, hurry-up offense, the Saints had their best playmakers at the skill positions on the field: running back Alvin Kamara; tight end Jared Cook; and wide receivers Michael Thomas, Ted Ginn Jr., and Tre'Quan Smith.

As he broke the huddle and surveyed the defense, Brees processed several factors in his mind: personnel matchups; pass rush; defender leverage in coverage; route access by his receivers.

For years now, Brees has run the two-minute offense largely by himself. Payton ceded the duty to him to expedite the play-calling and save valuable time. The Saints coaching staff trusted Brees implicitly to diagnose the defense and get the offense into the proper play at the line of scrimmage via a series of predetermined hand signals. Payton will make suggestions to Brees through the headset, but for the most part he's standing and watching the sequence play out just like everyone else in the stadium.

"That's something that Drew has done for a long time, and he's real good at it," Payton said. "Drew has got a real good clock in his head. He understands where we are at time-wise."

At the snap, Brees retreated into his five-step drop and saw his first option, Thomas, double-covered by Roby and Reid on the left side of the formation. He immediately looked right and saw Joseph backpedaling in outside leverage on Ginn, a tactic designed to prevent an outside-breaking route. Bingo! He launched his pass just as Ginn was cutting inside on a 12-yard dig route. Brees never saw the pass land as end Jacob Martin swarmed him to the ground just after he released the ball. Ginn snared Brees' pass at the 36, quickly dodged a diving tackle attempt by Gipson, and ducked ahead for another four yards to the 40. The entire sequence took less than five seconds. Ginn scrambled to his feet and tried to find umpire Alan Eck amid the chaos of players running to and from the line of scrimmage. Saints receivers had been drilled to run to the closest official and directly hand him the ball to expedite the spotting process. But on this occasion, Ginn failed to immediately find Eck amid the mayhem and a couple of extra seconds ticked off the clock. Brees finally spiked the ball at :20.

The Saints would realistically have time for only two more plays, barring a defensive penalty.

The Texans employed the same defense on second down, but this time Colvin aligned aggressively in press coverage against Thomas on the left side. Colvin was in his second season with the Texans after a disappointing four-year run in Jacksonville. The Saints had picked on Colvin all night, completing 7-of-8 passes on him for 106 yards. The All-Pro Thomas versus the journeyman

Colvin is a matchup Brees takes every time, and Thomas delivered. With Colvin playing outside leverage, Thomas needed to be physical to separate from Colvin and access his out route. At the top of his break, Thomas quickly cut left, swam his right arm over Colvin's shoulder, and deftly pushed him to the right. Brees didn't hesitate. He threaded his pass into a five-yard window behind Crossen's head and before the onrushing Reid could close on Thomas from his safety spot. Thomas snagged the ball at midfield and was snowed under at the Texans' 49.

As the players scrambled to the line for the next play, precious seconds ticked off the clock. Payton almost signaled to the officials to take his final timeout but hesitated at the last moment as he watched Brees direct traffic on the field. Payton understood how valuable a timeout was in this situation. With it, the Saints could call any play in their offensive game plan and still have time to stop the clock. Without it, they were handcuffed. The Texans could align their defense along both sidelines and funnel the Saints receivers into the middle of the field, forcing them into another frantic scramble to get aligned and clock the ball. Payton didn't like those odds, so he allowed the clock to run, and Brees spiked the ball with six seconds left.

"I understand what he is trying to do, but he wasted too much time," NFL color analyst Anthony "Booger" McFarland said on the ESPN *Monday Night Football* broadcast. "He's got time now with six seconds left and one timeout for a quick play. But it's got to be quick."

The game now essentially boiled down to one play. Lutz had converted field goals from 60 yards out during pregame warm-ups, so the Saints needed to gain six or seven more yards to reach his range.

Brees quickly gathered the offense into a huddle and rattled off a handful of possible plays he might call once he was able to diagnose the defense at the line of scrimmage.

"You're looking at so many things," Brees would say later. "You're looking at leverage. You're looking at matchup. You're looking at access. You're assessing all of these things and I have this checklist of plays in my mind that I'm going through until I land on the one—ding, ding, ding!—that is the best option based on what they're giving us right now."

What Brees saw was a different defense than the one the Texans played on the previous two snaps. This time they were in man-to-man coverage across the field, each defensive back aligned opposite the Saints' five receivers at the line of scrimmage. Linebacker Zach Cunningham manned the middle of the field as a rover. Three safeties were positioned 20 yards downfield on each third of the field.

"It was basically a prevent-type defense," Brees said. "They did not want to give up something big."

But the Saints didn't need something big. They only needed seven yards.

With 20 seconds on the play clock, Brees scanned the defense and quickly eliminated one of his options. The stick route to Cook over the middle wasn't going to work because he feared the rover might blow up the play.

With 17 seconds left, Brees signaled a route combination to the receivers by raising his right index finger above his head. Then, just as he was ready to take the snap, he noticed a flaw in the Texans coverage. While Roby and Crossen were tightly aligned opposite Thomas and Kamara to the left, Colvin unwittingly stood seven yards off the line from Ginn in the right slot.

"The Texans are playing loose coverage, I don't agree with this," McFarland said on the ESPN broadcast. "Too easy to get a quick completion."

Brees saw the same thing. With 10 seconds on the play clock, he audibled again, waving off the earlier play call and signaling a new one with a waggle of his hand toward Ginn.

"He's checking it," McFarland said. "Brees sees it."

Erik McCoy snapped the ball with six seconds on the play clock. Brees backpedaled into a three-step drop and fired a quick strike to Ginn, who was wide-open on a nine-yard hook route at the Houston 40. Ginn immediately fell to the turf to give himself up on the play, and Brees and Payton bolted to separate officials to call timeout. Two seconds remained on the play clock.

Brees had done it. Three plays. Three completions. Thirty-five yards in 35 seconds.

"Surgical by Brees," ESPN play-by-play announcer Joe Tessitore said. "Absolutely surgical."

Moments later, Lutz drilled his 58-yard field goal attempt, and the Superdome erupted in euphoria. Brees stood on the sideline, raised his right arm above his head, and pumped his fist in the air. The Saints had snapped their league-high five-game losing streak in opening games. And they had done it in dramatic fashion before a national television audience.

"Just a phenomenal job by Drew Brees," McFarland said on the broadcast.

On the field, Texans players and coaches walked around in a daze. ESPN sideline reporter Lisa Salters found Lutz for a postgame interview and asked him what was going through his mind as Brees marched the offense down the field.

"Look, when he's our quarterback I knew we were going to get a chance," said Lutz, speaking for Saints fans everywhere.

None of this happened by chance, of course. The victory was the result of months of planning and preparation. It validated everything Payton and Brees believe in. Preparation. Attention to detail. Confidence, aggressiveness, and poise in the clutch.

The analytics gave the Saints a 27 percent chance to win the game. But the analytics didn't factor into the equation Payton and Brees, the most prolific quarterback-coach combination in NFL history.

1

Finding the Pilot

No one could have known it then, but Sean Payton's recruitment of Drew Brees in the winter of 2006 was an early indicator of the coach's brilliance. He had never met Brees, who was the top quarterback on the NFL free-agent market at the time. There was no Kevin Bacon-degrees-of-separation connection, no prior history to work with. Payton didn't know Brees at all. But he knew he needed him.

The Saints owned one of the worst quarterback legacies in the NFL and were coming off a grim 3–13 campaign with the inconsistent Aaron Brooks under center. The Saints hadn't started an elite quarterback since Archie Manning played in the late 1970s and early 1980s. Since then, a parade of journeymen and overmatched rookies had manned the position. In the 25 years since Manning left in 1981, none of the Saints' 20 starting quarterbacks earned a single Pro Bowl invitation.

If the Saints had any hope of turning around their fortunes in their first year under Payton, they would need a top quarterback to lead them.

Having played quarterback at Eastern Illinois and coached the position previously with the Philadelphia Eagles, New York Giants, and Dallas Cowboys, Payton understood the importance of the role, especially in the NFL, where rules have tilted heavily in favor of the passing game. The NFL had essentially evolved into a league divided into the haves and have-nots: teams that had franchise quarterbacks and those that were trying to find one.

"The position touches the ball 65 to 70 times a game," Payton said. "Everybody gets on the plane, and the quarterback gets on last. He gets up in the cockpit, and everyone else waits for him to land it safely or fly the whole thing into a mountain."

Bill Parcells, who served as Payton's mentor during their tenure together in Dallas and advised Payton to take the head coaching job in New Orleans in 2006, was famously hard on quarterbacks. But he understood their importance in the game. He even made a list of requirements for the position, a Commandments of Quarterback Play, that he maintained and followed throughout his coaching tenure:

I. *Press or TV agents or advisers, family or wives, friends or relatives, fans or hangers-on, ignore them on matters of football; they don't know what's happening here.*

II. *Don't forget to have fun, but don't be the class clown. Clowns and leaders don't mix. Clowns can't run a huddle.*

III. *A quarterback throws with his legs more than his arms. Squat and run. Fat quarterbacks can't avoid the rush.*

IV. *Know your job cold. This is not a game without errors. Keep yours to a minimum. Study.*

V. *Know your own players. Who's fast? Who can catch? Who needs encouragement? Be precise. Know your opponent.*

VI. *Be the same guy every day. In condition, preparing to lead, studying your plan. A coach can't prepare you for every eventuality. Prepare yourself and remember, impulse decisions usually equal mistakes.*

VII. *Throwing the ball away is a good play. Sacks, interceptions, and fumbles are bad plays. Protect against those.*

VIII. *You must learn to manage the game. Personnel, play call, motions, ball handling, proper reads, accurate throws, play fakes. Clock, clock, clock, don't you ever lose track of the clock.*

IX. *Passing stats and TD passes are not how you're gonna be judged. Your job is to get your team in the end zone and that's how you're gonna be judged.*

X. *When all around you is in chaos, you must be the hand that steers the ship. If you have a panic button, so will everyone else. Our ship can't have panic buttons.*

XI. *Don't be a celebrity quarterback. We don't need any of those. We need battlefield commanders that are willing to fight it out every day, every week, and every season, and lead their team to win after win after win.*

Payton knew how difficult it was to find a player with all of the qualities on Parcells' list. Franchise quarterbacks are the most valued positions in the NFL. It's why they earn CEO-like salaries in the range of $25 million to $30 million a year.

Payton knew a team could have success without a franchise quarterback in a given year, but to achieve the kind of sustained success he wanted in New Orleans, he knew he needed a special player at the position.

To find their franchise quarterback, Payton and Saints general manager Mickey Loomis considered two options: they could pursue a veteran quarterback in free agency or select a prospect with the No. 2 overall pick in the NFL Draft. Southern Cal's Matt Leinart was considered the top quarterback available, but the brain trust knew drafting one so high was a risky proposition. Loomis was an executive in the Seattle Seahawks organization in 1993 when the club used the No. 2 overall pick in the draft to select Notre Dame quarterback Rick Mirer, who spent most of his eight-year NFL career as a journeyman backup.

The Saints preferred a veteran signal-caller, but the free-agent market was a collection of veteran journeymen like Jeff Garcia, Jon Kitna, and Josh McCown. Brees, who had made the Pro Bowl in 2004, was the most credentialed player on the market, but even he was a question mark. In the final game of the 2005 season, he suffered a 360-degree tear of the labrum, the ring of cartilage around the joint of his right shoulder, and a partial rotator cuff tear. For an NFL quarterback, it was a career-threatening injury.

Renowned orthopedic surgeon Dr. James Andrews repaired the labrum with 11 surgical anchors, about eight more than is common for the procedure. The San Diego Chargers, who selected Brees in the second round of the 2001 NFL Draft, were leery, and they elected to make Philip Rivers their starter, sending red flags across the league about Brees' health status.

The Chargers weren't the only team concerned about Brees' shoulder. His only serious suitors in free agency were the Saints and Miami Dolphins.

For obvious reasons, the Dolphins were widely considered to be the favorites for Brees' services. They had the tradition, a sunny location, and a high-profile coach in Nick Saban, who was entering his second season in Miami.

Payton, though, was undaunted.

From his research and film study, Payton loved everything about Brees, from his on-field decisiveness, accuracy, athleticism, and quick release to his off-field intangibles—his work ethic, intelligence, leadership skills, and winning pedigree.

"He won a state championship as a high school player in Texas, and at Purdue he led his team to three bowl games and a Big Ten title," Payton said. "Then he went to San Diego and was able to turn that program around."

Payton aggressively targeted Brees in free agency as one of his first orders of business in 2006, even though Brees' surgically repaired right shoulder was a major question mark. For Payton and the Saints, it was worth the risk. And as a former college coach, Payton loved a good recruiting battle. He was confident, despite New Orleans' disadvantages at the time, he could win over Brees.

Brees, meanwhile, was drawn to New Orleans' loyalty. While other teams were backing off, the Saints were coming after him. Their confidence in him was attractive. And post-Katrina New Orleans appealed to Brees' and his wife, Brittany's, civic-mindedness. They saw an opportunity to make an impact on a community that desperately needed help.

But Brees knew little about Payton, the young head coach putting the full-court press on his recruitment.

"I knew he was a first-time head coach, young, energetic, a great offensive mind," Brees said. "But besides that, I had never heard of Sean Payton prior to getting a call from him on the phone."

The Saints scheduled the first visit with Brees and rolled out the red carpet. On Saturday, March 11, Payton and Loomis flew on

Saints owner Tom Benson's private jet to Birmingham, Alabama, where Brees was rehabbing his shoulder at Andrews' clinic. They returned to New Orleans with Brees and Brittany for a two-day courtship that included a lavish dinner at Emeril's and tours of the city—potential neighborhoods and top golf courses. During the visit, the Saints also made it clear to Brees they would be the highest bidder for his services.

Brees returned to Birmingham on Sunday afternoon and flew to Miami that night for his official visit with the Dolphins. Miami had gone 9–7 in Saban's first season and team officials there believed they were a quarterback away from contending for a Super Bowl. Brees was their top target. The Dolphins had graded Brees highly as a prospect in the 2001 NFL Draft, and several of the team's scouts and personnel executives remained high on him behind closed doors. Miami signaled its interest by having Saban call Brees at the stroke of midnight to start free agency. Saban and Dolphins general manager Randy Mueller even flew to Birmingham to meet briefly with Brees on Saturday morning before he left for New Orleans.

The Dolphins wined and dined Brees, too. They flew him and Brittany to Miami on a private jet and put them up at the Harbor Beach Resort and Spa and threw a big waterfront dinner for them at Grille 66 & Bar in Fort Lauderdale. While Brees was getting his physical and visiting with Dolphins coaches, Saban's wife, Terry, was taking Brittany on a boat cruise up the intracoastal waterway.

The Dolphins medical staff, though, was less enthusiastic. After evaluating Brees' shoulder, Miami doctors said it was a long shot Brees would fully recover from the surgery. And even then, it would probably take a year for him to return to 100 percent.

"It was more than a gut punch," former Dolphins general manager Randy Mueller said. "It was a kick below the gut if you know what I mean."

As a backup plan, Miami entered into trade negotiations with the Minnesota Vikings for quarterback Daunte Culpepper, who faced a similar career crossroads as Brees after suffering a severe knee injury the previous season. Andrews also performed Culpepper's surgery, and Culpepper was told he would make a complete recovery and be ready to play football for the 2006 season. Believing they were close to making a Super Bowl run, the Dolphins pitched their tent with Culpepper.

Faced with a major rebuilding job, Payton and Loomis were in position to roll the dice. As a first-year coach, Payton owned a long leash with fans after the grim 2005 season. The Saints weren't pressured to make a playoff run like Miami. They could afford to take a chance on Brees.

"In our mind, even if it doesn't work out in Year One, then we're just waiting for two years," Loomis said. "If it didn't work out this year, hey, look, this guy's got another opportunity in Year Two."

The Saints offered Brees a six-year, $60 million contract, the largest in franchise history. While the offer was a tangible commitment by the team, it also included an escape clause after Year One in case things didn't pan out. Brees would earn $10 million in the first year and was due a $12 million roster bonus on March 2, 2007. If Brees struggled or was reinjured, the Saints could cut him and the only cost would be a relatively minor $6.67 million hit against their salary cap in 2007.

When Brees accepted the offer a day later, Saints fans were excited but far from over the moon. They had experienced their share of bad free-agent signings over the years. Saints fans were used to broken-down quarterbacks parachuting into New Orleans on the back ends of their careers. They were hopeful Brees would be the exception, but many of them remained skeptical.

At his introductory press conference in New Orleans a few days later, Brees tried to assuage fears and quell the skepticism about his injured shoulder.

"I don't mind talking about it," Brees said to a packed room of reporters. "I've got a big smile on the inside because I know where I'm going to be in about four months. So all this speculation, especially during this process where people just like to kind of drag you down...they'll be eating their words. It's not the first time somebody said I couldn't do it."

Payton loved every word of Brees' speech. The Saints had their pilot. It was the first win of Payton's tenure. No one could have known it then, but it was a positive early sign of the young head coach's talent, a testament to his intelligence, instincts, and competitiveness. The little-known Payton had gone head-to-head with the great Nick Saban and won.

2

Aligning in New Orleans

NEW ORLEANS WAS A NEW EXPERIENCE FOR SEAN PAYTON AND Drew Brees both. Neither had any connection to the city before joining forces there in 2006.

Even though he was born and raised in Austin, Texas, just a short plane ride away, Brees had been to New Orleans just once, for the wedding of his college roommate, Jason Loerzel, in 2003.

That same year Payton coached in the Superdome as an assistant with the Cowboys. The 13–7 loss was a day he would just as soon forget. The only other visit Payton had made to New Orleans was for a coaching convention during his days as a young college assistant. One of the few things he remembered from that trip was going home "with a lot of ATM receipts in my pocket and not a lot of sleep."

New Orleans is the United States' most unique city. Geographically, it is located in the Deep South. But the city's ethos is firmly rooted in Europe and the Caribbean because of its rich immigrant history. In nearly every way, culturally, spiritually, and philosophically, New Orleans is much closer to Toulouse, France, than Talladega, Alabama. But in one aspect, New Orleans is very much a Southern city: its people are religious about football.

A unique American city like New Orleans needs a unique football team, and the Saints certainly fit the bill. Everything about the Saints is distinctive. Their black-and-gold color scheme, a tribute to founding owner John Mecom Jr.'s oil business interests (black gold, Texas tea), is unique in professional sports. Their nickname, derived from New Orleans jazz great Louis Armstrong's song "When the Saints Go Marching In," is also distinctive, a nod to the city's deep Catholic roots. And their fleur-de-lis logo is also the city of New Orleans' symbol.

Located on a sliver of sinking, mosquito-infested silt in the middle of a swamp, New Orleans' very existence grows more precarious by the day. Coastal erosion claims a football field of Louisiana land to the Gulf of Mexico each day. To cope with this inconvenient truth, New Orleanians lean on certain customs: Mardi Gras, Jazz Fest, drive-thru daiquiri shops—and the Saints.

Few teams have such intrinsic ties to their hometown, both spiritually and aesthetically. The relationship between the city and team extends beyond the normal team/community dynamic.

For the team's fans, affectionately known as Who Dats after the colloquial chant "Who Dat Say Dey Gonna Beat Dem Saints," Saints games are more than mere athletic contests. They are communal events, three-hour revivals where all races, religions, and creeds of the citizenry converge, rally, and unite. New Orleanians attend games dressed in costume and Carnival regalia. They name their children after Saints players and regularly meet the team at the airport after its return flights from big road wins.

If something bad happens to a Saints player, the city rallies to the cause. When linebacker Steve Stonebreaker was fined $1,000 for starting a fight in a game against the New York Giants in 1967, a group of fans collected money to pay the fine. When Marcus

Williams missed the tackle at the end of the 2017 NFC divisional playoff game, a local couple bought a billboard downtown with the message: DAT'S OK MARCUS, WE [BIG PINK HEART] OUR SAINTS.

And this love affair has existed since the franchise's inception in 1966.

Unfortunately, the on-field product wasn't as impressive as the off-field support during the club's early years.

It took the Saints two decades to record their first winning season and another 13 years after that to win their first playoff game. Owner Tom Benson had raised the standards of the club when he bought the team in 1985 and hired general manager Jim Finks and head coach Jim Mora. But the Saints still were considered one of the league's also-rans. Before Payton arrived, they had registered only seven winning seasons and a record of 244–361–5 in 39 years. Of Payton's 13 predecessors, only Mora managed to post a winning record in New Orleans.

Before Payton left his position as Dallas Cowboys offensive coordinator to take the Saints gig, his mentor, Bill Parcells, offered him some final advice: "It was, 'Hey, real quickly, you've got to figure out what has kept that organization from winning and make those changes," Payton said. "Otherwise, they'll be having another press conference three years from now to introduce another someone in a navy blazer at the podium."

Payton said Parcells compared him and his rookie coaching brethren to penguins jumping off an iceberg into the dangerous Arctic waters.

"There's nine of you in that class," Payton recalled Parcells' message to him. "Everyone is swimming for the iceberg and the truth of the matter is maybe two or three of you will get to that other iceberg and climb up [and] the rest are eaten. Because typically those [coaching] changes are going on at those places that haven't experienced success."

While Payton respected Parcells and other Super Bowl–winning mentors like Jon Gruden and Mike Ditka, he also knew nothing they said could truly prepare him for the challenge he faced in New Orleans.

When Payton took over the Saints in January 2006, New Orleans was only five months removed from Hurricane Katrina's devastation and still in the early stages of the massive recovery. In the wake of one of the worst natural disasters in American history, the long-term future of the Saints was uncertain, as were New Orleans' prospects as a regular host site for Super Bowls, Final Fours, and college football championship games.

Even before Katrina, New Orleans already was one of the smallest and poorest markets to boast two professional sports franchises. Its metropolitan population of 1.3 million was the fifth smallest in the NFL. Its corporate base ranked ahead of only Buffalo. Saints season-ticket sales had dipped to about 35,000 before Katrina, down more than 33 percent from a franchise record of more than 53,000 in 2003. And it didn't help matters that the 2005 team finished 3–13, the club's worst record since Coach Mike Ditka's swan song in 1999.

This was the bleak situation that confronted Payton early in his tenure. During his first month on the job while holed up at the Airport Hilton Hotel on Airline Drive, a few miles down the road from Saints headquarters in suburban Kenner, Payton noticed the looks on the faces of assistant coaches he brought in for interviews. The hotel was surrounded by FEMA trailers, blue roofs, and construction equipment. The area's quality of life was not exactly a selling point to the spouses of potential coaching candidates.

"Everyone else was going out [of New Orleans]," Payton said, "and we were going in."

At his introductory press conference, Payton vowed to start "with a clean slate." Not only did the entire football operation need an overhaul, but the business side of the building also needed to be changed. The Superdome, meanwhile, was in the initial stages of a multi-phase $320 million renovation. For all intents and purposes, the Saints team that Payton and Brees took over in 2006 was a start-up operation.

"Let's be honest, we're in New Orleans, and it'd been under water [several] months earlier, and you drive through the city and you're seeing boats on top of houses and all these things," Loomis said. "You don't have all the services, the schools are closed, all those different things that happened."

The rebuilding task was daunting, but Payton remained unfazed. A year earlier he almost accepted the head coaching job with the Oakland Raiders but backed out at the last minute and returned to Dallas. Then he was the runner-up to Mike McCarthy for the Green Bay Packers head coaching job before settling on the Saints job. The Saints were his first head coaching job at any level of football, and he was excited about the possibilities.

"There were a lot of challenges," Payton said. "But we also knew there was a great opportunity here."

Payton knew he had to change the culture, and he set the tone early. Eleven starters from the 2005 season were shipped out, including popular wide receiver Donte Stallworth, a former first-round draft pick. Twenty-six new players made up the initial 53-man roster. He built the roster with average Joes who possessed high character, a strong work ethic, and a team-first attitude. He stressed teamwork over individual accomplishment. One of the first things he did as coach was show the players tape of the 2004 U.S. Olympic men's basketball team, which finished a disappointing third in the Athens Games despite a lineup that featured LeBron James, Allen Iverson, Tim Duncan, and Dwyane Wade.

"You have to look at why [the Saints] have only won one playoff game in 40 years," Payton said. "There's a reason. We're in a place where, within 10 minutes, you can get a daiquiri, sit at a blackjack table, and go to a strip club—and you can do it until four in the morning. If you've got the kind of people who are susceptible to that, they'll find trouble. So, yeah, character's important. New England showed us the model the past years."

Payton also made subtle changes. If a meeting was at 8:30 AM in 2005, it began at 8:00 AM during Year One. Instead of wearing black jerseys at home, the Saints wore white.

"Change is healthy," Payton said. "I felt the situation in New Orleans was right and I was ready for it. None of these jobs is perfect. Every one has strengths and weakness and challenges. You look at it and know it's going to present challenges. I flew back after the initial interview with Mickey and thought, 'This is a real good challenge.' Part of that is what's happening in the city. I think we can be part of that process and get the arrow pointing up in that area and for the people there."

The signing of Brees was the catalyst. The Saints hadn't had a Pro Bowl quarterback since Manning in 1979. And they hadn't had a great offensive-minded head coach since Hank Stram in the mid-1970s. The Saints' previous head coaches were all defensive-minded tough guys: Mora; Mike Ditka; Jim Haslett.

Payton and Brees ushered in a new era of hope and possibility to New Orleans, arriving at a time when the city and franchise desperately needed strong, competent leadership.

It easily could have turned out differently. Payton could have landed in Green Bay. Brees could have signed with Miami. Yet, fate brought them together in New Orleans. And back in 2006, Saints fans, desperate for a return to respectability and competitiveness, turned their lonely eyes to a first-time head coach and a quarterback with a surgically repaired throwing arm.

"You go back to that time when a lot of us came here six months post-Katrina," Brees said in 2019, recalling those early days in New Orleans. "All of us leaning on one another. You know, this was this is a new environment for Sean. It was a new situation, first-time head coach. Man, he had his hands full trying to put together a staff and a team to try to put together a winner to give the people of New Orleans and this community something to cheer about. I think he drew the connection very quickly. He helped to create that bond. He had to create the culture here that fits the mold of this city and the Who Dat Nation. So I think he's always embraced that. So that's one of the big reasons why there's such a connection between the two."

3

Destined to Be a Saint

HISTORY WILL SHOW THAT PAYTON ENDED UP IN NEW ORLEANS after the Green Bay Packers chose Mike McCarthy instead of him during their coaching search in 2006. But fate might have played a role, as well.

On December 29, 1963, Thomas and Jeanne Payton welcomed their third-born child into the world in San Mateo, California, christening him Patrick Sean Payton.

A devout Irish Catholic family, the Paytons named the boy after the Rev. Patrick Peyton, an Irish-born American priest who had traveled the globe after World War II and the Korean War on what became known as "The Rosary Crusade," imploring people to pray the rosary and coining the phrase, "The family that prays together stays together."

Payton's parents were from Scranton, Pennsylvania, and he spent his grade school years in Newtown Square, a bedroom community 30 miles west of Philadelphia. Payton would play sandlot ball with his older brother, Thomas, and his friends before the family moved to Naperville, just outside of Chicago, when he was in his early teens.

"I can remember that Sean always hung out with kids three to five years older than him," Thomas said. "They'd let him do stuff, watch them play football, touch or tackle. Kids his age would come over after school and ask my mom if Sean could come out and play. My mom [who died in 2002] wouldn't let my brother stay up late unless he took a nap. So the only way he could watch *Monday Night Football*—and we're talking about fifth or sixth grade here—is if he took a nap. Everybody else would be outside playing after school. He'd be taking a nap so he could watch *Monday Night Football* and talk about it with the older kids the next day."

From early on, Payton knew exactly what he wanted to do in life. He might not have been the most disciplined student at Naperville Central High School, but he had a clear sense of purpose in life. Don Zedrow, his eighth-grade teacher at Lincoln Junior High School, remembers telling the young, cocky Payton in shop class that if he didn't stop goofing around, he'd never amount to anything.

"I kid you not, he looked at me and said, 'Mr. Zedrow, I'm going to be a professional football player,'" Zedrow told the *Chicago Tribune* in 2007. "I said, 'Yeah, I've heard that one before.'"

Payton derived his early sense of direction from J.R. Bishop, his high school coach at Naperville Central High School, where Payton was a star quarterback. Bishop arrived at Naperville Central during Payton's sophomore year to reverse the football fortunes of the public high school in the Chicago suburb that had not experienced much success.

Bishop was an early mentor for Payton. He was the head coach at Wheaton (Illinois) College from 1982 to 1995, where he compiled a stellar 84–43–1 record. In semi-retirement, he served another decade as offensive coordinator and was inducted into the school's athletic hall of fame in 2004.

"He was a father figure to me and was very important in my development," Payton said. "I think that with myself, and a lot of other players, he probably stimulated our interest. When I got to high school, I think I was just aspiring to fit in. I always enjoyed sports, played basketball, football, baseball. I think the thing he did was he had a way of making sure you knew if you wanted to play football past high school, there probably was a college for everybody. He used to say that. I think six or seven guys went on to play college football, some major college, some Division III level. I think some of [my interest] was stimulated by him; the interest on still wanting to play when you went to college. He had a big impact on my life early on, as well as my parents."

Payton made an early impression on Bishop, as well, immediately identifying himself as someone with a future.

"You know, some of them just stand out," Bishop said. "They hit you right away. Here's someone who's just different than everyone else because of his interest, his eagerness, his depth of the game at such a young age. He wanted to learn more. He was in my hip pocket all the time just wanting to know more. You just knew through his own work ethic he was destined to be somebody good in some area. You didn't know at the time he was going to be a football coach, to come to the place he is right now. He had such a positive attitude. You couldn't get him down. You could hit him over the head and he'd come back for more. I always respected him for that."

Bishop was ahead of his time as an offensive coordinator. He ran a wide-open aerial attack on offense, built around the quarterback. And in the offseason, he conducted a popular passing camp in Franklin, Indiana, which was an early forerunner to today's 7-on-7 competitions.

Repeatedly, Bishop said, Payton would surprise him with his grasp of the intricacies of the game. He quickly became Bishop's eager pupil and spent hours watching game film and studying the playbook. By the time Payton was a senior, the All-DuPage Valley

Conference quarterback was helping finalize game plans and calling his own plays.

"He was one of those young men you could tell was something good," Bishop said. "He was always willing to try things and was one of the few players I've coached through the years that when he talked to me, I listened.... As a coach, I didn't always do what he said. But when he said something, I knew he thought it out, and he knew what he was talking about."

Payton's dream school was Purdue, which had a storied legacy as a producer of elite quarterbacks, among them Bob Griese, Len Dawson, Gary Danielson, and Mike Phipps. But the Boilermakers showed no interest, and Payton picked Eastern Illinois over offers from Southern Illinois, Northern Illinois, and Southwest Missouri State. At EIU, Payton set several passing records for Coach Al Molde's high-powered passing attack, which was nicknamed Eastern Airlines. Payton had passing games of 461 and 509 yards, the latter a school record, and eventually topped the 10,000-yard passing mark in his career. He recorded 20 300-yard passing games and set 11 school records, before they were eventually broken by Tony Romo and Jimmy Garoppolo.

"Sean was an intense competitor, an infectious leader, and one of the most confident players I had the pleasure of working with in my career," Molde later told the *Chicago Tribune*. "He was a player who loved watching film and preparing for the next game.... So many times he would check into a play at the line [of scrimmage], drop back, and throw a strike to one of our receivers for big gains and touchdowns."

Despite his impressive résumé, Payton wasn't selected in the 1987 NFL Draft. He tried out for the Kansas City Chiefs that spring but wasn't offered a contract. There wasn't much demand for a 5'11", 180-pound quarterback from a Division I-AA program.

Over the next 18 months, his professional playing career took him to three different leagues in three different countries. He started in the Arena Football League for the Chicago Bruisers and Pittsburgh Gladiators and then went to the Ottawa Rough Riders of the Canadian Football League. After being cut by Ottawa, he played briefly as a replacement player for the Chicago Bears during the 1987 player strike. Payton started three games for the Bears, who were coached by Mike Ditka. He won the first two before losing his finale to none other than the New Orleans Saints.

"It was my first year out of college and I had just been cut from the CFL. It was an easy decision," Payton said. "It was an opportunity. I wanted to play and possibly get evaluated. I've always thanked Coach Ditka for getting me on with my life's work [coaching], because I wasn't good at [playing]."

Before hanging up his playing career, Payton made one last stop. He played for the Leicester Panthers of the Budweiser National League in England. It was during his time in rural England that Payton began to consider a career change. He began to pursue leads for a graduate assistant position in the college ranks.

"My mom would give me a hard time because I didn't have health insurance at the time," Payton said. "You're at that stage where some of your friends are getting married, some already have, and they're all kind of established in their early parts of their careers. I'm like, 'God, I'm living over in England, and I don't have a savings account.'"

One of Payton's many calls went to Steve Devine, then the offensive line coach at San Diego State, who also was in charge of hiring and overseeing graduate assistants. Devine was skeptical at first, but after checking Payton's references, he offered him the job with one caveat: he needed to be there in three days.

"I'll get there," Payton said.

Payton flew to Chicago, loaded up his Chevy Cavalier, and made the cross-country drive west. His car broke down outside Denver and the mechanic jury-rigged the broken fan belt because Payton lacked the funds to pay for the full repair. Payton eventually made it to San Diego and lived with Devine for a couple weeks before finding an apartment of his own.

"Steve is the one who stuck me in a coaching shirt with armpit stains, put a hat on me, and said, 'This is what you've got to do to be a coach,'" Payton said. "He was real instrumental in the process."

Devine later became a scout for the New York Giants thanks, in part, to a recommendation from Payton. He retired in May 2019.

"Obviously, he had some talent," Devine said of Payton, "but he was a bright-eyed guy who was always looking for a way to win and get it done. He kept at it until people gave him a chance. He came to San Diego State full of ideas and ready to do anything you'd ask, from making coffee to running an errand. Good things always seem to happen to him. He's a guy I really admire."

Payton spent two years at San Diego State, then landed his first full-time job as the running backs and wide receivers coach at Indiana State. He returned to San Diego State as running backs coach in 1992 and 1993, where he coached All-American Marshall Faulk. He served as the offensive coordinator at Miami (Ohio) for two seasons, then was the quarterbacks coach at Illinois in 1996 before he finally got his break in the NFL.

Jon Gruden hired him to coach the quarterbacks on Ray Rhodes' Philadelphia Eagles staff in 1997–98, and it was there, under the direction of Gruden and offensive line coach Bill Callahan, that Payton laid the foundation for his knowledge of NFL offenses.

"It was my first opportunity in the NFL and it gave me a chance really to learn," Payton said. "I learned a lot in a short period of time working with Jon and that offense. It was a foundation for me that I still hold on to.

"It was a little bit like law school. There were a lot of late nights and a lot of early mornings. I learned about preparation. You come out of college and you get into this league, and you realize that there's a lot of football that you don't know. It can be humbling, but yet it was important."

Working as closely as they did together, Payton and Gruden developed a strong relationship. Payton would often sleep on the couch in Gruden's office. The two remain close to this day.

"He's been a big part of my development," Payton said of Gruden. "When I got hired [in Philadelphia] in '97, just for me to really be a blank tape is what they were looking for, for me to study and learn. It afforded me a great opportunity.... He's got a great mind. He's a unique guy, and he's very talented."

In 1999, Payton moved to the New York Giants staff as quarterbacks coach and was promoted to offensive coordinator a year later. He was dubbed the "Boy Wonder" of the Giants offense in 1999 and 2000, but two years later he was reeling after having the play sheet ripped from his hands. After several subpar offensive performances during the 2002 season, head coach Jim Fassel took away Payton's play-calling duties. The Giants scored just seven touchdowns in seven games with Payton calling the shots, and three of those scores came in one game. The move appeared to work. The Giants made a run to the playoffs, and Payton, his role diminished and reputation tarnished, started to look for work elsewhere.

"I told Sean when this happened, this isn't going to affect your career," former Giants general manager Ernie Accorsi said in 2002. "How you react and handle this, that will be your legacy."

Accorsi was right. What happened next for Payton defined his career.

4

The Parcells Effect

BILL PARCELLS HAD NEVER MET SEAN PAYTON WHEN HE HIRED him in 2003. He just knew Payton was considered a rising star in the coaching ranks and had a strong reputation as a quarterbacks guru. Despite the shaky finish to Payton's tenure in New York, Giants personnel director Chris Mara, whom Parcells knew from his days in New York, had given Payton a glowing recommendation. Parcells wanted to add him to his new coaching staff in Dallas and hired Payton over the phone.

Payton didn't know Parcells, either, but he certainly knew of him. He had led the New York Giants to two Super Bowl victories and took New England to the championship game. Parcells was football royalty, and Giants general manager Ernie Accorsi told Payton that working for Parcells would be like earning a graduate degree in coaching.

Payton jumped at the chance to work for Parcells, turning down the Arizona Cardinals offensive coordinator job for a position as assistant head coach and quarterbacks coach in Dallas.

"When you think about that opportunity for a young guy to work for a Hall of Fame coach, it's invaluable," Payton said. "The very last thing we discussed [over the phone] was salary and benefits and any of that stuff. I hadn't even met him. All of the other things were more important to him. The football and the passion. Those were the things that he got excited about."

Parcells wasn't initially sure that Payton had what it took to become an NFL head coach, but he quickly discovered Payton's passion for the sport and thirst for knowledge were traits that might ultimately make him successful.

Parcells quickly became a mentor and, eventually, a trusted adviser. When the Raiders tried to hire Payton for his first head coaching job in 2004, Parcells privately advised Payton to turn it down and wait for a better gig in the future. And when the Saints called two years later, Parcells gave Payton his blessing.

"He was very, very energetic, bright, with high energy," said Parcells, who referred to Payton as Dennis after the cartoon character Dennis the Menace. "He was intelligent and was a good listener. That's the best way to describe him. I enjoyed my time with him."

Payton compared his three seasons working under Parcells to graduate school. His influence on Payton went beyond Xs and Os. Parcells taught Payton how to manage a game, run a team, and lead an organization. He taught him the value of attention to even the smallest detail, a trait Payton has maintained throughout his coaching tenure.

"What I remember from Bill was that he never stopped thinking how to win," Payton said. "For Bill, fresh analysis beat conventional thinking every time. He was brilliant at analyzing every opponent individually and then figuring out what it would take to win the game." When Payton took the Saints job, he brought the Parcells Way to New Orleans. While he adopted Fassel's practice schedule from the New York Giants, he borrowed almost everything else from Parcells. He used Parcells' conditioning test, weightlifting regimen, disciplinary system—almost everything had Parcells' fingerprints on it. Payton took Parcells' approach to training camp, moving it from the team's home facility in suburban Metairie to Millsaps College, 180 miles away in Jackson, Mississippi. He also removed the Saints' fleur-de-lis logo from rookies' helmets. He hung signs at the facility with another Parcells mantra: Saints players will be Smart, Tough, Disciplined, and Well Conditioned.

During the early years, members of the Saints football operations staff would joke that they needed to buy "What Would Bill Do?" bracelets because of Payton's constant references to Parcells and his method of operation. But there was a method to Payton's strategy. By continuously referring to Parcells, Payton was surreptitiously establishing his philosophy, using the future Hall of Famer as a way to validate his approach in New Orleans.

"Having the chance to work for Bill Parcells for three years, you learn a lot more about all the things that are necessary to be the leader of a team," Payton said. "When you're around someone like that for three years, it's an on-the-job, day-to-day learning experience. There are things that come up daily that you can't help but take notice of. Those are the benefits of working under someone like that rather than just go hear him speak at a clinic."

One of the many Parcells coaching methods Payton continues to employ in New Orleans was to introduce three to five keys to victory to his players at the initial team meeting on Wednesdays of game week. He also adopted many of Parcells' legendary motivational tactics. After a big win or a long winning streak, he would plant mouse traps around the football facility to remind his players, "don't eat the cheese" from friends, family, and the media. Another time, he had staffers paint several life-size fake exit doors on the walls of the facility to deliver the message to his players and coaches: there are many ways out of the NFL—don't make excuses.

"Sean was a no-nonsense, hard-nosed coach, and I think he definitely took that from Parcells," said former Saints linebacker Scott Fujita, who played for Parcells' Cowboys in 2005 during Payton's third and final season as Parcells' primary offensive assistant. "Sean would come around and take time out to B.S. with guys here and there. And Parcells did that same thing. But Sean also wasn't afraid to put a lot of pressure on guys. Certain people need that to bring out the best in them. Bill did that, too."

Parcells taught Payton that change and confrontation are healthy.

"I had an Italian mother," Parcells said. "My mother was a very loving person, but she was highly confrontational. She and my father believed in doing things the right way. My experience growing up was that confrontation could be healthy. It gets things out in the open. Hopefully when you get them out there you can solve them. I believe that strongly."

Payton learned from Parcells to challenge people, even his coaches and superiors. If a player or coach is not pulling his weight, Payton won't hesitate to address it.

"Sean is always honest with you," Brees said. "He doesn't sugarcoat it. If you want to know the truth, he has an open-door policy where he says, for example, to end the season at every exit meeting, I've heard him say the same thing. 'You're going to hear a lot of stuff in the media about who we should keep and who we should, who we should get rid of, and for what reason. Don't allow that to get you upset or even give you false hope about certain things. If you want to know the truth, you can come into my office right now, and I'll tell you the truth.'"

If Payton feels like a player is not giving full effort during practice or is going through the motions during his week of preparation, the coach will let him know. He's also a stickler for body language and energy level. Just as Parcells did, he demands that his coaches and players carry themselves with positive energy and be enthusiastic at work. Everyone—coaches, players, staff—needs to be passionate about work and winning.

"Bill valued confrontation," Payton said. "It was eye-opening at first, but nothing was ever tabled. And the older and wiser that I got the more I appreciated why he was like that. You want to be true to who you are, but it is important to address things and not table them, especially in a team environment. I think that once that's done, I think the players, coaches, and everyone involved understand that that's just how it is. That can be healthy, rather than letting things fester or not addressing certain things at all. That's something that I think he was very good at."

One of Payton's favorite Parcells lines is, "Some of these coaches and players have retired on the job." It's his not-so-subtle way of keeping everyone motivated and maintaining an edge.

"Sean is a great communicator, but at the same time, he believes in controversy," said Dan Campbell, the Saints tight ends coach who played three seasons for Parcells in Dallas from 2003 to '05 and began his coaching career in Miami in 2010, when Parcells was still in the Dolphins' front office. "He believes in airing things out. Let's get this out on the table. If something bothers him, he's not going to keep it to himself or say, 'I don't want to hurt the guy's feelings.' He's going to get it out in the open, and we're going to clear the air.

"And believe it or not, that in itself is a huge deal, because there's a lot of coaches in this league that won't do that. They're just afraid to do that. It takes freakin' guts, man. They're afraid to go talk to that defensive tackle that was just a little late to a meeting or a guy who is just not giving the effort in practice. Sean's not going to let that stuff slide. And that's another reason why we've won around here."

"Some coaches are afraid to address certain things, like maybe afraid to address the elephant in the room or afraid to tell you the truth because they're afraid it's going to hurt your feelings," Brees said. "Sean's not that way. What I find though is that the way that he presents it to you is not something that's going to make you feel bad. It's going to challenge you."

Payton received a bachelor's degree in communication from Eastern Illinois, but he received his PhD in football communication from Parcells. The latter taught Payton how to run and lead an organization.

"The one thing with Bill was there were never any hidden punches," Payton said. "You always knew where you stood with him. I think players appreciate that. So it's just telling them the truth.

"Sometimes, even if it's a veteran player, it may not be what they want to hear. But it might be what's necessary for them to hear. With Bill, there weren't any protected, pet cats or anything like that. Everyone was above the radar, and he was fair. It was a lot easier that way than trying to pretend to be fair."

Payton has an entire wall of his office dedicated to Parcells. Among the framed pictures and letters is one large photograph of Payton and Parcells coaching on the Cowboys sideline, with an autographed inscription from Parcells: "I am grateful for your help and prideful in your accomplishments and looking forward to your future. My best, Bill Parcells."

And to this day, Parcells' influence remains with Payton and throughout the Saints facility. He remains Payton's most trusted adviser and even makes recommendations on personnel. It was Parcells who tipped the Saints to the talents of undrafted free agent Tommylee Lewis before the 2016 NFL Draft. Payton usually talks to Parcells at least once a week during the season, often on Monday morning phone calls.

"I've said this before," Payton said. "There's a lot of on-the-job training. Daily, there might be something personnel-wise from an organizational standpoint, practice schedules, training camp schedules, whatever. He knows how to win, and I learned an awful lot in a short period of time. I look back on my career and I was touched by so many people that were successful and they're a big reason why I'm here right now. I'm humbled by that."

5

Child of Destiny

ON JANUARY 15, 1979, ANDREW CHRISTOPHER BREES WAS BORN into the sport of football.

His maternal grandfather, Ray Akins, was a legendary coach at Gregory-Portland High School and finished his career as one of the winningest coaches in Texas prep history. His uncle, Marty Akins, was an All-Southwest Conference wishbone quarterback at Texas, where he started for two years in the same backfield as Earl Campbell. Both are members of the Texas High School Football Hall of Fame.

Football wasn't just a sport to Brees. It was a way of life.

Brees' parents, Mina and Eugene "Chip" Brees, were lawyers and excellent athletes themselves. Mina was a four-sport standout and all-state basketball player at Gregory Portland High School. Chip, meanwhile, played basketball at Texas A&M, where he met Mina when she was a cheerleader.

With a heritage like that, athletics were a part of Brees' life from the outset. And there was hardly a sport he couldn't master. Mina, a singles player for Austin city championship teams in 1995, introduced Drew to tennis, and he became one of the best junior players in Texas, earning a No. 3 ranking in the USTA's age-12 group. That same year he set an Austin city record with 14 home runs in Little League and was chosen to play on a youth soccer select team.

Drew and his younger brother, Reid, would spend their summers attending two-a-day preseason practices at Gregory-Portland. But Drew didn't start playing football until high school, primarily because Mina was leery of the sport. She had seen how a knee injury derailed her brother, Marty's, career and didn't want something similar to happen to her boys.

"I had witnessed my brother's career come to a screeching halt," Mina Brees told the *Austin American-Statesman* in 2002. "I was a little leery of...kids playing tackle football too early."

Chip and Mina divorced in 1987, when Drew was eight and his brother Reid was six. Both parents remarried. Mina was married for 10 years to Harley Clark, a state district court judge and former Texas yell-leader who is credited with inventing the famous Hook 'em Horns salute. Chip married Amy Hightower, whose father, Jack, was a congressman from north Texas and later a state Supreme Court judge. The couple received joint custody of the children, and the boys split their time between both homes.

"There's absolutely no way that a divorce cannot affect children or any of the people who are intimately involved," Mina said in a 2000 Lafayette *Journal and Courier* story. "I do think they became more adaptable and more mature earlier because of that. They had to become more responsible."

In 1993, Brees enrolled at Westlake High School, located in West Lake Hills, an exclusive suburb west of Austin. Westlake was an academic and athletic powerhouse. The Chaparrals won state titles in seven different sports before Brees arrived, and the school regularly was listed among the top high schools in the nation in rankings by *Newsweek* and the *Washington Post*.

Brees played football, basketball, and baseball, where he was a power-hitting infielder and a right-handed pitcher with an 88-mph fastball.

Brees was not an immediate football prodigy. As a freshman he played on the B team, and as a sophomore he found himself stuck behind Jonny Rodgers on the junior varsity. Rodgers was the younger brother of Jay Rodgers, a star who went on to play at the University of Indiana, and the son of Randy Rodgers, then in charge of recruiting for John Mackovic's staff at the University of Texas. That August, Brees grew so discouraged he threatened to quit the team so he could concentrate on basketball and baseball. Brees was dissuaded by a pep talk from his mother, and a few days later Rodgers injured his knee during a scrimmage.

"If Jonny hadn't got hurt, I don't know if Drew would have ever had a chance," Westlake varsity coach Ron Schroeder told the *Austin American-Statesman*. "I never heard anyone talk about him as a starting quarterback, then all the sudden he had to be the starter when Jonny got hurt."

In Brees' first JV game he completed 9 of 10 passes for 315 yards and four touchdowns. The Westlake JV didn't lose a game that season. The next season he led the Chaparrals varsity to a 12–0–1 record before suffering the first major injury of his career. In a regional playoff game at Alice, Texas, Brees tore the anterior cruciate ligament in his left knee while running a bootleg. His season was over and so was Westlake's a week later.

"That was a big, defining moment," Brees said. "I had seen other athletes tear their ACLs and not come back the same. It really scared me at the time. At the time, it was the hardest thing I ever had to do, both mentally and physically. It was more so mentally getting over the hurdle of coming back from something that I thought at the time was pretty devastating and coming back and having my best year."

Brees had surgery in January 1996 and attacked the rehab process. He was fully recovered when his senior year started but still wore a large brace on his surgically repaired knee as a precaution. Brees led the Chaps to a 16–0 record and the Class 5A Division II state title, the first in school history.

The night of Westlake's 55–15 state championship romp over Abilene Cooper at Texas Stadium in Dallas, the team returned to Westlake High and there were throngs of people waiting outside the locker room, including autograph-seeking youngsters. One by one, his teammates came out to sign the championship T-shirts, but Brees was nowhere to be found.

"Drew was so sentimental about his last time in that locker room as a player, he did not want to come out," Amy told the *Journal and Courier.*

As a senior, Brees passed for 3,528 yards and 31 touchdowns with a 63 percent completion rate. He was named the Class 5A offensive MVP award and finished his career with 5,416 passing yards and 50 touchdowns.

"My biggest memory is that there was never a down or distance so foreboding that we didn't think we could get it," Westlake team doctor and longtime family friend Newt Hasson told the *Waco Tribune-Herald* in 2011. "We always knew Drew could come through. If it were third-and-30, he'd get 31 yards. If it were fourth-and-14, he'd get 15 yards. There was never any doubt that he would get whatever yardage we needed to keep the chains moving."

College scouts and recruiting analysts were less impressed. Despite his gaudy numbers at the highest level of Texas prep football, Brees was not listed in SuperPrep's Texas 102 as a senior, nor did he make the 100-player All-Southwest Team in Tom Lemming's Prep Football Report.

Hometown Texas didn't recruit Brees at all. The Longhorns sent him just one form letter and never called him once. Texas A&M,

his dream school because of his parents' ties, flirted with him for a couple of months but showed more interest in his Westlake teammate Seth McKinney. Texas A&M coaches told him he was their backup plan in case their top target, Major Applewhite, a highly ranked prospect from Baton Rouge, chose elsewhere. Mina Brees even took it upon herself to personally call some college coaches, but every coach told her he was set at quarterback.

"I was a skinny, runt-looking kid," Brees said. "I just had my knee surgery a couple of months before and had this big ole brace on [my leg]. I wouldn't have recruited me, either."

In the end, Brees' only Division I scholarship offers came from Purdue and Kentucky, a pair of schools known more for their basketball programs than football prowess. Brees picked Purdue because of its Big Ten affiliation and strong academic reputation. Even when Applewhite spurned A&M for Texas and the Aggies made late advances, Brees stuck with his decision. It proved to be a fortuitous call.

The Boilermakers' new coach, Joe Tiller, was an offensive guru, one of the innovators of the spread offense. When he took the job, he promised fans the Boilermakers would play an exciting brand of offensive football. He called it "basketball on grass."

When Brees arrived at Purdue, there were six quarterbacks on the roster. His goal was to redshirt and maybe make the travel squad. But one by one, the players ahead of him fell by the wayside. Senior John Reeves switched to defense, redshirt freshman Clay Walters and true freshman Jim Mitchell transferred, and true freshman Ben Smith switched to the secondary.

That left senior Billy Dicken as the starter and Brees as the backup. Brees played sparingly as a freshman, but by the spring of his sophomore year, he was the only experienced quarterback on the roster and he took 90 percent of the snaps in practice.

When it was time to make his collegiate debut, Brees was more than ready. With his pinpoint accuracy and quick decision-making, Brees thrived in Tiller's pass-happy offense and burst on the college scene. Tiller's innovative attack and Brees' innate field generalship were a match made in passing heaven.

In his first season as a starter, he threw for more yards (3,983), more touchdowns (39), and a better completion percentage (63.4) than more heralded peers Donovan McNabb of Syracuse, Akili Smith of Oregon, Cade McNown of UCLA, Joe Germaine of Ohio State, and Michael Bishop of Kansas State. And he led Purdue to a 9–4 season, capped by an Alamo Bowl victory over Bishop and K-State.

He took the offense to another level in his junior season. In a 31–24 loss to Wisconsin, Brees attempted an NCAA-record 83 passes, completing an NCAA-record-tying 55 of them for 494 yards. In a 56–21 win against Minnesota, he went 31-for-36 for 522 yards and six touchdowns.

As a senior, he led Purdue to its first Rose Bowl appearance in 34 years and its first Big Ten title since 1967. And along the way, he set two NCAA records, 13 Big Ten records, and 19 school records. Brees won the Maxwell Award as the nation's top collegiate player and was a two-time finalist for the Heisman Trophy. He finished his career as the Big Ten's all-time passing leader with 11,792 yards and 90 touchdowns, numbers that still stand atop the conference's career rankings today.

In the spring of 2001, as Brees prepared for the NFL Draft, he encountered similar criticisms to the ones he heard as a senior at Westlake. Once again, Brees found himself in prove-it mode.

NFL scouts worried about his lack of height, pedestrian speed, and average arm. Some believed he was the product of Tiller's system, which tended to turn average quarterbacks into world-beaters. Billy Dicken, who started during Brees' freshman season, played sparingly before Tiller arrived, but passed for 3,136 yards and 25 touchdowns in his one season as a starter under Tiller and was named first-team All-Big Ten.

Years earlier, Tiller's offense had produced another record-setting quarterback named Josh Wallwork. At the University of Wyoming in 1996, Wallwork led the nation in total offense but never cracked the NFL. Instead, he toiled in the Arena Football League.

At the time, the comparisons to Brees seemed valid. Both were undersized, athletic quarterbacks with quick decision-making skills. But off the field, the two quarterbacks could not have been more dissimilar. Wallwork lacked the intangibles that made Brees so special. Wallwork's drug problems eventually destroyed his career and led to an eight-month jail sentence for meth possession.

Still, Wallwork's success caused some football people to wonder if Brees was also a product of Tiller's system.

"I think it's a combination of both [the system and the player]," Minnesota coach Glen Mason said at the time. "I don't have as short a memory as a lot of people. That offense didn't take off just when Drew Brees came. The senior [Dicken] that didn't play [prior to Brees]. He really performed well in that system. I think it's a combination of a really talented quarterback that's running an offense that's suited for him. It's a great marriage."

Tiller, though, insisted Brees would star in any system and told every NFL scout as much when they visited campus in West Lafayette, Indiana, to evaluate Brees.

"Certainly our system is user-friendly and he happens to be the user right now," Tiller said in 2001. "If you want to put a percentage on it, I really don't know. I just know that he's the right guy for our system, particularly at this time. But the system is not making Drew Brees."

Brees fared well at the NFL Scouting Combine in Indianapolis. He measured 6'0⅛" in bare feet. His time of 4.85 in the 40-yard dash was below par but far from awful. His vertical jump of 32 inches was above average, and his hand size (10.25-inch width) ranked in the top 10 percent of quarterbacks. His ball speed of 68 miles per hour on his passes topped the quarterback class that year, according to Tom Braatz, the director of college scouting for the Miami Dolphins.

"Drew has been a very productive quarterback in college," Rick Spielman, the Dolphins' vice president of player personnel, told the *Fort Lauderdale Sun-Sentinel* in 2001. "Everybody knows the biggest question on Drew is whether you can live with the height or not. We're going to have to sit down and make a decision on that if it's Drew Brees or whomever may slip down to where we're at."

That year, Atlanta (No. 5 overall selection), Carolina (No. 11), Kansas City (No. 12), and Miami (No. 26) were all in need of quarterback help in the draft. All passed on Brees. Only Atlanta, which traded into the No. 1 slot to select Michael Vick, took a quarterback. Brees slid out of the first round. Brees had heard pre-draft scuttlebutt that the Dolphins would select him at No. 26, but they chose cornerback Jamar Fletcher instead.

The San Diego Chargers were the beneficiaries. General manager John Butler orchestrated a draft-day trade with Atlanta to send the No. 1 overall pick to the Falcons for the No. 5 and No. 67 picks. The Chargers used the No. 5 selection to take running back LaDainian Tomlinson and the No. 67 pick to take cornerback Tay Cody. With their future franchise running back in their pocket, they rolled the dice that Brees would fall to them in Round 2. Their gamble paid off. The Chargers selected Brees with the first pick of the second round, No. 31 overall.

The selection of Tomlinson and Brees will go down in history as one of the best draft hauls in NFL history. Two overlooked prospects from the state of Texas. One a Hall of Fame running back. The other a future Hall of Fame quarterback.

6

Alike Yet Different

IT DIDN'T TAKE LONG FOR PAYTON TO REALIZE HE HAD A KINDRED spirit in Brees. During the bye week of their first postseason together in New Orleans, Payton and his staff were working on a Friday afternoon at the team's practice facility in suburban Metairie. Coaches use the open date in the schedule to self-scout tendencies and evaluate their offensive and defensive efficiency. The Saints staff was breaking for the weekend around 1:30 PM when Payton looked out the window of his second-floor office and noticed a lone figure on the practice field. It was Brees, dressed in a T-shirt and practice shorts and holding a football near the far end zone.

Curious, Payton and offensive coordinator Doug Marrone scrambled downstairs to inquire. As the coaches approached the field, they noticed him conducting passing drills on air, dropping back, going through his progressions, and throwing to imaginary teammates.

"What are you doing?" Payton asked.

"I'm just trying to stay in my routine so my body is still in condition," Brees explained. "I'm going through a game in my mind, visualizing our offense against the Eagles defense. I'm just going through different reads and throws and putting myself in different situations."

Payton looked at Brees incredulously. In 20-plus years of coaching, this was a first.

"Well, I hope we're winning," Payton said.

As the coaches walked away, Payton shook his head. Bye weeks are sacred for NFL players, a time to escape the mental and physical grind of the season and recharge their batteries. It had been a long season so far for Saints players and coaches. They had endured a grueling training camp at Millsaps College in Jackson, Mississippi, a Bataan Death March of practices in the unrelenting heat and humidity. The exhibition season and early regular season schedule had taken the Saints to Denver, Phoenix, Washington, D.C., Charlotte, and overseas to London. The open date before the divisional playoff game against the Philadelphia Eagles was only the second extended break the team had enjoyed in five months. And yet, here was Brees, alone on the practice field, throwing imaginary passes to imaginary receivers on his day off.

"I'm glad he's on my team," Payton said to Marrone.

One of Bill Parcells' coaching edicts was to find coaches and players who loved the game. Payton knew right then he'd found the right pilot to lead his football team, a grinder who shared his passion for the game. Payton, after all, was the guy who regularly slept in his office, someone who could watch film for hours trying to find a crack in the opposing defense's armor. In Brees, he had found his football soulmate.

That 2006 afternoon was one of the first signs that the Payton-Brees marriage would be a special one. Brees and Payton didn't know each other before joining forces in New Orleans. They had no idea if they would mesh or succeed when they cast their lot with each other back in 2006. But they were starting to figure out that, at least in terms of football, they were a perfect pairing.

"There's definitely a synergy between them," said Luke McCown, who served as Brees' backup in New Orleans for three seasons from 2013 to 2015. "There's just a like-mindedness that is uncommon. Drew thinks more like a coach than any player I've ever seen, and Sean sees the game through a quarterback's eyes more than any coach I've ever played for. It's just the perfect storm."

Fifteen years apart in age, the similarities between the two men are striking. Both are highly intelligent and highly competitive. Both own aggressive mindsets and an unwavering confidence in themselves. And both possess what Saints quarterback coach Joe Lombardi refers to as rare mental stamina, the ability to process loads of information over an extended period of time. When most coaches and players reach a peak of mental exhaustion, Brees and Payton are just getting started.

"Personality-wise, I think they're both big-time grinders," former Saints right tackle Zach Strief said. "Sean is legendary for meeting until 2:15 AM, and Drew's the same way. Now he's more regimented in his approach, but Drew's at the facility two and a half hours before you do anything as a team, and he's there four hours after everyone has left. They both kind of have that grinding mentality and I think it gives them a platform in that relationship. Because Drew spends so much time preparing, they're on the same information level, and it allows them to both have a say and it be justified and reasonable. Having those two guys looking at every game the same way has allowed them to grow tighter. They both feel like every week there's this plan that we have built together that's going to win."

In that regard, Marrone compared Payton and Brees to flight directors at a NASA Mission Control Center because of their leadership skills, authoritative knowledge of the offense, and inherent ability to command a room.

"They both know every single thing that's going on," Marrone said. "They can coach, correct, do everything. I mean they can speak to coaches, they can speak to each other, they can speak to the team. They're great communicators and great leaders. It's unique to have both your head coach and quarterback have all of these qualities in common. It's very difficult to replicate that."

It's also difficult to find a pair as competitive as Payton and Brees. Both are famous around the Saints facility for turning everything into a competition. Brees and Payton routinely go at each other during the post-practice quarterback challenges waged daily between the Saints quarterbacks and offensive coaches. They have also taken their competitions outside the building to the golf course and baseball field.

"I've been around a lot of people now, and I don't know if I've ever been around anyone as competitive as Drew Brees," Marrone said. "Sean's the same way. If I said, hey, I bet you I can take this penny and pitch it to this wall and get it closer to you. I'll bet you $5. They're ready to go. I mean at the drop of the hat, anytime, anywhere. They're all in. It's unbelievable."

Yet, as competitive as they both are, Brees and Payton said they have never really experienced a major argument in their 14 years together. If Payton and Brees ever had a major falling-out, Saints coaches and players said they weren't aware of it. Their disagreements have been reserved for play calls and in-game situations.

"There were moments during games where Sean would say, 'All right, Drew, pick it up, body language,'" said former Saints backup quarterback Mark Brunell, recalling communications over his headset. "He would coach Drew and be firm with Drew, and Drew never got pissed off or disrespectful. He understood the pecking order there, who was an authority, who was the head coach and who was the player.

"I was impressed with Drew's ability to handle that and understand that as good as he is, he still needs to be coached. And I was also impressed with Sean understanding, 'Hey, listen, I'm the guy around here. I'm the head coach, and if I feel my star quarterback, my future Hall-of-Fame quarterback needs to get his ass yelled at a little bit, then I'm going to do it.'"

Payton's background as a quarterback allows him to understand Brees on another level than most coaches. And Brees, being the grandson of a former coach and World War II veteran, has an abiding respect for organizational chain of command. He appreciates the coach-player dynamic and is a willing student of the game.

"There's a mutual respect there," Brees said. "Sean having played the quarterback position, there's a perspective there. He knows what it was like to be in those shoes, and he respects that. And he understands that so much of playing the quarterback position is confidence, and so he is constantly doing things to bolster your confidence."

That's not to say Payton won't jump Brees during a game if he makes a mistake. Just like any other player on the roster, Brees will feel Payton's wrath if he throws a silly interception or takes an ill-timed delay of game. But Brees said Payton has never yelled at him as vigorously as his first NFL coach, Marty Schottenheimer, did in San Diego.

"If I miss a throw or make the wrong read, I'll look to the sideline and he'll shake his call sheet and he'll give me that face, like saying, 'What are you doing?!'" Brees joked about Payton. "And listen, plenty of times [during games], the clock's ticking down, and I'm wanting the play and it's not coming in, and he's getting it right back from me. But there's a respect between us."

Over the years, Payton and Brees have brought out the best in one another. In Payton, Brees found a coach who instilled even more confidence in him than he already had, a football savant who saw and coached the game through a quarterback's eyes. In Brees, Payton found a quarterback with the perfect combination of intelligence, athleticism, and talent to operate to his offense at the highest level of efficiency.

Brees was a good player in San Diego. He won 30 of 58 games as a starter and made the Pro Bowl in 2004. But under the tutelage of Payton, he blossomed into one of the game's elite players, a perennial Pro Bowler and MVP candidate.

Too, Payton was a respected coordinator for the Giants and Cowboys. His offenses regularly ranked among the league's top 5 through 15 in total offense and passing yards. But no one was calling him the league's next great offensive mind until he joined forces with Brees.

"He's very intelligent, and from a leadership standpoint and all the other things that go into playing that position, that's something he's very comfortable with, and something he's done successfully for a long time," Payton said. "He's played extremely well for us and been such a staple in everything we've done. He's a big reason why we've achieved what we have so far."

For Saints players and coaches, especially those who have been with other teams, the relationship between Brees and Payton is special. They marvel at their like-minded, almost telepathic connection during games. They've worked together so long they can often finish each other's thoughts during film study. Over the years, their minds seemingly have melded into one.

"That relationship may be as good as I've ever seen," Carmichael said. "They're two similar people. They believe in themselves. They love challenges; that's what drives them. They have an inner drive to win. Both of their brains are always working, you know, looking to attack, attack, attack. They're very similar in that aspect."

In a league where the average playing career lasts 3.5 years, Brees and Payton have operated and produced at an elite level for nearly a decade and a half. While other teams cycle through head coaches and quarterbacks every few seasons, the Saints have enjoyed the same quarterback-coach battery for 14 years and counting. Add in Carmichael, who's been with the duo the entire time, and mainstays Lombardi and receivers coach Curtis Johnson, and you have the most stable situation of any offense in the league. No other team comes close to matching that level of continuity.

"They're joined at the hip," Saints tight ends coach Dan Campbell said. "They've been together so long they know how each other thinks. There is a trust issue. Coach has a ton of trust in Drew. He knows Drew thinks the exact same way he does. He understands the situations of the game. That's why there's been this rapport between these two and this great working relationship. They're unique human beings. He's a phenomenal coach, and he's a phenomenal player. They're the best at what they do. And you just don't find those guys every day. They come around every 20 years maybe. To have both of those guys here at the same time is phenomenal."

Payton and Brees are alike in many ways, but the one overriding personality trait they share is confidence. Each has an unshakeable confidence in himself. Regardless of how dire the situation, they both believe they can overcome the odds.

Former Saints linebacker Scott Fujita once called Brees "annoyingly optimistic." Payton, too, is often at his best in times of crisis. When the Saints are mired in a losing streak, he turns into the team's biggest optimist. He thrives on chaos, and his steely-eyed confidence trickles down to his players and fellow coaches during adverse times.

"There could be a news report that says there's a meteor that's coming for the Saints facility that's going to knock out a 10-mile-wide radius, and everyone in the area is going to be dead, and he would be like, 'This is perfect. This is just what we want,'" Lombardi joked. "He's got a way, regardless of how tough things are going, to remain upbeat."

This confidence manifests itself on game days. Payton and Brees' aggressive mindsets feed off each other. Both are willing to take calculated risks. Their tenure together has been highlighted by countless instances of bold decision-making.

With the Saints trailing Miami 24–3 in their Week 7 game in 2009, Brees convinced Payton to go for the touchdown on fourth-and-goal at the 1-yard line with five seconds left in the second quarter. Brees' sneak for a touchdown helped fuel an epic 46–34 comeback victory.

Payton's famous "Ambush" onside kick call to start the second half of Super Bowl XLIV will be remembered as one of the great play calls in Super Bowl history.

This aggressive mindset doesn't always work out. In the final minutes of the 2018 NFC Championship Game, with the Saints driving for the go-ahead score inside the Rams' red zone, Payton famously told Brees on the sideline that he did not want to settle for a field goal, eschewing conventional wisdom and going for a touchdown instead.

"I don't want to take 55 seconds off the clock and just kick a field goal," Payton said during a timeout at the two-minute warning, with the score tied at 20. "We're going to be smart, but we're going to try to score a touchdown."

Brees enthusiastically agreed. "Yeah, absolutely!" he said. "Absolutely!"

But Brees' uncharacteristic misfire on a routine slant pass to Michael Thomas stopped the clock and allowed the Rams to save a timeout they would later use to help set up a game-tying field goal in a game the Rams eventually won in overtime.

The loss in the 2019 NFC Championship Game was one of the most heartbreaking setbacks of the Payton-Brees era, but the aggressive mindset Payton and Brees displayed down the stretch is what has propelled the duo to such great heights in their careers. More often than not, their aggressiveness is rewarded.

"They are both kind of gunslingers," Strief said. "They're both so aggressive in the way that they see how to attack a defense. And so because of that there is no conservative sounding board off of them. You see them stand on the sidelines during a game and talk, and it takes a lot for one of them to be like, 'No, we better not go for it.' That's both of their mentalities. A lot of the stuff that they want to do makes sense to each other because they're both highly aggressive and both highly confident that that aggression will pay off and not come at a price."

Another similarity: both thrive under pressure. The more intense the moment, the better Payton and Brees perform. Both embrace the spotlight. Neither wilts in the moment.

"They both are extremely bright and [have] extremely strong work ethics," Joe Brady said. "But at the end of the day, they are two competitive guys, and I think that that is what makes them dynamic. When it's game day and the lights are shining, that's when Sean Payton and Drew Brees are at their best."

As alike as they are on the field, Payton and Brees would be the first to tell you they own different personalities and lifestyles off it.

Friends describe Brees as quiet, conservative, and reserved away from the Saints facility. While he can be just as driven and focused in his business and community interests, his laid-back Texas personality is more prevalent away from the football field. He spends most of his free time with his family: wife Brittany and the couple's four children, daughter Rylen and sons Baylen, Bowen, and Callen. A big night out for Brees is a visit to the local trampoline park with the kids.

A devout Christian, Brees was raised in a Protestant church and professes to live by two fundamental Christian maxims: "Love the

Lord with all your heart, mind, and soul. And love your neighbor as yourself." He spends part of his private time each morning reading Bible scripture.

Payton, meanwhile, is much more of a free spirit. Brees describes him as "outgoing and rowdy" away from the office. And while Payton has mellowed considerably from his freewheeling post–Super Bowl days, he still knows how to have a good time when the situation calls for it.

Payton has a touch of OCD symptoms. He is prone to tangents and regularly dips smokeless tobacco. For several years, he religiously wore the same visor on the sideline and chomped sticks of Wrigley's Juicy Fruit gum during games. More than one reporter who has visited him in his office has watched him go down a 20-minute rabbit hole while trying to find a play on his laptop computer.

"Sean will tell the same story to you over and over," said marketing agent Mike Ornstein, a longtime friend of Payton's, who has worked with and for the team in various capacities during Payton's tenure. "Pete [Carmichael] and Joe [Lombardi] do a good job of playing along. They laugh every time like they've never heard it before."

Payton and Brees are different people with different personalities and lifestyles. They express themselves in different ways and go about their business differently. But after 14 years and countless hours of collaboration, they are one and the same when it comes to football.

"I can't think of another great quarterback that has had a relationship with the head coach that goes beyond just a work relationship," said Brunell. "There's a legitimate, sincere, real friendship there, just a deep mutual affection for one another. When you have two guys like that, typically there is one trying to up the other. They're not interested in that. They both realize that I'm not Drew Brees without Sean Payton and I'm not Sean Payton without Drew Brees."

7

The Sean Payton Offense

THE PHILOSOPHICAL ORIGINS OF THE SAINTS OFFENSE CAN BE traced to Bill Walsh, Jon Gruden, and the West Coast system. But, physically, the offense was born during a meeting of the offensive staff on February 6, 2006.

On the day after Super Bowl XL, the recently hired Payton brought a copy of the Cowboys playbook he used the previous three years in Dallas and a copy of the Giants playbook he used in New York and told offensive assistant coach Pete Carmichael to make 10 copies of each. The books were dispersed to each coach at the table, and the coaches opened to Page 1 and went to work. Plays were either kept or discarded, depending upon Payton's plan.

The playbook was still being built a month later when Brees was signed in free agency. Payton asked Carmichael, who worked with Brees the previous two seasons in San Diego, to integrate some of Brees' favorite plays into the offense.

"Sean had a vision of where he wanted this offense to start, and we pulled plays from each playbook," Carmichael said of the Giants and Cowboys. "Then, when we signed Drew, Sean wanted to know some of the concepts and plays that he really loved, and we incorporated those into the offense. Then, when Drew got here, we listened to his input and that's how the playbook progressed."

Most modern NFL passing offenses can be traced to one of two classic systems—Walsh's West Coast offense or the Coryell system originated by Don Coryell, who coached at San Diego State in the 1960s and later with the San Diego Chargers. Traditionally, the West Coast system featured a horizontal passing attack, relying primarily on short, timing-based passes to the backs, tight ends, and receivers. The Coryell offense was more of a downfield passing game, attacking with deep and intermediate throws to the receivers.

Initially, Payton incorporated different parts of each system into his offense. Most of the passing concepts come from the West Coast system he learned during his tenure with Gruden in Philadelphia. A lot of the Saints' initial running game was adopted from Parcells' offense in Dallas. The pass protections came from the Giants and Cowboys.

Many differences exist between the Walsh and Coryell systems, but the most obvious is terminology. Walsh used code words to identify plays and numbers for protections. Coryell used numbers for plays and words for protections.

Just about every college and NFL team uses a passing tree numbered 1 to 9 to identify basic individual pass patterns. The different pass routes in the Coryell system are assigned digits 1 through 9.

When Brees was in San Diego, for example, one of Chargers quarterback Doug Flutie's favorite plays was 678, which featured a dig route (No. 6) by the X receiver or split end, a corner route (No. 7) by the tight end, and a post route (No. 8) by the Z receiver or flanker. When the Saints added the play to their offense, they simply called it "Flutie."

Payton compared the difference between the West Coast and Coryell systems to the difference between using a Mac operating system and Windows.

"All systems can give you the same type of plays," Payton told ESPN.com in 2018. "It's just, 'How is it communicated? Are we naming the formation? Are we numbering the protection and then naming the route?' It varies—and all are effective. All of us, though, are searching to streamline that constantly, so you find yourself with words that you're implementing to be one syllable—you know, 'wasp'—or those terms that come out of your mouth cleanly and quickly. In your hurry-up or no-huddle [offense], you might just say a word, and then everyone's understanding, 'It's this play.'"

When tagging the plays, the staff tries to employ some logic or familiarity to make them easier to learn. Some are references to players. One of receiver Robert Meachem's key plays during his time was called "Volunteer," the nickname of his alma mater, the University of Tennessee. One of the Saints' key plays to receiver Michael Thomas is tagged Buckeye. Another Saints play is called Shark because it features four routes: a skinny post, a hook, an alley read, and a cross.

"S.H.A.R.C." Lombardi said. "It's easy to learn that way. You try to come up with something that makes it learnable or relatable."

Regardless of the terminology, the basic philosophy of Payton's offense is to attack the defense on all three levels—deep, intermediate, and short—with all five skill position players on every play. The backs, both halfbacks and fullbacks, are incorporated into the passing attack and are targeted as often as the receivers and tight ends.

Where the Saints offense differs from most West Coast attacks is in their downfield attacking philosophy. Payton calls them "shot plays," and he tries to set up and call a handful of them a game to keep defenses honest. That's why former Indianapolis Colts defensive coordinator Larry Coyer described the Saints offense before Super Bowl XLIV as "a mix between dinkin' it and lettin' 'er go." It's also why the Saints almost always have a speed receiver like Devery Henderson, Robert Meachem, or Ted Ginn Jr. on the roster.

"Sean has a very aggressive approach," said Marrone, who was the offensive coordinator on Payton's original staff. "When people hear West Coast they think horizontal passing, and you really don't see that in the offense. Sean is always looking to attack you deep."

Because Brees throws so often to spots in anticipation of where his pass-catchers are going to break, the Saints receivers, backs, and tight ends must be good at reading defenses—especially on option routes, which are a staple of the Saints offense.

More than perhaps any team in the NFL, the Saints obsess over the details of their pass routes. Every factor is considered down to the minutest details: splits; alignment; personnel on each route.

The routes are synchronized to the quarterback's drop. Three-step drops are married to quick pass routes, five-step drops to intermediate routes, and seven-step drops for deep passes. Ideally, the receiver will be breaking open at the same time the quarterback plants the last step of his drop.

Payton has a phrase for this sophisticated choreography: "Painting the picture for the quarterback."

"Quarterback is a funny position," Payton said. "The other 10 guys on offense need to paint the picture for this player, be it the receivers, the protection, the back. And when they're able to do that, you can see him function very well."

Few NFL offenses are more reliant on the synchronization of this timing than the Saints. Brees' hallmark accuracy and innate anticipation skills allow him to fit balls into tighter windows than most quarterbacks who have ever played the game. The Saints' sophisticated use of receiver splits and alignment creates leverage against opposing coverage schemes.

"This whole offense is about precision, timing, execution," said Rich Gannon, a former NFL MVP quarterback who now serves as an NFL analyst on CBS.

The Saints do such a good job of exploiting defensive weaknesses with their scheme that they don't necessarily need a fleet of elite players at the receiver positions. Receivers still need to be athletic enough to get open, but intelligence, discipline, and reliability are valued almost as much as athleticism. That's why undrafted players like Lance Moore, Willie Snead, and Austin Carr have been able to carve out productive careers in New Orleans.

"It's all about spacing," Lombardi said. "There's this timing to how plays develop for a quarterback. That's why for so long we had super smart, good route-running receivers, but not necessarily guys that you could just put outside the numbers and say, 'Go win a 1-on-1 matchup.'"

Because Brees has never had a particularly powerful passing arm, he relies on timing and anticipation to make his throws. The Saints' entire passing attack is built around this facet of Brees' game. It's why every detail of the offense—the splits, alignments, and timing of the routes—is fine-tuned to the smallest detail.

When Brees leaves, Payton will morph the offense and tailor the playbook around the strengths of the next quarterback. If it's Taysom Hill, for example, the offense will feature more read-option runs and downfield passing.

"Everything we do offensively is predicated by who's in the building," Payton said. "You're looking for certain pieces. When we drafted Reggie [Bush] and had Deuce [McAllister] we had certain packages that took advantage of those guys. It all goes back to, what do these guys do well, and it's up to us to have them try to do those things."

This customization is a key ingredient in the Saints' success. When new receivers come to the Saints, Payton will have them run every route in the route tree with the quarterbacks during practice to identify their strengths and weaknesses. The offensive staff then marries the route concepts to the specific receiver when compiling the game plan for a given game. This is also true of the backs and tight ends.

"Sean will always say, 'Hey, this route is not for everybody,'" Carmichael said. "He'll figure out that some guys can run this specific route and then other guys have other routes that they can run. He puts guys in spots that are doing things that they can do well.

"Sean is very specific about personnel. What kind of receiver do we need? Those inside routes that Lance Moore, Marques Colston, and Michael Thomas run, those inside routes aren't for everybody. The guy has to a feel for or a knack for finding the void or running a route off a certain defender."

Meachem was Exhibit A in this case study of the Saints' successful customization. The 6′2″, 214-pound Meachem came out of the University of Tennessee as a highly coveted speedster, but when the Saints got him on the field they quickly learned he lacked the natural hip flexion to make quick cuts and change directions. When he ran routes that required him to break down and change directions quickly—hooks, comebacks, outs—he was easy for NFL defensive backs to cover. So during his time in New Orleans, the Saints only ran him on routes that didn't require those kinds of movements: posts, seams, and corners.

Meachem thrived as a complementary piece in the Saints system. During his first four years, he averaged 35 catches and six touchdowns a season and posted a healthy average of 16 yards per catch. In March 2012, the San Diego Chargers signed him to a four-year, $25.5 million contract and made him their No. 1 receiver. But the Chargers lacked the Saints' vision, and the marriage proved to be a disaster. Meachem failed to land a starting job. He caught only

14 passes for 207 yards and two touchdowns and was released a year later.

The Saints re-signed Meachem and plugged him back into their system. He enjoyed two more productive years with the Saints before retiring after the 2014 season.

"San Diego thought Robert Meachem was terrible, and they threw him out after a year," Lombardi said. "Well, Robert did some things very, very well. He had speed, and he was strong, and he was excellent at tracking a ball downfield. He was not a great transition guy, breaking down and changing directions. For him, the route always needed to be a 200-yard dash or rounding second to third, where he can kind of make circular cuts. The minute he had to break down he'd get covered. So we just said, let's never have him do the things that he's not good at. It's all about moving the chess pieces around."

The Saints have stayed true to this maxim over the course of the Payton-Brees era. Over the years, the Saints offense has strayed from its West Coast roots and morphed into its own unique system, but it will always play to the strengths of the players on the roster in any given season.

When the Saints had star running backs McAllister and Bush in 2006, the offense morphed into a more run-based attack. When they won the Super Bowl in 2009, the offensive plan featured the team's quartet of receivers: Colston, Meachem, Moore, and Devery Henderson. When Jimmy Graham came on board, game plans were highlighted by plays to the tight end. In recent years, the staff added a read-option run package to the playbook to take advantage of quarterback Taysom Hill's skill set.

"Coach [Payton] and Pete [Carmichael] and Joe Lombardi and the rest of that offensive staff put so much time and attention into every little detail," Hill said. "What makes those guys special is they never ask anybody on our team to do something that they can't be successful at."

When players leave the Saints, the plays are not discarded entirely. The plays remain in the playbook. But the game plan changes year to year, according to the available offensive personnel.

"When you watch the Saints, you're not seeing necessarily seeing the old-school, West Coast–type offense," said former Saints offensive assistant Joe Brady, who is now the offensive coordinator for the Carolina Panthers. "You're seeing more conventional plays. You're going to see a little bit of everything in terms of a Sean Payton's vision for an offense molded with what you know Drew and players on that year's particular team are good at.

"When you're game-planning and you're watching Coach Payton, Pete [Carmichael], and Joe [Lombardi] put together these plays, it's fascinating how they find ways to put their players into positions to be successful," Brady said. "They know this is what this guy does best, let's get him on this spot on this play. It sounds simple but it's really difficult to do at the level they do it at."

Of course, none of this Xs and Os wizardry works if you don't have time to execute it. Brees and the receiving corps can be world-beaters at their respective crafts, but if the opposing defensive line is dominating the Saints offensive line, none of Payton's offensive mastery will matter.

Consequently, the Saints have always fielded strong offensive lines in the Payton-Brees era. Payton learned the importance of having a dominant offensive line from Parcells, and the Saints have invested heavily in this area throughout his tenure. Guard Andrus Peat, tackle Ryan Ramczyzk, and center Cesar Ruiz were first-round draft picks. Center Erik McCoy was a second-round pick. Pro Bowl left tackle Terron Armstead was selected in the third round. The Saints traded for center Max Unger in 2015 and made guard Larry Warford a priority signing in the 2017 free agency period.

"[Payton] totally understands the importance of the offensive line, the front office understands it, Mickey [Loomis] understands it," Strief said. "And I think a huge part of it, too, is you want to make Drew's career go as long as you can and the single best way to do that is to have him not get abused every week."

But everything starts with Brees. It all works because of his rare ability to process the information overload, adapt seamlessly to the changing personnel, and execute flawlessly during the heat of battle on game days.

"The system is great because he's so great; it's because of Drew," Lombardi said. "There's a lot of good stuff we do, but it's all predicated on him. Just like we try to put this receiver in this spot and that spot. Drew can do this, so let's do it."

What started out as a pure West Coast offense has become its own distinct entity in the Payton-Brees era. The offense has morphed and expanded and changed so often over the years and become so customized to Brees' strengths, it's become its own unique system.

When Lombardi left New Orleans to become the offensive coordinator of the Detroit Lions from 2014 to 2015, he tried to take some of the concepts and philosophy with him. But the system he ran there looked and operated nothing like what Brees and Payton ran in New Orleans.

"It's really Sean Payton's offense now," Mark Brunell said. "If you look at his DNA and the influences he's had and the people that he's been around, it's very much West Coast, but it's really evolved, and Sean has put his own stamp on it. It's just years of Sean just kind of coming up with his own system and how he wanted to do things, how he wanted to name things.

"And I think also, too, that Sean and the offense benefit from having a quarterback that's always going to make things right. That's why I would call it the Sean Payton offense with Drew Brees. That's what it has become."

8

The Winchester Mystery House

Late in the 2018 season, Drew Brees wanted to have a little fun. So he asked the offensive coaching staff to dig up a call sheet from Payton's first season. They were stunned at how much had changed in 13 seasons.

The 2006 play calls were simple, many with just three to five words as opposed to the lengthy, almost comical 10- and 12-word calls Brees uses today. And the call sheet itself looked rudimentary, nothing like the massive document Payton has employed in recent seasons.

"Everything was so basic," Brees said.

Lombardi joked that the Saints "couldn't score a point" with the 2006 offense in today's NFL.

The Saints offense today, Brees said, is "light years" from where it was when he and Payton started. He compared the 2006 offense to elementary school. The offense they run now, he said, "is like freakin' Calculus 303." Lombardi took it even further: "We're at PhD level with this quarterback."

How did it get here? Many factors played a role in the evolutionary process, but the rare continuity the Saints have enjoyed during the Payton-Brees era is the main reason they have advanced their offense from freshman orientation to graduate level sophistication. The Saints have had the same quarterback with the same head coach and the offensive coordinator in the same offensive system for 15 consecutive years. And in Carmichael, Lombardi, and receivers coach Curtis Johnson, they have three longtime assistants who know every detail of the system and how it's supposed to work. It's a unique situation. Even Tom Brady, who quarterbacked the New England Patriots for 20 years, went through three different offensive coordinators during his tenure.

In addition to the collective experience and familiarity, the group shares a high level of football IQ, an almost nerdy passion for Xs-and-Os play design. The continuity and expertise afford the Saints a level of experience and knowledge unmatched by any other offensive staff in the NFL.

"It's never gotten stale between Sean and Drew and the other coaches on staff," Lombardi said. "There's always this drive. 'Hey, we can't just keep doing what we've done. How do we improve and evolve?' And so, there's been this consistency combined with the creativity."

The evolution of the offense is partly born from necessity, the natural order of competitive sports taking its course. As defenses have evolved across the NFL, the Saints have needed to adapt their scheme to try to stay ahead of the competition.

"There's a lot of research that goes into it," Lombardi said. "We spend a lot of time in the offseason studying other teams, looking at our offense and seeing how defenses have evolved to play us. We've run this play and it's been so successful for us, teams are starting to see this formation and checking to certain defenses to counter-punch. So we then say, 'Okay, they are going to play this play like that, what's another play that we can use to attack the defense?' It's a constant process."

This creative mindset has kept the Saints offense ahead of opposing defenses and allowed the team to rank among the top 10 in yards gained for all 14 seasons of the Payton-Brees era. It's also prevented it from going stale the way it did on Mike Martz in St. Louis and Mike McCarthy in Green Bay.

"They always want to improve, they always want to look to see how they can get better," Marrone said. "They always want to grow, so it's never, hey, this is what we do, and we're going to do it. It's, hey, this is what we can do and how can we get better? The mindset is always progressing, of wanting more, give me more so I can be more productive. There's really no limit to where we want to go."

And where the Saints offense has gone over the course of 14 seasons is to the extreme edge of offensive football. Today, the Saints run one of the most complicated and sophisticated offenses in the NFL. The play calls are among the longest in the NFL, some containing as many as 17 words. The playbook binder is now four-to-five inches thick. And the call sheet Payton takes into a given game looks like a Cheesecake Factory menu with literally hundreds of plays.

"We started with our offense, and it's just grown and grown," Carmichael said. "There's been tweaks and some stuff eliminated and added, but the majority of the stuff we were doing in '06 still exists but it's just gotten bigger because you're spending time in the offseason seeing what other teams are doing. Oh, man, what a great idea. That fits our personnel. Let's work on it in the offseason and see how we like it."

McCown estimated that Brees and Payton probably add 30 to 35 plays to the playbook throughout a given season. But most alterations involve subtle changes to the core concepts within the

Saints' established menu. New plays have to fit within the scheme of the offense for players to digest and understand them easily.

"A lot of times you have video looks where you can show them, 'See, take a peek at this,'" Payton said. "And you show them a picture: 'Picture if we do [that].' And so we try not to come up with a lot of new inventions. Might be formation, might be personnel grouping, but I think there's a balance there of things that they know well."

More new plays are sometimes added when new players are signed to the roster. For example, the Saints incorporated a read-option run package in the offense when Taysom Hill came on board in 2017. When Mark Ingram was drafted in 2011, the Saints started to run more outside zone run plays. These new plays might drop out of the playbook once the player moves on, but they stay in the offense. So the inventory just continues to build.

"Sean looks at it and says, 'What fits our personnel best?'" Carmichael said. "Is it the power schemes? Is it the zone schemes, and is it inside or outside zone? We've always had those kinds of concepts in our offense, but it's more like what are we making our focus on this year based on our personnel and then we incorporate them into the offense.

"I can remember the night before the [2006] draft we found out we were going to end up with Reggie Bush, and the next day there was 10 new formations on everybody's desk."

Where the Saints offense has taken on a life of its own, though, is in pre-snap adjustments they've added to counter opposing defenses. The Saints use a series of code words they call tags to communicate these adjustments on each play. Many of the plays also have run-pass options, meaning two plays are actually called in the huddle, giving Brees the option to change the play according to the defensive look he sees at the line of scrimmage.

"The offense has become so complex because the answer isn't always so easy as, well, check to this run," Strief said. "Instead, it's we need to have a mechanism now to bring this receiver down, and what does Drew do to motion him down? He's going to cover the force, and it's going to change this scheme over here, so do we have to signal it? Do we have to call it something? Can Drew handle it? Do the other guys even have to even know about it? And then once you have that mechanism, it's now a tool in the offense and it can be used whenever. All those adjustments and these little solutions that have been found over the years do certain things and they add up."

As the Saints have incorporated these nuances into the system, the in-huddle play calls have grown lengthier and lengthier over the years.

Just a few examples:

Full Left Twin Y Orbit Q8 Kill Toss 39 Michael

Bunch Right Tare Slash 37 Weak F Kill Q8 Solid Z Speed Smash

Gun Flex Right Stack 394 Dragon Smoke Kill Turbo Sucker Right

The code words indicate different things to the offense.

Full Left Twin Y is the formation, an alignment with two tight ends (the "Ys") on the left side.

Orbit is a pre-snap motion.

Dragon Smoke designates a route concept by the receivers.

The numbers—39, 37, 394—are pass protections, with the 3 signifying a three-step drop by the quarterback.

In general, the longer the play call, the more information Brees is communicating to the rest of the offensive players.

"[Brees] can call a little bit lengthier play call in the huddle, but it's letting everybody else know what to do," Payton said. "It takes some of the pressure off the other guys but puts a little bit on Drew's plate. That's why our vocabulary is expanded on in-the-huddle calls."

Former Saints quarterback Garrett Grayson, the team's third-round pick in 2015, admitted that he struggled to master the verbose calls and communicate them with authority in the huddle during his first few years in New Orleans.

When Teddy Bridgewater took over the offense after Brees was injured in 2019, the play calls weren't as long. And they wouldn't be as involved if Hill took over the offense, either.

"It's a coaching maxim and it's probably a good one: Keep it simple," Lombardi said. "We don't do that here."

Over the years, the challenge for the Saints has come in trying to keep the offense at the PhD level for Brees while still making it work for the other players, who don't have the same mastery of the system. It's one of the reasons new players, especially rookies, struggle to make an impact early in their Saints careers. The learning process can be formidable and, in some cases, confounding.

"When you're building the playbook, everything makes sense and there's a logic to the terminology," Carmichael said. "These formations are all called this for a reason. Then, all of a sudden, you make a tweak the week you're playing the 49ers, and we call it '49er Right.' Well, that formation just stays in the playbook, and sometimes it's a little bit more of a challenge for a new player coming in, saying, 'That makes sense. All these terms start with [the letter] T if you're in 13 personnel. Wait, 49er Right? Where did that come from?' Giant Panther, what's that?' Well, they've stayed in the playbook because they work. And that could be a challenge for new players."

The Saints offense has morphed and evolved so much over the years, Lombardi jokingly compares it to the Winchester Mystery House, the infamous California mansion with architectural oddities such as doors and stairs that go nowhere, windows overlooking other rooms, and stairs with uneven risers.

"One of the things about an offense that has evolved like ours is there are a lot of hallways that lead to nowhere," Lombardi said. "We've just become so much more complex."

The danger with becoming so complex is a potential breakdown in efficiency. More offense doesn't necessarily translate to better, more efficient offense. Information overload can often paralyze players and lead to mental errors. The extra bells and whistles might look great on the whiteboard, but they can prove counterproductive if they cause pass-catchers' heads to swim in the lineup.

The reason this hasn't happened in New Orleans is largely because of Brees. In addition to being one of the smartest quarterbacks in the NFL, someone capable of processing the myriad nuances added to the offensive package, he's also someone who has an almost insatiable desire to learn, who can't get enough of the process. Former Saints offensive tackle Jon Stinchcomb refers to Brees as "the supercomputer" because of his staggering ability to process information and then transfer it to the playing field.

The analogy Payton uses to describe Brees is that he's the guy who, when buying a new car, always gets the deluxe model with the bells and whistles on the dashboard. Where he differs from most people is "he actually learns what each button does and then masters how to use it."

"It's almost to a fault with him," Payton said. "He's going to know the line calls and the assignment of everyone on offense. If you're not careful, he's got the filet on the grill at Emeril's but he's taking a peek at the banana cream pie. You're like whoa, whoa, whoa. But we have a lot of volume here because we can put a lot on Drew, and he's able to handle it."

The Brees Supercomputer gives the Saints the ability to construct offensive game plans that seem brand-new to their opponent each week but are still easily digestible for their offensive players. The plays stay the same, but the Saints make them look different by tinkering with the alignments or changing the formation. Along with varying their formations and alignments, the Saints also get creative with the routes themselves—both the combinations and the players who run them.

The idea is to keep defenses guessing. And the staff leans heavily on Brees to communicate these nuances to the other 10 offensive players before the snap and get the Saints in and out of the right play at the line of scrimmage.

"We have a base offense, and then we evolve, and build off of that offense," Brees said. "We are very game-plan oriented, so each and every week, there are very few calls replicated from the week before, and if they are, it's new shifts, motions, formations, personnel groups potentially."

These modifications create a heavy burden for the Saints offensive personnel during game-week preparation. It's one of the reasons the Saints personnel department places such a heavy emphasis on football IQ and intelligence in their scouting reports on prospective offensive skill-position players.

"We change our formations up quite a bit, just to try to disguise looks, whether it's a shift or a motion to make it look different even though it's the same to us," Carmichael said.

Former Saints quarterback Luke McCown played for four teams in the nine seasons before he joined the Saints in 2013. He said he's never seen anything like the offensive complexity the Saints employed on weekly basis under Payton and Brees.

"It's not like they call the same plays every week," McCown said. "Sean comes up with a whole new game plan every week for that particular defense and those schemes that he's seeing. And then for the execution to work out the way it does on Drew's end is remarkable. I played for a bunch of different teams and offenses, and I'd never seen that before. It's remarkable."

Strief estimated the Saints add six to eight new tag concepts each season. Multiply that by the 14 years Brees and Payton have been together in New Orleans, and it's easy to see why the Saints offense is a massive learning challenge for players, especially newcomers to the system.

"It can get complicated very, very quickly, and that is the evolution of the offense, because all of those answers, all of those problems are still in the offense," Strief said. "[Former Saints receiver] Lance Moore talks all the time about how this offense is so different than anywhere else. And there's just so much stuff. They're not in the playbook, but they're in the offense because those two guys [Brees and Payton] remember that. Once it's in, it's in. Those two guys have been building the same offense for now [14] years, and that has made this very complicated for a lot of guys."

This offensive evolution wasn't intentional and it certainly didn't happen overnight. The process is 14 years in development. As Brees grew more familiar with Payton's scheme during his early years in the system, the playbook gradually expanded. His learning capacity staggered the Saints offensive staff. The more the coaches gave him, the more he ate it up. The staff quickly started to realize Brees was a different animal than anyone they had encountered before. His brain was seemingly incapable of being overloaded. And so they kept adding more to the playbook until they came up with the sprawling amalgamation they have today.

"There's a lot of people in the NFL that believe less is more, and that's okay—that works, too," Campbell said. "But not when you've got a quarterback like ours. The candy shop is open with him. More is more with him."

DOME-INATION:
2008 Green Bay Packers

While the New Orleans Saints led the NFL in total offense and advanced to the NFC Championship Game in the first season of the Payton-Brees era, the offense didn't fully come into its own until Year Three. By 2008, Drew Brees had full command of the offense and Sean Payton had added a fleet of playmakers to the attack: Reggie Bush, Marques Colston, Robert Meachem, Lance Moore, Pierre Thomas, and Jeremy Shockey. And while the 8–8 record didn't reflect it, the Saints were building into an offensive machine. That year, the Saints led the NFL in total yards (6,571) and scoring (463 points), the first time in franchise history they'd led the league in both categories in the same season. And Brees became just the second quarterback in NFL history to pass for more than 5,000 yards in a season. He fell just 15 yards shy of Dan Marino's then-NFL record of 5,084 yards and was named the NFL Offensive Player of the Year, the first Saints player to ever win the award.

The first real glimpse of the Payton-Brees juggernaut came on November 24, 2008. In a Monday night game against the Green Bay Packers, the Saints delivered a 51–29 beatdown before a national television audience.

The Packers were coming off a 13–3 season in Mike McCarthy's third year as head coach. They entered the game on the heels of a 37–3 rout of the Chicago Bears eight days earlier. And they were helpless against the Saints.

After going three-and-out on their opening drive, the Saints didn't punt again until the final 3:45 of the game. They scored on eight of their next nine drives. Brees completed 20 of 26 passes for 323 yards and four touchdowns. His passer rating of 157.5 established a career best and was the second-highest rating ever recorded against the Packers in their illustrious history.

"They just beat us, can't make any excuses, what happened here or there, they came out and beat us like we've never been beat," Packers defensive tackle Ryan Pickett said afterward.

Brees lit up a Packers pass defense that was ranked third in the NFL and had returned six interceptions for touchdowns in the previous 10 games.

"We got our [expletive] whupped tonight," Packers cornerback Charles Woodson said. "Thoroughly. In front of the whole country."

It was the first major offensive outburst of the Payton-Brees era. The 51 points tied a Saints franchise record and were more than the Packers had allowed in the previous three games combined. In fact, they were the most allowed by the Packers in nearly 22 years. The game also marked the first time a Saints quarterback had ever recorded a passer rating of 150 or higher in a game. If there was a coming-out party for the Payton-Brees Saints offense, this was it.

"We had gotten some pieces to the puzzle that you felt like, 'Okay, we're poised to make a run,'" Brees said of the 2008 season. "It was our third-year comfort level in the offense. We had added some difference-makers to the offense. We had the four horsemen [receivers Colston, Henderson, Meachem, and Moore], and we were rolling."

9

Blitzing the Defense

THE VOLUME OF THE SAINTS OFFENSE GIVES BREES AND PAYTON myriad options to work their magic on game days. But what has made the Saints attack so unstoppable over the years is its multiplicity and the aggressive philosophy behind it. And that starts with Payton, whose offensive approach is to "blitz the defense" with an array of formations, alignments, and personnel groupings. He also takes advantage of quick counts, no-huddle and hurry-up tactics—anything he can to gain an edge over the enemy. The idea is to apply pressure on the defenders and stress the opposing defensive coordinator as much as possible from play to play.

From a defensive perspective, it's nearly impossible to keep up with and prepare for everything the Saints throw at opponents. It's not uncommon to see the Saints line up in 30 formations or personnel groupings before halftime. The Saints have used as many as 60 different formations and personnel groupings in a game before. They used 44 in their game against the Dallas Cowboys in 2019.

"They give you a lot to get ready for," New England Patriots coach Bill Belichick said before playing the Saints in 2009, a game the

Saints would eventually win 38–17. "If we took the other 15 teams we play and put all the formations and personnel groups together, it would probably be about the same as the Saints. It's that many. Over the course of 70 plays, there are hardly any repeat formations in the game. Sometimes you end up making mistakes, blowing a timeout or something like that, and that's an issue, too. And the Saints really try to stress you on that, probably as much as any team I can remember. It's hard."

The Saints leave no stone unturned in their quest to blitz the defense. During timeouts, they keep their five perimeter players on the sideline so opposing coordinators have less time to match their personnel. They even use a unique verbal system to employ their personnel groups for each play to expedite the process.

The Saints create additional stress and confusion for opposing defenses by breaking the huddle quickly before each play, preferably at or before the 19-second mark on the play clock. They often huddle four yards behind the line of scrimmage, one yard closer than most teams, to save time getting to the line of scrimmage.

"We really harp on the tempo of in and out and up and down and on and off in trying to apply pressure offensively," Payton said.

And the Saints don't slow down once they reach the line. Brees uses a variety of pre-snap motions and movements to keep defenses on their heels. And if catches the opponent in the midst of aligning or calling out the play, he'll audible to a quick count and snap the ball.

"When you shift and move, really that's your way as an offense of blitzing the defense," Brees said. "You make them have to adjust quickly, make decisions quickly. At times, defenses will have checks to certain formations or certain looks, whatever it might be, depending on the personnel you have on the field or the formation you're in. So when you're able to switch guys up and move them around a lot, all of a sudden it puts the defense in a tough spot where maybe they blow a coverage or a guy pops wide open, and you get a matchup that favors you."

Further, the ball comes out quickly in the Saints system. Brees' ability to read defenses and process information allows him to make quick decisions in the pocket. He annually ranks among the NFL leaders in time-to-throw statistics, regularly averaging about 2.5 seconds from the time of the snap until the time he gets rid of the ball.

"Everything they do offensively is at a breakneck pace," former Seattle Seahawks head coach and longtime NFL assistant coach Jim Mora Jr. said. "The way they get on and off the field in substitution. The way Drew Brees gets into the huddle, calls the play, and gets to the line of scrimmage. The way they shift. The way they go in motion. And it puts tremendous stress on, not only the defensive coordinator to get a call in, but on the defensive personnel to react."

Before Super Bowl XLIV, then–Indianapolis Colts defensive coordinator Larry Coyer described the Saints as "the masters of hiding personnel groups. That's where their genius lies. They move them around all the time. It's problematic because they do it so quickly and they do it every play. You have to weather the storm, really."

Though the Saints often repeat some of the same plays, they'll run them from different alignments with different players to confuse defenses and keep them from identifying what they're looking at.

"They window dress [the offense] a thousand different ways" to create confusion in the defense, Ravens Coach John Harbaugh said.

The Saints pull off these elaborate disguises because of the versatile way they employ their perimeter players. Most of their skill-position players can and will play more than one position. The receivers can play split end, flanker, or slot. Tight ends can play fullback. Running backs align at wide receiver. Fullbacks play tight end.

The players come and go, but the packages carry over year to year. The Pony package, featuring two running backs, was used extensively during the early years of the Payton-Brees era, when Reggie Bush and Deuce McAllister were in their primes. It was highlighted again when Mark Ingram and Alvin Kamara teamed up in the same backfield for the 2017 and 2018 seasons.

"You've got to have versatile players to do that," Brees said. "When you have that type of versatility, these are things that defenses have to stress about. How are we defending this guy or that guy? They're the ones who have to react to us."

This hybridization creates more prep work for the Saints players, but it has several benefits for the Saints. First and foremost, it allows the offense to be malleable from play to play and create confusion for the defense, depending on how they choose to defend the Saints. Second, it helps the offense withstand injuries that might decimate other clubs. And third, it forces opposing teams to prepare for myriad possibilities, all the while knowing that only so many of them will be used during a game and there will likely be new ones they haven't seen before.

"It really adds into the preparation part of it, because you have to, although they won't use all those packages in a game, you certainly have to have calls ready in preparation for it," Atlanta Falcons coach Dan Quinn said. "They've got a big playbook, and when you go through the years and different matchups in different ways they feature the guys, you have to have a bunch of calls ready."

No player better exemplifies this multiplicity than Taysom Hill, the backup quarterback Payton has turned into a star since signing him as an undrafted free agent in 2017. Hill is a quarterback by trade, but he has become a Swiss Army knife in New Orleans thanks to Payton's creative mind. In the 2019 season, Hill lined up at five different positions: wide receiver (116 plays), tight end (85), quarterback (41), H-back (17), and fullback (5). His versatility creates a guessing game for defensive coordinators every time he breaks the huddle. Do coordinators defend him with an extra linebacker to try to stop the run? Or do they deploy a safety to cover him as a tight end or receiver?

One of Payton's favorite ways to use Hill is in three-tight-end sets with Jared Cook and Josh Hill, a grouping the Saints employed 22 times in 2019. They used a similar personnel package in 2010 with Jeremy Shockey, Jimmy Graham, and David Thomas. The three-tight-end sets put defenses in a quandary because the Saints can either run or pass out of the package depending on how the opponent elects to defend it. If the defensive coordinator plays more defensive backs to guard against the pass, then the Saints can quickly motion into a heavy formation with both tight ends in-line and run the powerful Hill at the undersized unit. If the defense goes heavy with extra linebackers, then the Saints can use motions to get the fleet Cook or Hill matched up against a slower linebacker in space.

"They can get into a three-wide [receiver] package with all tight ends in there because they've got some good, [athletic] tight ends," former Ravens defensive coordinator Greg Mattison said. "What they do by doing that is it forces you sometimes on defense to stay more basic in what you're calling. You can't load up a run defense when you say [their] tendency is [running the ball], because they could spread you all out, and now you've got a disadvantage."

Former Buffalo Bills head coach and longtime NFL defensive coordinator Rex Ryan said the Saints' multiplicity forced him to drastically reduce his play call sheet during games when he coached against them.

"We realize it puts defenses on their heels," Lombardi said.

Once teams go simple, the Saints are masters of taking advantage of defensive tendencies and dictating matchups to the opponent by employing certain personnel packages. To that end, the Saints use every active skill-position player available each game.

"We spend a lot of time in our meetings talking about personnel groupings, not only talking about [receiver] splits and areas of the field they're going to get to but as we're going through each play, we discuss who exactly will be running those plays," Carmichael said. "We do a great job of making sure that the right 11 players are on the field for each play. That is one of the most unique things we do. After all this time, we have a feel for each play and what kind of bodies and characteristics are needed to run it effectively."

For example, Lombardi said most defensive coordinators will call certain plays with specific personnel groupings to counter an offense when it uses 11 personnel, NFL terminology for a popular personnel grouping featuring three wide receivers, one tight end, and one running back. But against the Saints, the 11 personnel grouping is more complicated than most teams.

"With us, it's 11 [personnel] but with these receivers and this tight end and there's three different forms for that," Lombardi said. "And 21 [personnel], well, it's different with Alvin Kamara and Latavius Murray. There's so many different personnel variations, they [the opponent] don't have time to let the play-caller know who's on the field and they just have to cut down their calls. They're not going to chase us around the field and try to match our personnel."

And when defenses go simple against a quarterback as talented and experienced as Brees, he often has a field day. Therein lies the conundrum.

"They force you to simplify," Mora said. "When you get simple, Drew Brees knows where you're going to be, and he knows where to go with the ball."

If a defense has a weakness, Payton and Brees will find it and attack it, using players and positions like chess pieces to force the hand of the defense and create mismatches.

A 2010 game against the Los Angeles Rams exemplified the Saints' blitz-the-defense strategy. From the opening snap, the Saints had the Rams on their heels with an aggressive, up-tempo attack. The Saints used a different personnel grouping on their first six plays. They alternated backs and receivers on almost every down. By the eighth snap of their opening 13-play drive, all 12 skill-position players had been on the field for at least one play. The rundown of running backs on those eight plays: Reggie Bush, Pierre Thomas, no back, Chris Ivory, Bush and Thomas, Thomas, Bush and Ivory.

"We moved in and out of a lot of different personnel early on—three tight ends, one tight end, three running backs, no running backs," Payton said later. "The personnel was constantly changing early to create indecision and to slow down any type of plan they might have."

While the plan was impressive, the execution was even more remarkable. There were no dropped passes or mental errors. Despite the fast pace and hectic substitutions, the Saints committed only one penalty on the first two series.

The Saints averaged six yards a play and compiled 12- and 13-play touchdown drives to start the game. The Rams saw that three-tight-end package Mattison talked about on seven of their first 21 plays. Brees completed 13 of 15 passes in the first quarter for 97 yards and two touchdowns. Eight of his completions were to backs and tight ends. Before the Rams could catch their breath and make their defensive adjustments, the Saints led 14–0 and were on their way to an easy 31–13 victory.

"I think you spend so much time trying to figure out what the exact personnel group is in the game and what you want to be [in defensively to defend it], and then you are late getting in the play call," said Tennessee Titans coach Mike Vrabel, a former star linebacker for the New England Patriots. "And they operate so efficiently in and out of the huddle. The way Drew commands the huddle and operates, then you're behind, you're scrambling. You've just got to get a call in and get ready and get adjusted."

Payton unveiled an unconventional play against the Philadelphia Eagles in 2018 to have just such an effect. The play featured all three of the Saints quarterbacks—Brees, Hill, and Teddy Bridgewater—and only resulted in a one-yard run by Hill. But that wasn't necessarily the point. The unusual look forced the Eagles defenders to scramble.

"Part of it, really, is thinking of something that they [the Eagles] haven't seen," Payton said. "That's the job of a game-planner. You want eight heads to turn to [Eagles veteran safety] Malcolm Jenkins and be like, 'What do we do?'"

ESPN analyst Ron Jaworski calls it "renting space in the defense's mind."

In that same game, Payton built his game plan to target the Eagles' injury-ravaged secondary. Philadelphia entered the game without three of its four starters in the defensive backfield.

Further, starting cornerback Sidney Jones, who began the season as a backup, was coming into the game with a hamstring injury. The Saints attacked him from the opening snap. Payton ran three of their first four plays right at Jones. He lasted 22 plays before leaving the game with an injury. The Eagles' other starting cornerback, Avonte Maddox, left even earlier than that, hitting the sideline after 18 plays. Payton mercilessly attacked their inexperienced backups for the rest of the game. They employed a heavy diet of multiple-receiver sets to stretch thin the Eagles' defensive backfield and Brees carved it up, completing 23 of 30 passes for 363 yards and four touchdowns. His quarterback rating for the game was a near-perfect 153.2. The Saints routed the Eagles 48–7, the worst loss ever delivered to a defending Super Bowl champion.

"The thing that I've always respected about Sean competing against him [when Payton was with] the Giants and the Cowboys is that he forces you to play against every personnel group known to man," said longtime NFL defensive coordinator Gregg Williams, who coached on Payton's staff for three seasons from 2009 to 2011. "He forces you to put every personnel group you have on the field. And then if he can figure out, 'Hey, that fourth corner, that third corner, that third linebacker isn't really as good,' then he forces you to keep that group on the field."

The Saints were the only team in the NFL to start a different offensive lineup in all 16 games for each of the 2017, 2018, and 2019 seasons. In the past decade, they have annually ranked among the league leaders in most unique offensive lineups. They are the only team in the NFL to rank in the top five in this category each of the past six seasons.

"They throw the whole sink at you early with their personnel groups and formations, their shifts and motions and different concepts," said Rich Gannon, the CBS Sports NFL analyst, who won the NFL's Most Valuable Player award in 2002 while running a similar version of the Saints offense under Coach Jon Gruden. "It's really their way of blitzing the defense. It's personnel that come on and off the field. It's formations. It's motions and shifts. It's a quarterback that's been in this system for 14 seasons. It's a lot to prepare for and it puts a lot of stress on a defense in terms of their ability to make adjustments and communicate."

10

The Grind: Putting Together the Plan

THE TIGHT ENDS ROOM IS LOCATED ON THE FIRST FLOOR OF THE New Orleans Saints training facility, across the hall from the squad room. As rooms go, it's nondescript—four gray cinder block walls, a black door, and a black-gray carpet. It could pass for a classroom in your neighborhood elementary school if not for the floor-to-ceiling photographic mural of Jeremy Shockey on the wall behind tight ends coach Dan Campbell's desk and the two motivational signs on each side of the room: NEW ORLEANS SAINTS TIGHT ENDS MUSTS: SMART. TOUGH AND AGGRESSIVE. COMPETITIVE. RELENTLESS.

For the leading passer in NFL history, this is where the weekly grind of preparing for the upcoming opponent begins. For all intents and purposes, this is Drew Brees' office at 5800 Airline Drive.

"Officially, it's the tight ends room, but really it's Drew Brees' room," Campbell joked.

Brees isn't sure when the tight ends room became his de facto office, but he knows it was early in his Saints tenure. And he knows why: necessity and convenience. Since the quarterbacks are the only offensive position group without their own meeting room, they were forced to become wanderers for office space throughout the building. They'd alternate between meeting in Carmichael's office or the offensive staff meeting room on the second floor. They eventually found themselves diving into the tight ends room every Wednesday, Thursday, and Friday morning after the main team meeting when the tight ends attended special teams meetings. Its central location saved them time and energy from traversing the stairs to the main film room on the second floor during game weeks.

Over the years, Brees adopted it as his preferred spot to evaluate film. During the season, he spends a good portion of his weekday mornings breaking down game tape here. Consequently, the tight ends room is now outfitted with an espresso machine that serves Brees' favorite coffee and has a large cardboard cutout of his smiling face displayed on the wall, a prop Campbell preserved from one of Brees' post-practice quarterback competitions.

NFL work weeks follow a similar schedule. Tuesday is a long day for the coaching staff, a full day of film study and meetings to compile the plan for the base offense, the first- and second-down plays that will be run against the upcoming opponent. It's an off day for the players: time to rest, recover, and enjoy with family and friends. For Brees, it's a full day of work. He typically gets to the facility before dawn and doesn't leave until after dark.

While Campbell and the rest of the offensive staff are meeting collectively upstairs on the second floor, Brees is one floor below with the other quarterbacks, studying video of the upcoming opponent's last three games and any other games coaches deem relevant.

Wednesdays, Thursdays, and Fridays begin at 6 or 6:30 AM to account for practice sessions in the afternoon. The film study sessions on these days corresponds to the specific daily install of the game plan. Wednesdays are what is known as base offense—first and second down—so the group will not only watch all the video of every first and second down the opposing defense has played in the past three games, but also specialized cut-ups of every blitz or pressure package they've run during those downs over a longer period of time. They do the same thing on Thursday for third downs and Friday for specialty situations: red zone, short yardage, goal line, and two-minute. The idea is for the film study session to inform the quarterbacks of the plays the coaching staff will install for practice that afternoon.

Film study is serious stuff for Brees. He takes notes in a journal throughout the sessions and forbids any conversation that doesn't pertain to the task at hand. If the other quarterbacks want to talk about the great dunk from the Pelicans game the night before or the great restaurant they plan to hit with their wives that evening for dinner, they need to do it before or after film study. As the unquestioned leader of the group, Brees sets the tone.

"Once we turn the film on, it's all business," Hill said.

Brees is so locked in during his film study sessions, he often doesn't even notice when Campbell ducks in to grab something from his desk or file cabinet.

"I have my routine and I really just zone everything else out," Brees said.

The intensity and breadth of Brees' film study sessions often stun newcomers and rookies when they encounter them for the first time. The tedious attention to detail and sheer time involved require extraordinary mental stamina. Some quarterbacks simply can't handle the grind, Daniel and Hill being the exceptions.

"It's intense," Daniel said. "He takes what he does very seriously, and a lot of guys that come into the league or that come from different teams, they just they don't get it, and they don't understand it. But his intensity makes everyone around him want to be that way because they understand how much he cares. That sets a tone for the team and people feed off that. Some quarterbacks are these happy-go-lucky guys. That's not Drew. He's a guy that you can go to war with."

Brees doesn't simply watch film. He scrutinizes it with the precision and intensity of a gem cutter. He methodically goes through each play, scanning the defense for any kind of "tell" he can find in a defender's body language or alignment. During video cut-ups of an opponent's third-down defense and blitz packages, he might rewind a single play two dozen times as he studies each of the 11 defenders and their alignment and positioning and jots down notes to himself in his journal. It's a tedious, time-consuming task and Brees takes no shortcuts—not even after 19 years.

"I remember my rookie year, Chase [Daniel] and I would look over at each other and be like, 'What is he looking at? Why is he rewinding this play again and again?'" Taysom Hill said. "But the longer I've been with him, what I've realized is he's watching every single player on the defense. How is this corner going to play in this coverage? How is this linebacker going to play in that coverage? How's the safety going to play? He tries to break down tendencies so he knows how a defender is going to react on any given play based on what the route is, what the coverage is. And he does that throughout the entire week."

Over the years, Brees has become fluent in body language. He has a thorough understanding of defensive concepts and coverage responsibilities in a particular scheme. He has developed scouting reports on various defensive coordinators and knows their tendencies and personnel preferences. Consequently, he has become an expert at reading a defender's pre-snap behavior and body language, especially in rookies or inexperienced players.

"It could be anything," Brees said. "More often than not, there's at least one guy on the field who's telling you what everybody else is doing. Ten guys can put on a great disguise, a great poker face, be winning an Oscar with their disguise. And then there's one guy who's maybe a little nervous because he's disguising something here, but he's responsible for this area way over there, and he starts cheating that way. When I see that, I'm like, all right, thank you, you just told me what everybody else [on defense] is doing or where the pressure is coming from, or any number of things."

Any tell or tendency can give Brees an edge and keep him one step ahead of the opponent on game day. In this way, Brees isn't much different from most experienced quarterbacks. What makes him special, coaches and teammates say, is his ability to take what he finds during film study and apply it during the chaos and heat of battle on game day.

"I'm always looking for opportunities because I know that in any given game there could be that one play that's the difference maker, whether it's the result of that play, the momentum that it creates, if it prevents something bad from happening," Brees said. "That could be the difference in the game. And I want to make sure that we are taking advantage of every one of those opportunities when they come."

The Saints offensive coaching staff takes the same mindset into its work week, which is even longer and more laborious than the one Brees puts in.

For Payton and his staff, a normal work week in the NFL schedule begins on Monday afternoon for a Sunday game. After players and coaches meet as a team and in positional groups to review the previous game, the attention quickly turns to the next opponent.

Under Payton, game-planning is a collaborative effort. The entire offensive coaching staff is involved, along with Brees and the other quarterbacks. Campbell, offensive line coach Dan Roushar, running backs coach Joel Thomas, and assistant offensive line coach Brendan Nugent are in charge of the running game. Carmichael, Lombardi, Payton, and receivers coach Curtis Johnson collaborate on the passing attack. The staff meets as a group to brainstorm ideas and share initial thoughts, then they scatter to their offices to watch film and individually focus on a different aspect of the plan: empty formations, play-action passes, etc.

"Sean is always popping his head into your office, 'Hey, I'd like to have this rep this week. Or did you see that?'" Carmichael said. "On Monday there's a list of plays being created by guys' thoughts on that week's game plan."

Throughout this time, offensive assistants Declan Doyle and D.J. Williams tabulate the run and pass plays onto separate lists for review and consideration on Tuesday morning. Before them, this was one of the tasks Joe Brady performed for the Saints in the 2017 and 2018 seasons. These are the beginning stages of the massive call sheet that Payton will use on game day.

"You get together and there's crossover between the coaches doing the running game and passing game," Lombardi said. "Hey, you're running this run play out of this formation; okay, let's change this pass formation so there's play-action. Sean is watching film on his own and he will come in and give us his thoughts, as well."

After a late night of film study, the entire 11-man offensive coaching staff meets at 9 AM Tuesday morning to begin the tedious process of compiling the game plan. Under Payton, these game-plan sessions are collaborative, democratic affairs. All opinions are encouraged and heard, from the coordinators down to the offensive assistants.

Roushar starts the meeting by presenting the plan for the running game to Payton, who jots ideas to himself on a notepad throughout the session. Every play on the list is evaluated and discussed in detail. It's not unusual for the group to spend an hour on a single play and then determine it won't make the cut and eighty-six it.

"Some weeks, Sean will see the plan and say, I love it," Lombardi said. "Some weeks, he's like, I don't like any of your ideas and we're starting from scratch. But regardless, we're still going through every play on that game plan with a fine-tooth comb. And whether it changes or not, we're looking at it. Show me the film. Why do you like this? There's just all of this input that comes in."

Lombardi, who served as the offensive coordinator in Detroit in 2014 and 2015, and Campbell, who spent six seasons on the Miami Dolphins coaching staff before coming to New Orleans, say Payton's inclusiveness makes the process stimulating and unique.

"I know when we put together a third-down plan, I might have a few ideas, but I'm gonna ask Pete Carmichael or Joe Lombardi what they think, too," Payton said. "That interaction helps you arrive at better decisions."

The long hours aren't great for the coaches' family lives, but they know they are one of the keys to the team's success. It's the way Payton does business. Coaches who can't accept it don't last in New Orleans.

"Nobody grinds like we do—nobody," said Campbell, who is considered one of the top head coaching prospects in the league and interviewed for head coaching positions with the Arizona Cardinals, Cleveland Browns, Green Bay Packers, and Indianapolis Colts in the 2017, '18, and '19 offseasons.

When Lombardi was the offensive coordinator in Detroit, he said Lions head coach Jim Caldwell wanted the entire running game plan for that week's game completed by 8:00 AM Tuesday and the passing game finished by 9:30 AM. By comparison, the Saints often are not finished with the game plan for the running game until 4:00 PM on Tuesday and the passing game will often take them deep into the morning hours of Wednesday to complete.

Lombardi said he tried to institute the Saints' method of operation during his two-year tenure in Detroit, but it didn't take under Caldwell, who was more comfortable with a less-is-more approach. And Lombardi stresses that it's not in any way a criticism of Caldwell's coaching ability or process, just a different way of doing business.

"There was a totally different way of playing offense there," Lombardi said. "In Indy, which Jim [Caldwell] was really comfortable with, one receiver would line up on the left side and the other on the right, and they had much fewer formations. I assumed the process would change a little bit [in Detroit], but it did much more than I thought, just because we had less time and less input, and there wasn't that same culture of the game-planning we did here [in New Orleans]."

In New Orleans, Payton subcribes to a more-is-more approach, primarily because the Saints have the luxury of Brees, a quarterback capable of handling the massive mental workload. This is where the intelligence, experience, and continuity of 14 years together pay off for Brees and Payton.

The Saints often will go back through three years of an opponent's game tape during their film preparation on game-plan days. All the opponents' games from the current and previous seasons are reviewed. The plays are inventoried by down-and-distance situations so coaches can get an understanding of tendencies and preferred concepts.

If the opponent has a new coordinator, the staff will review tape of the coach's previous team to see how his teams operated there. When Dan Quinn became the head coach of the Atlanta Falcons in 2015, for example, the Saints studied tape of the Seahawks' 2013 and 2014 seasons, when Quinn served as Seattle's defensive coordinator.

"We'll go back two or three years if it's relevant," Campbell said. "And we're going to watch that tape, and we're going to see how he likes to play these plays versus a good tight end. What's he going to do against an X receiver like Mike Thomas? Are they going to double over here? And we're going to watch the game until we feel like we have every situation covered. We know exactly how they are going to play us. What does he like to do? Where are their strengths? It's fourth-and-1, what's he going to call? We don't want to ever feel like we're going to get caught with our pants down."

Throughout the day, Brees will text his thoughts to Payton or Carmichael from what he sees during his film-study sessions. Over the years, Brees' role in the game-planning has grown. The pre-snap check-with-me plays he makes at the line of scrimmage are his main focus. But in recent years, Brees has gone from suggesting a tweak to a route to scheming entire play concepts.

"We'll have our phones in there and all of a sudden it will be—ding!—'Hey, go to Kansas City and watch Play 27 against Atlanta,'" Carmichael says, describing a text from Brees on the floor below. "He usually has his thoughts on some empty [backfield] stuff. He throws all of his thoughts [on the game plan] into a text message, and sometimes he might even come upstairs and poke his head into the offensive meeting room and ask, 'Hey, I know this guy is down this week. Who do you see the personnel playing in his place in the slot?' He does a great job also of studying how this DB plays his technique when he's in press [coverage]. That continues throughout the week. He looks for tendencies. He's got such a great memory, and he keeps such great notes he probably knows the majority of [defensive] guys in the league and has a feel for them."

Added Lombardi, "He's excellent at saying, 'Hey, we've got this guy running the route at this depth, and I think it fits better with my footwork if we can cut it down two yards or so. Or, 'I'd rather have this receiver on this route rather than this other receiver.' He's excellent at giving his input. Every detail, he's got a thought."

And even when Brees isn't physically present in the room, his influence is pervasive. His exacting high standards raise the bar for everyone. None of the coaches wants to be the one who gives him an incomplete answer when the game plan is introduced on Wednesday.

For example, Lombardi said the coaching staff might have a run play with a 99 percent chance of being successful in the upcoming game, but the opponent has shown one defensive look that could blow up the play for a loss. Most teams, Lombardi said, would be willing to live with those odds and keep the play in the game plan. Not the Saints. Not with Brees at quarterback. The staff will spend an extra hour trying to find a solution to the one percent.

"When you have a quarterback that is as smart as Drew is, he's going to find that look, and he's going to ask you about it," Lombardi said. "We know we have to come up with an answer. There is a responsibility that you feel. We have to give this guy an answer for every situation that he has. If you've left a hole in the game plan, he's going to find it and he's going to ask you about it."

Under Payton and Brees, the game plan is an evolving, weeklong process. The plan is formulated on Tuesday and introduced to the team on Wednesday, but it's constantly changing as the team starts practice to see how the concepts translate from the meeting room to the field.

One of Payton's pet sayings is, 'The hay's never in the barn.' In other words, it's never too late to add something to the plan. Coaches and players say it's not uncommon for Payton to introduce a completely new play to the plan on Saturday night or even Sunday morning.

But for the most part, by Saturday, the plan is largely intact. It has been tweaked and honed into a few hundred plays for roughly 18 situational categories: base runs and passes; third down; play-action passes; short-yardage; red zone; goal line; four-minute; two-minute; screens; draws; special plays or gadgets; etc. The call sheets are compiled by the offensive assistants and distributed to Payton, Brees, and the rest of the offensive staff. This is the script Brees uses to conduct his visualization session after the walk-through on the day before each game.

Later that night at the hotel, Payton presents the first 12 to 15 plays, or openers, to the offensive players. A short walk-through is conducted in street clothes to familiarize everyone with their assignments on the opening set of plays. The group then breaks for a snack before Payton, Brees, Carmichael, and Lombardi reconvene for a final meeting, which is referred to as the dot meeting, normally about 9:15 PM.

It's not unusual for NFL quarterbacks to meet with the play-caller on the eve of game day to synchronize their thoughts. But the Saints take it to another level. They break down every play in each situation of the game plan. It varies week to week, but Brees usually will identify four to six favorite plays per category during the meeting. His choices are based on how successful the plays were in practice and how comfortable and confident he feels in executing them on game day. Payton uses a yellow highlighter to identify each of Brees' favorite plays on the laminated call sheet, then he takes a black Sharpie and adds a single black dot to each one.

"Having played the position, Sean knows that if you like the play then you're going to go to great lengths to make sure it's successful," said McCown, who sat in many dot meetings during his three-year tenure as Brees' backup from 2013 to '15. "You really study it. You're going to know the ins and outs of it. You're going to understand the rhythm of it, the timing of it and where people should be. You're going to make that play go."

Like most things under Payton, the dot meeting is a collaborative effort. Brees and Payton dominate the discourse, but everyone in the room is free to weigh in. Brees will ask Payton how he sees a play working against certain coverage or when during the game or where on the field he might call a certain play. He might tell Payton he really likes a certain pass play but is a little nervous if the defense attacks it with a certain blitz. If Brees doesn't like a play, Payton might try to present a case for why he thinks it will work, but nine times out of 10 it's eliminated from the game plan. The meetings usually last about 40 minutes, but sometimes they can extend until late that night. By the time it ends, Brees has vetted, dissected, and probably practiced every play that he will run in the game.

"It's an exciting process," Brees said. "It's a bit nerve-wracking early in the week because you're sitting there watching film after film and you're trying to identify all the ways that you can attack that defense, but it all eventually comes together. I think some of our best ideas at times come late in the week, on a Saturday night or even Sunday morning. When the game starts, I can anticipate what he's going to call in every situation and why he's calling it."

The tedious, mind-numbing grind of film study and game-planning is the least glamorous part of an NFL coach's job. It doesn't make for compelling theater on NFL Films documentaries. Most fans don't understand the amount of work that goes into preparing for each game and most media members don't appreciate it. But for the Saints offensive staff, it's one of the reasons for their success, something that gives them an edge on their opponents. A lot of coaches and players talk about it. The Saints live it, because Payton demands it.

"It's a results-oriented business, so there's certain things that you have to get done on a Monday night and certain things that need to be done by Tuesday night and Wednesday night," Payton said. "We try to be prepared, to be ready, to be thorough, so I don't know how you define that. The fear of failure is sometimes what drives you the most, I think. The fear of not being successful."

A father of six, Lombardi wasn't sure he was ready and willing to make the sacrifice required to make it as a member of Payton's coaching staff. He remembers the culture shock of his first year on the job in 2007. The Falcons, with whom Lombardi worked as a defensive assistant the previous season, certainly didn't work this way. His mind was so boggled by the long hours and draining schedule that he called his father, a former coach himself, to vent. His father's advice resonates with him to this day.

"He said, 'Hey, who was the No. 1 offense in the NFL last year [in 2006]?'" Lombardi said, "'Why don't you just keep your mouth shut and learn everything you can learn, and then you can start piping up if you feel like you can do something better.' He was absolutely right. It's exhausting, and it's hard work, and I don't think most people are willing to do it. I'm not always happy about it. But I'm happy with the results."

11

Finding the Golden Nugget

HISTORY WILL REMEMBER THE 2017 NFC DIVISIONAL PLAYOFF
game between the New Orleans Saints and Minnesota Vikings as the
Minnesota Miracle game. Stefon Diggs' stunning 61-yard touchdown
catch on the final play of the game instantly earned a spot on the
list of greatest plays in NFL history. Minnesotans will relive it for
generations and tell their grandchildren where they were when Diggs
split Saints defensive backs Marcus Williams and Ken Crawley and
raced down the sideline for the dramatic walk-off score.

The stunning finish spoiled what should have been one of the
great come-from-behind wins in Saints history. If not for the divine
intervention of the gridiron gods, the game would have gone down
as one of the signature moments in the Payton-Brees era of Saints
football.

After all, the Saints had turned U.S. Bank Stadium on its
collective head with a furious fourth-quarter rally, outscoring the
Vikings 24–6 in the game's final 17 minutes to turn a 17–0 deficit
into a 24–23 lead. And they were only 25 seconds away from winning
and advancing to the NFC Championship Game, one play away

from becoming just the second team in NFL history to rally from a 17-point deficit in a playoff game's final 17 minutes.

Then fate intervened, and the heroics of Sean Payton and Drew Brees were long forgotten.

The Vikings had dominated the Saints for the first three quarters. Just about everything that could go wrong did go wrong for the Saints early. Brees threw two interceptions in a game for the first time in nearly three months. Ken Crawley gift-wrapped a field goal with a pair of pass interference penalties in the second quarter. A touchdown to Ted Ginn Jr. was called back because of a penalty. The Saints failed to convert a single third down. And the normally reliable Wil Lutz missed a field goal.

By the time Brees and the Saints offense touched the ball for the first time in the second half, they trailed 17–0 and only 23 minutes remained in the game. The Saints would need to score three times against a Vikings defense that allowed the fewest yards and points in the NFL that season. The Saints' win probability was 3 percent, and for those in attendance that day a comeback seemed even more remote.

On the first series of the second half, Brees found his rhythm. He completed 5 of 6 passes for 60 yards, the final 14 on a touchdown strike to Michael Thomas to trim the Vikings lead to 17–7 with 1:18 left in the third quarter. After spinning their wheels for two-plus quarters, the Saints finally had some momentum.

One of Payton's strengths as a coach is his feel for a game's pace. The quarterback in him still has an innate sense of the ebbs and flows of a football game. He constantly talks about gaining and losing control of a game as a play-caller. Payton knew this was the Saints' chance to get back into this one. They desperately needed to capitalize on the moment. And when Marcus Williams intercepted Case Keenum on the first play of the Vikings' ensuing drive and returned it deep into Vikings territory, Payton knew the door of opportunity had just swung wide open for the Saints.

As the Saints marched toward the Vikings goal line, he began thinking of a play he'd been waiting to call, something he discovered during the coaching staff's week of game preparation.

While studying film of the Vikings red zone defense in his office late Thursday night, Payton came across a play the Indianapolis Colts successfully ran against the Vikings for a touchdown a year earlier. The play itself—a six-yard touchdown run by Robert Turbin—wasn't what caught Payton's eye. What he noticed was the void in the Vikings secondary on the back side of the play. As the Colts tight end positioned himself before the snap to make a crackback block on the Vikings left defensive end, the Vikings linebackers and free safety all immediately diagnosed the play and attacked the line of scrimmage to stop the run. Unfortunately, their execution didn't match their play recognition, as Turbin slipped three tackle attempts by Vikings defenders and skirted into the end zone.

To Payton, the result of the play was irrelevant. What mattered was how the Vikings defense played it. And the large, undefended expanse of turf they left open in the back side of the secondary caused Payton to sit up in his seat. It was just the kind of weakness an offensive play-caller like Payton lived to attack, the Holy Grail of film study.

"I saw that," Payton said, "and thought: That's interesting."

Saints tight ends coach Dan Campbell refers to this discovery process as "finding the golden nugget." The code-breakers come in a variety of forms, but most are either personnel- or scheme-related: a cornerback's tendency to bite on play fakes; a linebacker's poor ball skills; a systematic flaw in a coverage scheme. This elusive cracking of the defensive code is what drives Payton and makes Saints coaches spend long, tedious hours in the office scanning videotape until their eyes glaze over the week before a game.

In the mind of the eternally confident Payton, there is always a flaw somewhere to exploit. It might take more time find it against disciplined, well-coached teams. But it's there. And in this case, the Saints head coach was going to take advantage of one of the Vikings' strengths: the intelligence and instinctiveness of the Minnesota defense.

Payton knew the Vikings' defensive tendencies well. He and Minnesota coach Mike Zimmer worked together on Bill Parcells' Cowboys staff in the early 2000s. Payton considered Zimmer one of the top defensive minds in the NFL and respected the discipline of his units. He also knew Zimmer's preference for smart, tough, veteran players like free safety Harrison Smith and linebackers Erik Kendricks and Anthony Barr.

From film study and having played the Vikings four months earlier in the regular season opener, Payton could see how quickly Smith, Barr, and Kendricks diagnosed plays, sometimes ambushing the opposing ballcarrier in the backfield just after the handoff.

Payton knew Zimmer implicitly trusted his veteran defensive leaders at key moments in the game and often aligned in a certain single-high safety zone defense during tight red-zone situations. Payton wanted to use that aggressiveness against the Vikings. To do that, he needed to create an illusion. So, using the Turbin run in 2016 as a guideline, the Saints designed a play late Thursday night, less than 72 hours before kickoff, that would exploit the Vikings' aggressive tactics.

The play was called *Full Left Twin Y Orbit Q8 Kill Toss 39 Michael* and it provided Brees two options at the line of scrimmage. If the Vikings blitzed, he would check to a quick pass to Mike Thomas, one of the Saints' favorite blitz-beaters. But if Zimmer did what he usually does and the defense aligned the way the Saints expected, in an aggressive zone look with man-to-man principles, then Brees would call their special pass play.

The key to the play was the window dressing. The Saints had to make it look exactly like the one the Colts ran against the Vikings a year earlier. And if the subterfuge worked, it would fool the Vikings' best defenders and attack two of their most vulnerable ones.

Strong safety Anthony Harris was a former undrafted rookie from Virginia who was primarily a reserve and special teams standout during his first three seasons with the Vikings. He has since developed into a Pro Bowl–caliber player, but at the time, he was only playing because starter Andrew Sendejo had left the game after being concussed during a collision with Michael Thomas in pass coverage. The Saints knew the inexperienced Harris might be overly aggressive from his position in the back center of the Vikings defense and were going to challenge him.

The other key target was slot cornerback Terence Newman, a Zimmer favorite, who, at 39, was the oldest defensive back in the league. The Saints loved the matchup of the physically gifted 24-year-old Thomas in the slot against the aging, slow-footed Newman. Payton was so confident in the matchup he told Thomas earlier in the week, "You're going to retire Terence Newman on this play."

The Saints broke the huddle and wide receiver Willie Snead aligned to the left side with fellow receivers Ted Ginn Jr. and Michael Thomas to the right. When Brees saw the Vikings defense align in the exact defensive look they wanted, he immediately checked into the pass option of the play by audibling at the line of scrimmage.

To the average onlooker, Brees' hand signals and audibles meant nothing. To the Saints offensive players, it was Go Time. Toss 39 Michael was on.

Brees quickly signaled for Kamara to move from a right off-set position in the backfield to the "I" spot directly behind him, then signaled for Hill to start his waggle motion from his alignment on the left side of the formation.

"We were giving the illusion that we were running a toss crack play to the left, and so what we did is we had Josh Hill do this little back-and-forth motion to make it look like, 'Oh, here I come to crack the [defensive] end,'" Brees said. "With smart, instinctive linebackers and safeties, the minute that they see and feel that motion, they're running to where they feel like you're going to toss crack because they know that if they can beat their block, then they're going to hit this thing in the backfield for a loss. So honestly, it's a play that you run against smart defenses. And that's a smart defense."

The Saints probably wouldn't have tried this tactic against an inexperienced defense. But against a savvy, veteran-laden unit like the Vikings, it was perfect.

"You're counting on them to do what you have studied [on tape]," Payton said. "It's hard to fool the dummy who's gotten fooled a bunch. He's inconsistent. You're looking for consistent behavior, and these guys [the Vikings] are smart, now."

To sell the ruse, Payton instructed Hill to shuffle his feet extra times and stare down the end, the exact opposite of his normal M.O. Hill's acting job worked like a charm. As he began his waggle motion, Smith, Barr, and Kendricks, on cue, immediately started to cheat that way.

"Josh sold the crack so much you can see Harrison Smith basically jump into blitz mode to get into the backfield," Payton said. "To him, this was kindergarten."

Except it wasn't.

After the snap, Brees enhanced the illusion by faking a pitch to Kamara, who broke to his left as if running a toss sweep. The play-fake caused safety Harris, aligned in the back center of the end zone, to take two quick steps toward Kamara, leaving a massive window on the backside of the Vikings defense where Thomas and Ginn were breaking into their pass routes from the right side of the formation.

Just as Payton expected, Newman was no match for the powerful Thomas, who easily beat the veteran cornerback on a quick slant. Brees' strike led him perfectly into the void vacated by Harris. Thomas scored standing up. No Vikings defender was within four yards of him in the end zone.

"That's as good as it gets," Payton said. "When it all comes together like that, it's like fuckin' Christmas."

Walk-in touchdowns in the red zone are rare commodities in the NFL, where the schemes are so sophisticated and the athletes so fast and well-prepared. When they occur, you know something unusual happened, either a busted coverage or a well-designed scheme.

"The pro report [from director of pro personnel Terry Fontenot]," Payton said, explaining the Vikings' setup play, "is going to give me what they do, their strengths and weaknesses, but the film study is going to show me, where are their eyes in this coverage. Are they playing the coverage the right way? They played this coverage well. Everyone did their job. Zimm will go back and watch this on film and say, 'All right, man. They got us on that one.'"

The touchdown was the culmination of hours of work by the Saints staff. Every detail of the play—the personnel grouping, the formation and alignment down to the width of the receiver splits, the waggle by Hill, the play-fake by Brees and Kamara, the route by Thomas—was hashed out in offensive meetings as the Saints compiled their red-zone game plan for the Vikings. Then it was put into motion and repped on the practice field that Friday afternoon. And it was all done knowing the situation might not materialize in the game or see the light of day.

"It was textbook," former Saints offensive assistant Joe Brady said. "It worked exactly like Sean said it would during the week. He painted the picture exactly like it played out. It was special."

Backup quarterback Chase Daniel admitted being dubious of the play when Payton installed it that Friday.

"I just remember thinking, 'What is this play? This play is like something out of Pop Warner. They're never going to fall for it. They're an NFL defense,'" Daniel said. "Sure enough, the first chance he gets, when we need it, when we're down there in the right situation, he calls it and it is wide open—like completely *wide open.*"

The touchdown silenced the U.S. Bank Stadium crowd and fueled a fourth-quarter comeback that should have gone down in Saints history. Instead, Diggs' heroics rendered it an afterthought. Regardless, it exemplified why Payton is considered one of the great offensive coaches in NFL history.

"He's been doing it a long time and he's very creative," Eagles head coach Doug Pederson said of Payton. "The thing is with Sean, too, he's going to exhaust the film, like most coaches. But I think he definitely goes above and beyond to exhaust the tape. He's going to find something that he can exploit in your defense."

One of Payton's favorite finds came in Week 12 of the 2018 season, when he noticed a weakness in the Atlanta defense during film prep for the teams' nationally televised Thanksgiving night game. The Falcons zone pass coverage had a flaw he hoped to exploit. When Atlanta opponents were in a 3-by-1 set with three receivers to one side of the offensive formation and changed the strength of their formation late against the Falcons defense, it put weak-side linebacker De'Vondre Campbell in a difficult spot. Not only was he expected to stop the run, but he also was responsible for covering the deep third of the secondary on the back side of the defense, an almost impossible task. The Saints installed a play that week to attack this weakness and planned to use it when they were just outside the Falcons 20-yard line, an area the Saints referred to as the fringe red zone on the call sheet.

To make the play even more effective, Payton installed it with Tommylee Lewis as the primary receiver. The diminutive speedster was activated that week for the first time since suffering an injury in Week 2 and probably would be overlooked in the Falcons game-planning. The idea was to use Thomas to attract the focus of the coverage and slip Lewis behind the unsuspecting secondary in the opposite direction. Further, the Saints threw in some window dressing, pulling left guard Andrus Peat and having Brees fake a handoff in the backfield to Mark Ingram to sell a run play. Payton was so confident in the play's potential success he told Thomas during the week he would have the best view in the Superdome of Lewis' touchdown as he ran his fade route into the right corner of the end zone.

Payton didn't waste any time in dialing it up from his extensive menu of plays. After the Saints marched to the Falcons 28-yard line on their opening drive, Payton sent in the call from the sideline.

Just as he anticipated, Brees' play-action fake lured Campbell into two false steps toward the flow of the play in the Saints backfield. Lewis, from his starting spot in the right slot, snuck unimpeded into the heart of the Falcons defense and raced past the Falcons linebackers on an over route to the left. Suddenly, safety Damontae Kazee, who was aligned alone in center field, was caught in a pickle, with Lewis racing in front of him to his right and Thomas and Keith Kirkwood running go routes to his left. It was one of the easiest pitch-and-catches Brees would make all season. Lewis hauled in the 28-yard pass untouched.

"When they drew up the play during the week, Coach [Payton] explained how it would play out and it played out the exact same way in the game," Lewis said. "We knew they would concentrate their coverage on Michael and he would hold that corner and safety (away from the play). All I had to do was beat the linebacker."

When describing the play later, Payton said wryly, "Connor [Payton's son] could have made that throw."

Payton values film study as much as any coach in football. He believes the process is a critical part of an NFL coach's job, the staff's inherent obligation to the rest of the team. It's why he requires his coaches to work 18-hour days during the season and why he built a sleep room on the second floor of the Saints training facility with bunk beds and curtains to aid the process.

Consequently, the Saints offensive staff has earned a reputation among its peers as one of the most creative, hard-working groups in the NFL. All NFL coaches grind, to some degree. But the Saints take pride in going the extra mile in their commitment to film study because Payton demands it. The staff rarely leaves the Saints facility on Mondays, Tuesdays, Wednesdays, or Thursdays before midnight.

"I don't know any other way to operate," Payton said. "I tell our coaches, Friday night is your night to go home. Our job is to find more plays to make the job a little easier for our players. We're trying to reduce their stress on game days. There's nothing like finding something late on a Wednesday or Thursday night, and it ends up being a difference-maker. That's what drives you."

Payton's assistants might grouse to each other from time to time, but they know the drill. It's all part of the Payton Way. As Malcolm Gladwell's 10,000-hour rule professes, there's no secret to the success. Successful golden nugget panning is about discipline, commitment, attention to detail, and countless hours of tedious film study. And when it all comes together on game day, there are no complaints.

"All of those hours that we're grinding we're trying to do one thing: we're trying to find the very best matchups," Campbell said. "We want to put our best guy on your worst guy. And you've got to freakin' work at it. Sometimes it may be [that] you can only use this personnel group. Or you can only use this formation. Or you can only use this shift to get that one or two plays of a matchup. But that one or two plays is the difference between seven points and three points or no points. And what's what makes the difference."

It goes back to Saints coaches' practice of evaluating film of opponents' games from two or three previous seasons in an effort to find an advantage—including, for new coordinators, studying games from the coach's previous stops to try to assess tendencies.

"We'll go through hours and hours of tape until we finally find the gold mine—there it is, we've found the golden nugget," Campbell said. "And that's what we do. And we do it better than anybody. We're not trying to be fancy. That's what some people may think that we're trying to be elaborate. We're just trying to get freakin' Mike Thomas on your worst guy. We're trying to get Kamara on one of your linebackers. We're trying to get Jared Cook on your freakin' donkey, and we'll see if you can cover him. That's what we do. And we do it better than anybody else."

DOME-INATION:

2009 New York Giants,
New England Patriots

The 2008 rout of the Green Bay Packers wouldn't be the first time the New Orleans Saints offense would devastate an opponent in the Payton-Brees era. Less than a year later, they would embarrass another proud franchise with another highly rated defense.

In Week 5 of the 2009 season, the New York Giants came to New Orleans with a 5–0 record and the league's top-rated pass defense. They were allowing just 210 yards a game and had trailed for a total of only 18 minutes and 31 seconds in their first five games combined. Their pass defense had allowed opposing quarterbacks to pass for only 104 yards a game, 61 fewer than any other team in the NFL.

Vegas oddsmakers installed the Saints as three-point favorites, essentially calling the teams even on paper. But the Saints had a built-in advantage they didn't factor into the equation: an open date the previous week. Payton and the staff used the extra time to decipher the Giants defense, and they fixed their crosshairs on cornerback Terrell Thomas and safety C.C. Brown, a pair of inexperienced players who were thrust into starting roles because of injuries to Aaron Rouse and Kenny Phillips.

It didn't take long for the Giants to realize they were in trouble that Sunday afternoon. After not allowing more than four plays on the opening drive of the first four games, they watched the Saints march 70 yards in 15 plays for a touchdown on their first possession. They followed that with touchdown drives of 80, 57, and 61 yards and finished the first half with 315 yards and a 34–17 lead. They scored touchdowns on five of six drives and it would have been a perfect six of six if not for a failed fourth-and-goal run from the Giants 1. At one point in the first half, Brees completed 15 consecutive passes.

It didn't get any better for the Giants in the second half as Brees continued to strafe their secondary. As lopsided as the 48–27 final score was, it could have been worse if Payton hadn't lifted Brees for the game's final six minutes. Brees finished with 369 passing yards and four touchdowns on 23-of-30 passing. While targeting Brown and Thomas, he was 9-of-13 for 180 yards and four touchdowns. All nine of his completions against the duo resulted in first downs.

"I didn't see this coming," Giants linebacker Antonio Pierce said.

Few did. It'd been a decade since the Giants had allowed so many points. In the modern era, they'd never allowed a quarterback to post a passer efficiency rating as high as Brees' 156.8. After allowing just six passes of 20 or more yards to their first five opponents combined, the Giants allowed seven to the Saints, plus another 19- and 18-yarder.

"It got to the point where it was almost comical," Giants defensive end Justin Tuck said. "We couldn't do nothing to stop them."

Payton's game plan was masterful. The Saints moved the pocket, used an extra offensive tackle at times to provide extra protection against the Giants' vaunted front four, and ran passing plays out of the formations that they had previously used for the run. They put the overaggressive Brown on a string and kept the Giants defensive line off-balance with play-action passes. In 33 pass plays, the Giants failed to sack Brees and managed to hit him only twice.

"I liked what [Payton] did from a design standpoint to create windows in the Giants defense, and very subtle things he did with his offensive line," said Fox Sports analyst Daryl "Moose" Johnston after reviewing the game. "He knew what the defensive principles of the Giants were, and he used that against them. Some of those plays were fun to watch. I just don't know how you win in a situation like that, because the Giants were doing what they were supposed to do, but it was what Sean Payton expected them to do."

Six weeks later, Brees and Payton produced an even greater display of offensive brilliance.

The 2009 New England Patriots were not a vintage Bill Belichick–coached team, but they still entered the game ranked second in the NFL in pass defense and scoring defense, allowing just 16 points a game. They had outscored their first 10 opponents by an average of 12.6 points a game, the second-highest margin in the league. And the game was viewed as a showdown between two of the league's best teams, the 7–3 Patriots against the 10–0 Saints. But the Patriots did not know what was in store for them against an unbeaten Saints team primed to prove its bona fides on the *Monday Night Football* stage.

From the opening kickoff, the Saints relentlessly attacked the Patriots defense in every manner and from every angle. They scored on long, methodical drives and a 75-yard strike. They scored on long sluggo seam routes, screen passes, and a dump to their third tight end, Darnell Dinkins.

Brees threw touchdown passes to five different receivers and led the Saints to scores on seven of their first nine series. He finished with 371 yards on 18-of-23 passing.

The Saints averaged a franchise-record 9.6 yards per play, and it would have been higher had they not called off the dogs on their final series. The beating was so bad Belichick removed Tom Brady from the game with 5:00 left in regulation.

"[The Saints] were better than we were in every phase of the game," Belichick said. "I don't know how to put it any other way. They were better coached, and they played better on offense and defense."

The Saints used a heavy dose of two-tight-end sets to give Brees extra protection, and Payton and Brees targeted overmatched Patriots cornerbacks Leigh Bodden and Jonathan Wilhite throughout the game with their trio of receivers: Marques Colston,

Devery Henderson, and Robert Meachem. Brees was pressured just twice in 23 passing attempts and the receiver combined to catch 12 of 16 targeted passes for 306 yards and three touchdowns.

The offensive onslaught was so devastating, ESPN NFL analyst Ron Jaworski said during the broadcast, "I'm running out of words and phrases to praise this offense. I'm speechless, there are so many wonderful things they are doing."

The Saints had gains of 75, 68, 38, and 33 yards against a defense that had allowed one pass play of 40 or more yards to its first 10 opponents combined. Their average of 9.6 yards per play remains the second-highest yards-per-play average ever recorded against a Belichick-coached team. It's also the only time one of his teams has allowed five touchdown passes in a game. The Saints' 480 total yards remain the third most yielded by the Patriots under Belichick and the highest total since 2001.

"We were able to accomplish something offensively that was pretty special," Brees said.

Statistically, it was the finest passing performance of Brees' career and one of the best in league history. He compiled a club-record 158.3 passer efficiency rating, the highest the system allows and one of only 21 "perfect" passer ratings ever recorded at the time. His 16.1 yards per pass attempt was a team record and is still considered one of the great statistical achievements in NFL history. It had only been done a handful of times in modern NFL history and never against a defense with the reputation of the Patriots.

"Quarterbacks simply do not average 16 yards per attempt in today's NFL," said Kerry J. Byrne of analytics site ColdHardFootballFacts.com. "It hadn't happened in 34 years. It doesn't happen on the big stage of Monday Night Football. It doesn't happen against [Bill] Belichick. It doesn't happen against the mighty New England victory machine. It doesn't happen for an 11–0 team that has never won a Super Bowl. But it all came together for Drew Brees Monday night in the single greatest regular-season passing performance in modern NFL history."

Chase Daniel still vividly remembers the locked-in look in Brees' eyes during the commute to the game that night from the team hotel.

"You could just tell from his mindset that it was going to be a really good game for him," Daniel said. "Brunell knew it, too. He said before the game, 'Hey, watch this. Watch what's going to happen.' And then early on, we were getting chunk plays and every read, every throw from Drew was just so accurate. I remember watching from the sideline that night and thinking, that's one of the coolest passing displays I've ever seen."

12

Calling the Shots

WHEN THE SAINTS ENTERED THE FINAL DAYS OF GAME-PLANNING for their 2020 divisional playoff game against the Minnesota Vikings, one issue stuck in Sean Payton's craw: Do we have enough explosive plays in the plan?

So late on the Thursday night before the game, the offensive staff designed a pass to produce a potential chunk play against the Vikings defense.

This was a common practice for Payton and his offensive staff. Over the years, they've installed countless special plays in the final days of game-planning. What made this one uncommon was who it targeted: Deonte Harris, a seldom-used rookie receiver from Assumption College.

Few people outside of New Orleans had heard of Harris, but the Saints coaches were enamored with the dimuntive speedster's big-play potential. His role had gradually expanded in the offense as the season progressed. And now, in the biggest game of the year, they wanted to call his number in a matchup against Vikings cornerback Xavier Rhodes. On the surface, this would appear to be a mismatch.

Rhodes was a three-time Pro Bowler; Harris an undrafted free agent who made his living as a return specialist. But the Saints knew the 6'1", 218-pound Rhodes struggled to cover faster receivers, especially ones like Harris who were quick in and out of their cuts. If the Saints could get the shifty 5'7" Harris one-on-one against Rhodes, they liked their chances of making a big play.

But to get Harris one-on-one, they would need to address Minnesota's safeties. Harrison Smith and Anthony Harris were both excellent in coverage. Smith was a perennial Pro Bowler, and Harris was enjoying a career year with an NFL-best six interceptions.

To address the safety issue, Payton designed the play with Hill at quarterback instead of Brees. There was a method to Payton's madness. The threat of Hill as a runner forced teams to defend the Saints with an extra man in the box, usually a safety. This tactic would leave the defense with a single safety in center field. By aligning Harris on the same side of the field as star receiver Mike Thomas and running Thomas across the field on a corner route, Payton's play design would put that safety in a quandary. He would have to choose between shadowing Thomas, the NFL's leading receiver, or Harris, an unknown receiving commodity matched up with the Vikings' Pro Bowl corner. Payton knew the answer. He also knew he would need to wait for the right time and situation to call the play—and he found it early in the second quarter as the Saints approached midfield.

Payton set up the play by calling for a Hill run on first down. His 11-yard gain had the Vikings on high alert. The trap was set. To enhance the ruse of a run option, backup offensive lineman Nick Eason was inserted into the lineup. The "heavy" personnel formation served the dual purpose of adding to the trickery while providing extra protection for Hill against the Vikings' formidable pass rush. As Hill aligned in the shotgun, nine Vikings defenders were within five yards of the line of scrimmage, including Smith.

Hill's play-action fake handoff to Kamara helped sell the run even further and lured the defense closer to the line of scrimmage. Hill then dropped back, looked at Thomas as he crossed the field on his corner route, and fired a bomb to Harris, who was streaking wide open down the middle of the field after beating Rhodes with a double move. Harris hauled in the bomb for a 50-yard gain. The Saints scored on the next to play to take a 10–3 lead.

"It took us a couple of reps in practice to get it down, but it worked almost perfectly," Payton said.

It played out almost exactly the way Payton described it to Harris and Hill during the team's installation of the play the previous Friday. Payton went into great detail, even identifying where Harris would eventually catch the ball.

"I told Deonte, you need to lean on Rhodes, exit door him and blow by him," Payton said. "I envision this ball traveling in the air a long ways, so keep running. Your path is going right between the uprights. Taysom had to move off his spot so he underthrew it or it would have been a touchdown."

The play was classic Payton. The biggest play in the game wasn't Brees to Thomas. Instead, it was made by a third-string quarterback and a reserve first-year receiver, a pair of former undrafted free agents. And Payton called it in the playoffs against one of the best defenses in the NFL.

"What I like is Sean calls plays without a great deal of fear," FOX Sports NFL analyst Troy Aikman said. "I think there's a time when you have to be careful and all that, but for the most part he calls plays expecting his players to make plays. And they have a lot of weapons they can go to."

Payton's imaginative play-calling has been a staple of the Saints offense since he took the reins in 2006. He ceded play-calling duties to Carmichael in 2016 and 2011 after he injured his knee in a freak sideline incident. Otherwise, Payton has been the play-caller for the entire Brees run. While an army of young offensive-minded head coaches have entered the league in recent years, Payton, along with Andy Reid and Matt McCarthy, remains one of the longest- tenured and most respected head-coach play-callers in the business.

"I think [Payton] is certainly one of the best play-callers in the league, and he plays wide open," said Steve Mariucci, the former head coach of the San Francisco 49ers, who called plays throughout his coaching career and now serves as an NFL analyst for NFL Network. "I like that about him. Sometimes a head coach might play it a little closer to the vest, because he has to be more broad-minded, worrying about resting the defense or things like that. But Sean just keeps it wide open all the time, and I really like that."

Like many teams, Payton scripts the first 15 plays as a way to feel out the defense. At times, he uses the early game plan to set a tone for his offensive unit by establishing the run or attacking a certain defender in coverage. The plan almost always includes a litany of formations and personnel groupings so Payton and the staff can gather information for future use.

"You want to have tempo in the first 15, and you want to be able to see what their adjustments are to certain formations and certain personnel groupings," Payton said. "You want to see how they're going to defense Alvin Kamara, and how they're going to play certain guys. There's a lot of information gained. All those things I think you look closely at in your early plays."

This strategy is one of the reasons why the Saints have traditionally been slow starters offensively. During the Payton-Brees era, they have scored an average of 8.6 points in the second quarter of games compared to 5.6 points in the first quarter, when they are executing their feeling-out process.

Strief said he could only remember a handful of times an opponent threw something at the Saints that they had not prepared for. In those rare instances, it doesn't take the Saints long to adjust.

Payton, Brees, and the offensive coaching staff can quickly adapt, drawing on their years of collective experience and knowledge.

"Their in-game adjustments are impressive," said Daniel, who was a Saints backup quarterback for four seasons (2010–12 and 2017). "It might take a drive for those guys to figure it out, where some teams it might take a quarter or two quarters. They're very keen on knowing exactly how the defense is playing and then what to do from there."

A famous example of Payton's in-game adjustments came in the 2019 NFC Championship Game. The Saints were having success passing to Alvin Kamara on choice routes out of the backfield. Kamara was the leading receiver in the game with 11 catches for 96 yards. So Rams defensive coordinator Wade Phillips countered by having his defensive ends and outside linebackers hit Kamara as he leaked out of the backfield to disrupt the timing of the play.

The famous NOLA No-Call play highlighted a Payton counterpunch: he inserted receiver Tommylee Lewis into the game and had Kamara and Lewis change positions. Kamara aligned in the left slot at receiver and Lewis positioned himself in the backfield as a running back. The switch confused the Rams defense, and the Saints snapped the ball quickly to take advantage of it. Nickell Robey-Coleman was scrambling to recover when he infamously collided with Lewis in the right flat on the play.

Just like the Minnesota Miracle, what should have been a highlight moment of the Payton-Brees era turned into heartbreak. The blown call and the ensuing controversy it spurred overshadowed Payton's brilliant maneuver. It became a footnote to history, one that likely will be forgotten with time.

"Sean sees things so fast," Saints tight ends coach Dan Campbell said. "And we can make those adjustments, and Drew doesn't even bat an eye. They've been together so long they know how each other thinks. There is a trust issue. Coach has a ton of trust in Drew. He knows Drew thinks the exact same way he does. He understands the situations of the game. That's why there's been this rapport between these two and this great working relationship."

Payton uses highlighters and Sharpie markers to jot notes to himself on his laminated call sheet during the game. Sometimes, he'll strike through a play because of injuries or personnel changes. Likewise, if an opponent loses a starting cornerback or safety to injury during the game, he might star a play and move it up on the call-sheet menu. If Brees has a hot hand, like he did the record-setting night he completed 29 of 30 passes against the Indianapolis Colts in 2019, he'll emphasize the passing attack. If the offensive line is winning the point of attack in the trenches, he'll lean into the running game.

"He's always adjusting," Lombardi said. "He does a great job of feeding guys that have the hot hand. And he's got a great instinct for when to take shots and when to be aggressive. I can't count the number of times when he's made a call and I cringed in the [coaches'] box and it turns out successful."

One of the reasons Payton's call sheet is so voluminous is because he wants to have options in every specific game situation so he can adjust during a game. These potential adjustments are discussed during the offensive game-plan meetings leading up to the game.

"If [the opponent] starts playing us in a bunch of this [defense] then we have got this package of stuff we can get to," Brees said. "You talk about these situations during the week, and obviously these are in his memory bank. So the minute he feels like this is the time, this is the situation, he is able to dial it up. We all know it is coming because we have talked about it, and so a lot of confidence comes with that."

During the week of preparation, Payton consciously tries to include a play or two in the game plan that will highlight each of his skill position players. It's his way of keeping defenses honest and keeping his players invested in the weekly game plan. Circumstances might prevent him from calling the play during the game, but he wants his players to feel included in the mission.

"It brings a little juice to the install [process]," Payton said. "It's important that there's a player's jersey number and name [each week], like that play is kind of your play. There's some ownership to it. And it creates some excitement and confidence when it works."

This inclusivity has been a hallmark of the Payton-Brees era. While both ardently believe in a "feed the studs" approach with stars like Thomas, Kamara, Graham, and Colston, they also are keenly aware of the importance role players have in the overall effectiveness of the offense.

When Philadelphia Eagles defensive coordinator Jim Schwartz elected to double-cover Kamara and Thomas in the teams' 2018 regular season game in New Orleans, Brees completed 18 of 26 passes to his supporting cast. Smith, Arnold, Kirkwood, and Carr—a third-round draft pick and three undrafted free agents— combined to catch 18 passes for 244 yards and two touchdowns in a 48–7 blowout. A week later, Arnold, Lewis, Kirkwood, and Carr accounted for all four touchdowns in the Saints' 31–17 rout of the Atlanta Falcons.

Hill noted this after scoring the Saints' only two touchdowns in a 26–18 win against the Atlanta Falcons in 2019, "When you have guys like Mike Thomas, Alvin Kamara, Jared Cook, the list goes on, it kind of creates opportunities for little ole' me because there is so much attention that is put on those guys and Coach [Payton] is one of the best at being creative and putting guys in positions to be successful," Hill said. "I got lucky because I was that guy tonight."

When Payton noticed a flaw in the Cowboys' defensive scheme in 2006, he famously targeted fullback Mike Karney throughout the game. Karney caught five passes for 39 yards and scored three touchdowns. In the 12 games leading into the Dallas game, Karney had a total of eight catches for 43 yards and six carries for 10 yards.

"Sean loves that because he's such a football nerd," Saints wide receiver Austin Carr told NBC Sports' Peter King in 2018. "He's the football equivalent of a coder."

Carr is a role player in the Saints offense. His main role is blocking in the running game, which explains why he caught a total of 10 passes for 106 yards and two touchdowns in the 21 games he played during his first three seasons. But that didn't stop Payton from calling his number for a couple of touchdowns in the 2018 season. Both scores exemplified Payton's ingenious play-calling.

Because Carr is an excellent blocker, the Saints use him on many running plays, both to give Mike Thomas a breather and to take advantage of Carr's physicality on the perimeter. Entering the Saints' Week 12 game against the Atlanta Falcons, Payton noticed on film that teams were overplaying the run when Carr entered the game, essentially ignoring him as a receiver. So he installed a play against the Falcons on Thanksgiving night to take advantage of it.

Payton planned to use the play in the red zone, so when the Saints approached the Falcons 20-yard line late in the first half, he set the hook. Carr was inserted into the lineup on a second-and-5 play and the Saints ran the ball with Mark Ingram.

When they reached the red zone two plays later, they used the same formation and personnel grouping, but this time, Carr slipped off his block and popped free into the right flat. Brees hit him for an easy 12-yard touchdown. No Falcons defender was within 10 yards of Carr. Another touchdown pass that Connor Payton could have thrown.

"That score was set up with the previous four or five weeks of play-calling," Carr said. "We had run that play tons of times with the same personnel grouping. If you ask someone a question and you know what answer they're going to give you, then you already have your response, right? That's why he's special as a play-caller."

Intel also contributed to Carr's score. The Saints took advantage of inexperienced Falcons safety Sharrod Neasman on the play. Neasman was a former undrafted rookie free agent who was thrust into a starting role because of injuries to Keanu Neal and Ricardo Neal earlier in the season. The Saints were familiar with Neasman from the time they had him in training camp earlier that season and knew some of his tendencies. Later in the Thanksgiving night game, Brees picked on Neasman again, hitting Arnold in single coverage against him for a 25-yard touchdown pass.

The aggressive way Payton targeted defensive weaknesses reminded former Saints wide receiver Devery Henderson of how Nick Saban would attack offenses during his coaching tenure at LSU.

"Sean Payton is a great play-caller and he sees the game through the eyes of a quarterback," Gannon said. "He likes to keep his foot on the throttle and continue to keep the pressure on the defense throughout the course of the game."

The former quarterback in Payton understands and appreciates the competitive mindset of his players. He knows the best way to keep his skill players invested in the plan is to get them the ball. And as the play-caller, he tries to call the number of as many players as possible early during a game.

Consequently, the Saints have rarely had players publicly complain about their usage or number of targets. The notable exception was Brandin Cooks, who openly expressed his frustrations about not being targeted enough in 2016. Not surprisingly, the Saints traded Cooks to the New England Patriots a year later.

"What's remarkable is how well Sean and Drew can manage those personalities through the game plan by putting them in situations where they can be successful," McCown said. "When you're shuffling personnel as much as Sean does, the genius of organizing a game plan that balances the goal of helping the team win and attacking the defense while also managing personalities and making everybody happy is beyond impressive. The amount of time that both of them put into the offensive game plan and managing people and scheming to get the ball to guys early in the game and keep them involved for that offense that really take their offensive genius to another level."

Brees makes a conscious effort to keep everyone involved. He regularly completes at least one pass to every skill position player on the active roster in a game. He rarely plays a game when he doesn't at least target every offensive weapon at his disposal.

In 2018, Drew Brees set an NFL record by throwing touchdown passes to 15 different players including the regular season and postseason. Of those 15 players, nine were former undrafted free agents: Arnold, Carr, Kirkwood, Lewis, Meredith, Garrett Griffin, Zach Line, and both Hills, Josh and Taysom. According to the Elias Sports Bureau, no team has had nine undrafted players catch touchdown passes since the draft came into existence in 1936.

"I think that's what makes Drew so great, is it doesn't matter who you are or where you went to school or if you're a first-round pick or undrafted. If you get open, he's gonna get you the ball," Griffin said.

Griffin is a perfect example of Brees and Payton's "if-you're-open" passing philosophy. The tight end from Air Force spent the entire 2018 regular season on the practice squad and was activated for the playoffs. The five-yard touchdown pass he caught from Brees in the NFC Championship Game remains the only touchdown catch of his career.

"If you look over the course of the [2018] season, some of the guys who have had touchdowns, it's like people had never even heard of them before," Griffin said. "I think that's what kind of makes Drew special."

This share-the-wealth approach by Brees and Payton has the added benefit of keeping defenses off-balance. As Seattle Seahawks coach Pete Carroll said before their Week 3 game of the 2019 season against the Saints, "I don't know what Sean's going to do. But rarely does anybody know what he's going to do come game time."

And that includes his own coaches and players. No idea is too crazy for Payton. He tells his staff he's in the "buying business" when it comes to play ideas. This inclusive approach also fosters buy-in from the staff.

"Sean always wants thoughts and ideas and input," Marrone said. "The mindset is always about being open-minded about trying to get better. There's really no limit to where we want to go. Sometimes the crazier the idea was, the better chance you had of getting it called in a game. The thought process was: Are we good enough to get this done?"

The answer for Payton, Brees, and the Saints offensive staff is always yes.

13

The Supercomputer

THE PLAY ON WHICH DREW BREES BROKE PEYTON MANNING'S all-time passing record is called *Hop to Gun King Trips Right Tear 52 Sway All Go Special X Shallow Cross Halfback Wide.* It's a derivative of one of the Saints' most popular route concepts, the All Go Special, one of their favorite zone beaters. It's designed to beat zone coverage by flooding one side of the field with four receivers. The route concept on the strong side of the offensive formation stresses the deep safety and flat defenders by running three receivers through the coverage on vertical routes and sending the running back into the flat on the same side. The defenders in coverage on that side of the field are forced to make split-second decisions on who to cover.

Precise spacing and route running are keys to the play. The receivers aligned wide—in this case, Tre'Quan Smith and Cameron Meredith—are positioned on each side of the numbers and run vertical go routes straight downfield. Smith is assigned to release outside his defender and fade his route toward the sideline. Inside of Smith, Meredith maintains his route down the numbers. And inside of them, Arnold, aligned in the slot just outside the right tackle, runs a post route designed to carry the safety in the middle of the field. Michael Thomas, the only receiver aligned to the left side of the formation, runs a shallow crossing route underneath the zone coverage to the right. Kamara provides the checkdown outlet by running a flat route to the right.

Brees' progression, known as a triangle read, is to the two inside receivers on the right—in this case, Meredith and Arnold—and then to Thomas, cutting across the field underneath from left to right.

The play stresses the zone coverage by sending three receivers deep on vertical routes—Smith, Meredith, and Arnold—and two receivers shallow on horizontal routes—Thomas and Kamara. If defenders don't communicate well and maintain proper discipline in their assignments, it can often produce a big play. Against the Redskins, the Saints ran this same play with the same personnel on the previous series to the left side of their formation. Brees hit his primary read, Meredith, down the numbers for a 46-yard gain to convert a second-and-17 play.

Now, on first-and-10 with Brees needing 35 yards to break the record and a national television audience watching, the Saints were calling it again, this time flipped to the opposite side of the formation.

During their week of preparation, the Saints noticed on film that the Redskins made an adjustment in their Cover 2 defense when the opponent aligned four skill players to one side of the field. The Redskins walked up their free safety—in this case, D.J. Swearinger—to cover the running back's route out of the backfield and rolled strong safety Montae Nicholson into a single safety alignment in the middle of the field. When this happened, the cornerbacks aligned on the boundary were responsible for deep coverage on their third of the field.

The Saints knew exactly how to attack this vulnerability. And they were going to try to make history while doing it.

When Brees motioned Kamara from the left side of the backfield to the right side before the snap, the Redskins responded accordingly. Swearinger immediately repositioned toward the line of scrimmage and Nicholson rolled left to the middle of the field. After motioning Kamara, Brees immediately called for the snap. The Saints were blitzing the defense, forcing the Redskins to adjust on the fly. And it worked.

As Brees backpedaled into his five-step drop and surveyed the field, he immediately noticed something awry. Josh Norman, the Redskins cornerback on the strong side of the field, was in the wrong place. Instead of retreating to cover the deep third of the secondary, he instead squatted in coverage near the line of scrimmage, eyes glued to Brees and Kamara.

"I'm turning and looking, I see that the corner, who's supposed to be deep third is not deep third, so immediately I know there's nobody in the deep third and that's where Tra'quan is," Brees said. "Look, throw. I didn't even look, throw. It was just...feel, throw."

Smith was wide open. Sixty-two yards later, he was in the end zone with the record-breaking catch.

Smith was as shocked as anyone that the ball came his way. As the outside receiver on the strong side of the play, his role is essentially to occupy the attention of the boundary cornerback and pull him away from Meredith and Arnold. In other words, he's the clear-out guy. In Saints jargon, this is known as a "bus ticket" route.

"We call it a bus ticket because if you don't have an outside release and carry the corner and mess up the play, then they're going to find you a bus ticket home," Taysom Hill said. "That gives you an idea of where [Smith's] route is in the progression on that play."

The play is one of the most popular in the Saints playbook. They've run it countless times over the years. Brees' first option is to Arnold on the post, then he looks to Meredith. If they are covered, he comes back to Thomas on the crossing route underneath. Kamara is the checkdown option if all else fails. But Smith? In all of the years the Saints have run the play during the Payton-Brees era, coaches and players said they can't remember a pass ever being thrown to the receiver on that route.

"I'm, like, the fourth read in the progression," Smith said. "I thought Drew was going to throw it to Cam again because he was also open."

It was a one-in-a-million throw. And fittingly, Brees delivered it on the play that made him the NFL's all-time passing king.

"I don't know how Drew saw him or felt him on that play," Carmichael said. "The Redskins had gotten a little confused and were in between one coverage and another coverage. Drew just threw it up. He didn't even think. To this day, I don't think we've ever thrown it to that guy on that particular play."

Over the years, Brees has developed an encyclopedic knowledge of NFL defenses. He's picked the brains of every defensive coordinator on the Saints staff over the years to learn the responsibilities of each defender in each defensive coverage. When Norman went off script and blew the coverage, Brees knew it the same way you or I would recognize the rearrangement of our living room furniture.

"He processes things extremely well," Payton said. "It's one of his rare traits. Where that ball went on that pass was uncanny."

This almost superhuman ability to process and execute in game conditions is why former Saints tackle Jon Stinchomb refers to Brees as "the supercomputer." His teammates and coaches marvel at his ability to compute on the fly and make split-second decisions.

"The amount of information that he can take out and process and react to is much more than anyone I've ever been around," Lombardi said. "His lens is wide, and he sees everything and processes it so quick."

Brees is constantly computing calculations in his head. When the Saints find a cornerback or safety they want to target in coverage,

Brees essentially becomes an oddsmaker in cleats. His mind calculates the chances of success on a play based on the matchups discussed during the week of preparation.

In Brees' mind, receivers like Colston and Thomas are rarely truly covered. Because of his confidence in his own accuracy and the trust he's developed with his receivers during practice, Brees is willing to throw passes many other quarterbacks won't attempt, especially if it's a matchup he and the staff have deemed favorable during their week of preparation.

"If Mike Thomas is one-on-one, I like our odds," Brees said. "Even when he's two-on-one, it had better be a really good two-on-one or else there's usually still a place you can throw the ball where he can get it and they can't. You assess that. That's my job as a quarterback. Be a great decision maker, get the ball in the hands of the playmakers, but you'll make those good decisions."

A 2009 game against the New York Giants illustrated this point. The Saints went after Giants safety C.C. Brown in coverage for the entire game. Brown was a backup strong safety who had been forced into a starting role at free safety because of injuries. He had three total interceptions in his four-year career. Football Outsiders referred to him as a player "with the range of a broken wireless router." The Saints targeted Brown seven times in coverage and completed five passes for 96 yards, five first downs, and two touchdowns.

"In that game specifically, I'm looking at a safety who isn't very experienced," Brees said, recalling, in detail, the strategy for the game almost a decade later. "I can tell [from film study] that he's maybe not in the right position a lot of times. Then when the ball is in the air, he has a hard time tracking it, a hard time playing the receiver. In my mind, the computation immediately goes up in our favor as to the percentage of something good that will happen. If any of my guys get one-on-one with this guy down the field, I'm going to throw it, because only three things can happen, and none of them are really that bad. The worst thing that happens is an incompletion. But we also might get a PI [pass interference penalty]. Or we might catch it for a touchdown. Immediately, in my mind, when I get that matchup, it's like, 'Ding, ding, ding.' That's opportunity."

In the Saints' Week 16 game against the Tennessee Titans in 2019, Brees made a similar calculation. He had tight end Jared Cook in single coverage against safety Kevin Byard. Brees went after him for a completely different reason than he did C.C. Brown a decade earlier. Byard, after all, was a Pro Bowler and All-Pro in 2017. He was regarded as one of the top ball hawks in the league, with 16 interceptions in the 2017–19 seasons. But none of that mattered to Brees. In his mind, it was basic math. Or in this case, physics. Cook stands 6'5". Byard is 5'11".

Byard jammed Cook at the line of scrimmage and ran stride for stride with him toward the goal line. By all accounts, Byard had Cook covered. Undeterred, Brees fired a pass high and over Cook's outside shoulder and Cook made a leaping grab in the back of the end zone. The 16-yard touchdown gave the Saints a 30–21 lead in the fourth quarter and helped seal a big road win.

"Cook is a big target obviously, and he has a big catch radius," Brees said later explaining why he targeted Cook on the play. "Any one-on-one matchup, there's not a guy on defense that's going to match his size, right? You always feel like there is a place where you throw the football where he can get it and other guys can't."

Brees has made these calculations throughout his career. It doesn't always work, of course. Sometimes the defensive back turns at the right time and intercepts the ball, as Cre'Von LeBlanc did on the first play from scrimmage in the Saints' 2019 NFC divisional playoff game against the Philadelphia Eagles. But more often than not, Brees' math skills have been rewarded.

"We're in the business of odds," Brees said. "When it comes to just one-on-one matchups in the passing game, you're really playing the odds. I'm constantly doing those computations in my head. That's the preparation during the week because you really don't have time to think on Sundays. It has to be a reaction. The reaction comes from what you've inputted into the computer throughout the week. It's if this guy or if these guys are one-on-one with this guy, I'm throwing it."

This ability to process under pressure is one of the most difficult traits for NFL scouts to evaluate in quarterbacks. Former Saints general manager Randy Mueller toyed with the idea of developing flight simulator software to facilitate the process for NFL personnel executives. Mueller selected Notre Dame quarterback Rick Mirer with the No. 2 overall pick in the 1993 NFL Draft and recalled how impressive Mirer was during the evaluation process while throwing on the field and breaking down Xs and Os on the whiteboard. But once the Seahawks played Mirer in a game, he struggled to execute. Mirer was highly intelligent, but he struggled to process the chaos at high speed. Mirer washed out as a starter in Seattle and ended his eight-year career as a journeyman.

Of all the many strengths Brees possesses, processing under pressure might be his greatest one. Saints coaches have learned over the years not to prematurely question his decisions during games. Each can cite a play where they have gasped incredulously into their headset as Brees makes an off-script delivery, only to see the pass connect for a big gain or touchdown.

"One of his great assets is he can think so quickly," Lombardi said. "He's smart. But there are plenty of guys that are as smart as he is. It's when that clock is running down and there's a linebacker up in the A gap, and he doesn't get nervous. He figures it all out. He's just a calm mind when the pressure is on. That's one of the most unique things about him. When it's go time, he thinks even more clearly than when he's sitting there in the meeting room. He's better in that environment."

Former NFL quarterback Trent Dilfer, the director of Nike's Elite 11 passing camps, remembers watching game film of Brees when Dilfer played for the Seattle Seahawks and being awestruck by his ability to stay one step ahead of the defense. Whatever the opponent threw at him, Brees always had an answer.

"It was like watching a surgeon," said Dilfer, who quarterbacked the Baltimore Ravens to the Super Bowl XXXV title in 2001. "He literally looks at every little detail, every minuscule aspect of quarterbacking and perfects it. As a quarterback watching it, you're like, man, I hope I can make that decision when I'm playing on Sunday. Man, I hope I see that. How did he know that? What did he study to figure that one out? How he did he make that throw? How did he know to throw it that early? You just sat there in admiration of he had all the answers to the test before the game started."

And it's not just matchups Brees is computing. He's also processing the opposing pass rush and working with the offensive line to set the protection scheme.

Stinchcomb recalled a 2009 game against the New York Jets where Brees consistently stayed one step ahead of head coach Rex Ryan and his unconventional pass rush schemes.

"Nine times out of 10 we would pick it up on the offensive line, but when we didn't Drew was always there to make it right," Stinchcomb said. "You've got a supercomputer behind you processing in a split-second. There are elite quarterbacks that would not be able to do what Drew does. There is so much that he does that he doesn't get credit for. Part of the reason our offensive line has looked so good over the years is because of him. He makes us look good. He makes everyone look good."

The Saints give Brees autonomy to change plays at the line of scrimmage. Many of the Saints play calls have run-pass options, which allow the quarterback to determine the play after he gets to the line of scrimmage and diagnoses the defense.

"Sean is a great play-caller, one of the best offensive minds ever, but he has always had the luxury of having a quarterback that's going to make him right," Mark Brunell said. "And it says a lot about Sean that he gives Drew the authority to do it. It's just one small example of why they work so well together. It's that trust."

Brees' ability to effortlessly make these high-pressure adjustments and get the Saints out of the wrong play and into the right one has become such a staple of the Saints offense, coaches jokingly say it can lead to complacency in their jobs. If they don't watch themselves, they'll find themselves resting on their laurels, knowing Brees will always do the right thing and make them look good.

"Part of our job as coaches is to put the players in situations that they're comfortable in and to not ask them to do what they can't do," Lombardi said. "That's never the case with Drew. He can do more than we can give him when it comes to that. I remember in our playoff run in 2009 against Arizona, we were in a play that was a run with a check to a pass and we got a [defensive] look that we hadn't seen. At first, we were like, 'Ah, they got us.' Then we were like, 'What's he going to do here?' He figured it out. He recognized that both options were bad and had a plan. He audibled out of it, and we scored a touchdown."

For this reason, Lombardi compares Brees to Harvey Keitel's character, Winston Wolfe, in the Quentin Tarantino classic *Pulp Fiction*.

"Drew is a great fixer," Lombardi said. "He's like the Wolf in *Pulp Fiction*. He solves problems."

14

Maxing Out

ON SUNDAY, DECEMBER 15, 2019, THE INDOOR PRACTICE FACILITY
at the New Orleans Saints training complex was almost empty. The
Saints had completed their walk-through practice in preparation
for their Monday night game against the Indianapolis Colts about a
half-hour earlier, and most of the players had retreated to the locker
room to undress, shower, and head home. This was essentially the
end of the work week. The only official team duties between now and
kickoff on Monday night were a few meetings at the team hotel in
downtown New Orleans later that night. But one Saint was still on
the field: Drew Brees.

Dressed in his red No. 9 practice jersey, shorts, and a baseball
cap, Brees stood at the 10-yard line of the south end zone and
worked through the script of plays in the game plan for the Colts.
He surveyed the imaginary defensive formation, then turned to his
imaginary teammates and audibled to a new play with a pair of his
hand signals. He then signaled to the imaginary center, took the
imaginary snap, and retreated into a three-step drop. At the top of
his drop, he looked left, checking off his imaginary receivers in the

route progression of the play. Then, he looked right, shifting his body and feet for optimal balance, all the while pumping the imaginary ball in his right hand. Brees' choreography was so true to form he even licked his fingers between plays, just as he does habitually during games.

For Brees, the visualization session is a vital part of his weekly routine. It's his opportunity to play the game before the game, to reinforce the game plan and mentally steel himself for the approaching battle.

He doesn't just simulate a successful completion. He also works through contingencies in each situation. *What do I do if the defense double-teams my first option? Where's my hot read if the linebackers blitz through the A gap? What if no one is open?*

Over and over, he systematically works his way through each play on the call sheet. Each rehearsal takes between 20 and 30 minutes to complete, and Brees doesn't stop until he's comfortable with each play sequence. It's a tedious, lonely process, but a critical one for Brees. The mental reps are just as important as the physical ones he takes in practice, a necessity for him to feel comfortable and confident heading into game day.

"I think when you can have a very defined starting point and ending point on every play, despite what is happening all around you, I think that helps create a calmness and a poise with you as a quarterback, which you have to have," Brees said. "I'd say that's very much controlling the chaos. How you determine that starting point and that ending point on every play is through preparation. When you've visualized everything that could happen, most importantly, when you've visualized the worst-case scenario—'If they do this, what's my answer?'—if you have all the answers, and you have all the tools, then you don't really go in worried. You almost want them to do it. You almost want them to throw you that change-up because you're like, 'Man, I've worked so hard to put myself in a position to combat this. Let's see it.'"

Brees honed his visualization process under Tom House, the former Major League Baseball pitcher who has built a second career as a coach, throwing specialist and sports psychologist. House, who holds a PhD in sports psychology, uses neurophysiological techniques to help athletes deal with the stress and anxiety of competition. He believes mental discipline and focus are as important to successful athletic performance as physical talent, maybe more so. House often has his clients perform drills while blindfolded or with their eyes closed to enhance their mental acuity.

"It's being able to draw on experience that when you see this, it's an outcome thing, when you see this, this is going to happen," House said. "[Brees] connects dots better than anybody I've ever seen."

Research has indicated mental rehearsal is helpful in various disciplines. A 2015 LSU study showed that surgeons who rehearsed their procedures beforehand performed better than those who didn't. Astronaut Chris Hadfield said it was an essential part of his preparation for spaceflight.

Countless athletes have also employed visualization exercises over the years. One of House's former teammates and pupils, pitcher Nolan Ryan, became a devotee of visualization during the last decade of his career. Early on the day of his starts, he would spend an hour or two going through the opponent's batting order, breaking down the strengths and weaknesses of each hitter, and visualizing how he got them out in past meetings. It was a ritual he repeated habitually throughout his career.

Alex Honnold, the renowned mountain climber and star of the Academy Award–winning documentary *Free Solo*, incorporated visualization into his prep work for his historic 2017 summit of Yosemite Park's famed El Capitan. Honnold meticulously recorded every move and technique required to scale the 3,000-foot granite face. He also mentally rehearsed contingency plans for bad weather or unexpected circumstances like falling rocks and wind gusts, the idea being, if you've already thought through how everything could feel, even when it goes wrong, you're prepared if things actually do go south. Rehearsing the way certain scary moments will feel means that those moments feel "right" when they happen, instead of feeling surprising.

Brees watched *Free Solo* twice and was fascinated by Honnold's preparation and mental stamina but noted one important difference between mountain climbing and football.

"The mountain is not changing, right?" Brees said. "He scripted his entire climb, but he knew where each of those cracks, crevices, and everything would be.

"There was a lot of things that you could see that maybe you didn't expect on game day, but very similar to that, when you have the answers to the test before you take the test—'If they do this, I'm going to do this, and if they do this, I'm going to do that'—then you feel like, 'Man, there's nothing they can do that I don't have a plan for.' You go in with a lot of confidence and a sense of peace, like, 'I put myself in the best position to succeed today, so whatever happens, happens, and I'm just going to turn it loose.'"

Brees started the visual walk-through sessions early in his Saints career and has religiously continued them on the day before games throughout his tenure in New Orleans.

Teammates and staff members often happen across Brees during one of his sessions on their way from the weight room to the team cafeteria and say he is so focused on the task at hand that he doesn't even notice their existence.

That was the case for Reggie Bush and some of his teammates from the Super Bowl LIV championship team on this particular Sunday. The players were in New Orleans to commemorate the 10th anniversary of the Super Bowl championship. The weekend was a three-day celebration of parties and public appearances. Payton invited the team to the Saints' walk-through practice and Bush, Scott Shanle, and Scott Fujita stumbled upon Brees going through his on-field rehearsal 40 minutes after practice.

Bush pulled out his cell phone, recorded a couple minutes of the session, and posted it on social media. The video went viral in minutes.

"This is what the leader of an organization, the leader of a football team looks like, right here," Bush narrated to his 651,000 Instagram followers. "This is what it takes. There's nobody in here but one man, getting his mind right, doing what he needs to do to prepare himself for greatness, for tomorrow's game. And this is what he does every week, every day [as long as he] has been playing football now. That's what it's about. You want to be great. This is what greatness looks like right here. Ain't no shortcuts in this world. You get what you put in."

The visualization exercise is just one facet of Brees' legendary weekly routine, which is planned almost to the minute, a regimen that amazes his teammates and coaches because of the discipline and mental toughness required to maintain it. Even after the birth of his four children and an expanding business portfolio, Brees has refused to take shortcuts or reduce his workload. Instead, he just started waking up earlier and adding more hours to his day. Brees believes the onerous daily schedule is necessary to adequately prepare his body and mind for game day. And the high standards he sets for himself have raised the bar for everyone else in the building—players, coaches, and staff members alike.

Brees' path to greatness started in San Diego. After his second season as a starter for the Chargers, Brees' career was going nowhere. He won only 10 of his first 28 games as a starter and threw more interceptions (31) than touchdowns (28). He knew he needed to overhaul his entire life if he wanted to reach his potential. In the 2004 offseason, he changed his diet, his strength training, his approach, and his attitude. He worked with performance specialist Jim Brogran on conditioning and balance work and consulted with House about throwing mechanics as part of a broad-based overhaul. He overhauled his diet after a nutritionist discovered he was allergic to wheat, barley, rye, all dairy, eggs, pineapple, and a variety of nuts. He even went online to complete a "Star Profile" to identify potential problem traits. That season, Brees led the Chargers to a 12–4 record and AFC West Division title, while earning the first Pro Bowl berth of his career.

"He realized he had more in the tank and went out and found a way to get more out of his gene pool," House said. "He grew up to be the individual he was capable of being. All we did was put the jigsaw puzzle together."

When Brees arrived in New Orleans as a free agent two years later, he brought his regimen with him and continued to perfect it. No stone was left unturned. He knew he needed to maximize everything within his control—conditioning, nutrition, game prep, mental stamina—to compensate for what he couldn't control: his lack of prototypical height, speed, and strength.

To that end, Brees developed a strict daily regimen—one for the season and one for the offseason. And from Day One, he committed himself to always being the first and last player in the building.

When Jamie Martin signed with the Saints in 2006 to be Brees' backup, he moved to the north shore of Lake Pontchartrain. On the first day of the offseason training program that April, Martin left home well before dawn, afraid that the infamous lake fog along the causeway would cause him to be late on his first day. His was the first car to arrive in the players' parking lot.

"Drew walks in a few minutes later and says, 'Hey, you get here pretty early, huh?'" said Martin, too chagrined to tell his teammate it was simply a case of overcorrection. "The next day I get there, and sure enough, Drew's car is already there in the parking lot."

All these years later, little has changed. He's always the first player to arrive at the Saints training facility in Metairie and the last to leave. He's tweaked his routine to adjust to changes in the Saints' practice schedule, but otherwise his weekly regimen has stayed largely the same.

For Brees, winning a game starts with the preparation. He firmly believes the work he does Monday through Saturday is just as important as what he does on game day. As a reminder, he keeps a plaque with a quote from Chinese military strategist Zhuge Liang on a shelf in his locker: THOSE WHO ARE SKILLED IN COMBAT DO NOT BECOME ANGERED. THOSE WHO ARE SKILLED AT WINNING DO NOT BECOME AFRAID. THUS, THE WISE WIN BEFORE THEY FIGHT, WHILE THE IGNORANT FIGHT TO WIN.

His week begins on Monday, which is usually a light day to review the previous game and get in some recovery work for his body. Brees grades himself on every play, as does Joe Lombardi. He gets in a workout and then calls it a day.

Tuesday is when the page turns to the next opponent. Brees awakes at 5:00 AM during the season and makes the 20-minute commute from his Uptown home to the team facility. He breaks down film in the tight ends room, which is located on the first floor of the building across the hall from the main squad room. He grabs a quick breakfast and then heads back to the tight ends room to meet with the other quarterbacks for more film study at 8:30 AM. He rarely leaves the facility before dark.

Wednesday begins at 6:30 AM with a film-study session. He then heads to the first full squad meeting of the week at 8:30 AM. Special teams and position meetings follow, then it's off to the locker room to get dressed for practice at noon. The Wednesday practice focuses on the game plan for what is known as the base offense and defense, first- and second-down plays, with a heavy emphasis on the running game. A weight-training session follows practice; then Brees heads to the locker room, where he meets with the media for his weekly press conference with local reporters around 2:45 PM. He then visits the training room adjacent to the locker room for any maintenance work he needs on his body, grabs a bite to eat from the cafeteria, and then heads to more meetings from 4:00 to 5:00 PM, where he and the other quarterbacks review practice with Lombardi. More film study follows with the other quarterbacks before Brees finally calls it a day around 7:00 PM. He gets home around 7:30 and spends time with his kids before putting them to bed at 9:00 PM. He then retreats to the kitchen and further studies the game plan over dinner until he goes to bed.

Thursday and Friday are structured similarly, but the game plan and film study change. On Thursday, the focus is third downs, and on Friday, it's situational work: red zone; goal line; short yardage.

The game plan is largely completed by Saturday. Brees and the quarterbacks meet to go over the script of plays for that week's opponents. The team conducts meetings in the morning, then holds a light walk-through session on the field for 45 minutes or so and breaks for the day. Brees gets in his visualization session after the walk-through, then the team reconvenes at the facility for the charter flight out of town or at the team's downtown hotel for home games. More meetings are held that night at the team hotel, including the "dot meeting," where, if you recall, Payton and Brees go over the final script and Brees tells the head coach what plays he likes best for each game situation.

"As I've gotten older, there's more and more hours devoted to the recovery [of my body]," Brees said. "There's no free time. I think my free time is maybe on the plane ride to fly to an away game or when I'm coaching my kids in flag football."

Brees' rigid adherence to his schedule allows everyone in the building to know his location at any hour of the day in the building. Lombardi kids that he can set his watch to Brees' routine. "If I walk in the film room on Wednesday morning at 7:00 AM he's probably going to be on the sub-blitz tape," Lombardi said.

Chase Daniel was so impressed by Brees' weekly regimen that he copied it and took it with him to playing stints in Kansas City, Philadelphia, and Chicago. Few other players have had the temerity to follow Brees' lead, although backup Taysom Hill had become the closest thing to an acolyte in recent years.

"It takes discipline and mental stamina to keep doing something over and over again, day after day, year after year," Lombardi said. "Maybe you could do it for football. I'm sure he does it for everything he does."

Brees indeed has a routine for almost everything, from his pregame warm-up to the way he puts on his uniform. His pregame warm-up always begins with a jog around the perimeter of the playing field. He then goes through the exact same exercise and calisthenic routine at the exact same spot on the field. Game after game, it's the same 20-minute warm-up. He never deviates.

He starts each practice the same way. After a quick warm-up, Brees goes to a specific spot on the sideline and touches his foot to it. He leaves his spot on the sideline, and waiting for him right where it is supposed to be is a water bottle left by a member of the staff. Brees picks it up and gives himself three squirts before starting practice. In the weight room, he does exactly the number of core-exercise reps to correspond to that year's Super Bowl. During the 2018 season, he did 53 reps. In 2019, it was 54.

Newcomers to the Saints program are often caught off-guard by Brees' habits. At first, they seem bizarre, borderline maniacal. How he wears his helmet during the daily post-practice quarterback challenge competition with teammates or climbs the pocket during non-padded, no-contact walk-through drills in practice. How he performs his stretches the exact same way every day at practice and jogs to one end of the field while everyone else is on the other end. How during his visualization sessions he barks out the cadence the exact same way he does to teammates during a game.

"When I got here, I was thinking, 'Is this guy a robot?'" Saints receiver Keith Kirkwood joked.

Hill had the same thoughts after he joined the Saints from the Green Bay Packers via waiver claim in September 2017.

"I thought, 'What in the world is he doing?'" Hill said, laughing. "When I saw the way that he prepared, I was shocked. I couldn't believe it. This guy still prepares this way when he knows the offense as well as he does, and he knows these defenses better than the defenders themselves. But that's just a testament to Drew. He always wants to be prepared. He's going to do everything he can to allow himself to be successful and his teammates around him to be successful."

But Hill and Kirkwood, like the rest of their teammates, quickly learned there was a method to Brees' madness.

"There's not any rock that is not overturned," Hill said. "Everything he does, every single throw in practice, is deliberate. That's what it boils down to. His ability to be deliberate in everything he does. If you think about it, that can be exhausting. But he does it."

Brees' zealous commitment to excellence reminds Lombardi of a phrase used in U.S. Army Special Forces: how you do anything is how you do everything.

"I don't think it's ever applied to anyone more than it does him," said Lombardi, a graduate and former tight end at the U.S. Air Force Academy. "I bet there's nothing that he doesn't do with the same approach. I bet he brushes his teeth with the same routine. 'How can you be the best tooth brusher you can be? I'm going to do it.' I'd like to say I've got a way of doing business, but when I go play golf,

I could give a shit. He cares a lot about everything he does. And there's a purpose. 'All right, how do I do this best?'"

Joe Brady, the Carolina Panthers offensive coordinator, said he constantly told his players at LSU about Brees' extraordinary work regimen and commitment to excellence. He used Brees as a role model to inspire his players and motivate them to adopt better practice habits. If Brees can do it, he says, they can, too.

"Everything matters to him," Brady said. "The way he watches film and how you know at 6 AM he's going to be in the tight ends room at that exact time watching film. How when he approaches that huddle for a walkthrough and OTAs it's just like he would be doing if it was the Super Bowl. Everything matters to him."

Payton compares Brees' preparation habits to a fighter pilot.

"His mental preparation during the week and just the exhausting nature of what that takes is amazing to watch," Payton said. "There has been a ton of great players that have played in this league and there's certain ways that they prepare and that's his formula. He's a tireless worker, and the attention to detail and the little things are important to him. He gets out of whack when the routine's off a little bit."

Brees' weekly focus and concentration set the example for the entire team—players, coaches, even people in the organization's business operations. His attention to detail and high standard of excellence are infectious and force others to raise their own standards to keep up with him.

"The way he does everything, how he handles his business, the way he's always the last one to leave the field—he never stops, he's just relentless," All-Pro receiver Michael Thomas said. "All of that is contagious to me. You want to try to perfect your game so that one day you can be an elite guy like him."

Alvin Kamara started following Brees' work and study habits shortly after he joined the organization in the spring of 2017. He'd never seen a player work as hard as Brees. His work ethic resonated with the star running back and motivated him to work just as hard at his craft.

"I kind of took a step back and was like, 'All right, well, if I want to be the best, then I gotta know what the best knows,'" Kamara said. "And I think Drew is probably one of, if not the, smartest people playing football right now, so I was like, 'All right, if I can get myself to try to be as in tune to the game as Drew...I can only get better. That's why he's been so successful, because it's like he has an answer for everything. It's like the kid you hate in class because he always knows the answer. That's Drew—but I love him, because he's my quarterback."

To reach the highest level of professional sports, players and coaches must have exceptional talent and work ethic. What separates Brees is his almost superhuman mental stamina, the ability to continue to study and process information, hour after hour, day after day, week after week.

"It's been the same way since he got here," said Strief, who joined the Saints at the same time as Brees in 2006 and has been with him as a teammate or coworker for his entire tenure in New Orleans. "It's how he was the day he got here in 2006. Some of the routines he has have not changed. You don't run into people in your life that can do that. Most people mentally just kind of exhale and let up. He doesn't have that mechanism in his body. It's a super unnatural ability that he has. He does the same stuff today that he was doing five years ago—at the same speed, at the same tempo, with the same intensity. It's the healthiest case of OCD I've ever seen. It's so productive. And it's something that most normal people could never maintain. I can't do that. It's what makes him exceptional."

House, Brees' performance coach, has scientific testing to confirm Strief's analysis. Using a device called a FocusBand, House and his staff have measured Brees' brain activity during various activities: workouts, practice, interacting with friends and family, playing with his kids. Remarkably, Brees' brain produced similar levels of output in each instance. There was no difference between the way he attacked his daily workout and the way he enjoyed time with his loved ones.

"When he works out with his new receivers [in San Diego], and he's in a teaching mode, his hertz of electrical activity in the teaching mode is the same as when he's working with his family," House said. "And his hertz of electrical activity when he's working with his family is the same as when he's playing on a Sunday afternoons. He shows up with X amount of motivation, X amount of effort and gives it to me every fucking time in whatever he's doing. We call it compartmentalization. He's a Renaissance man. He's special, not just in football. He's special in the big picture, in life, business, family, and fame."

This remarkable endurance has allowed Brees to maintain the same schedule for his entire tenure in New Orleans, 14 years and counting. Even after all the wins and records and accomplishments, he has refused to shortchange the process. Over the years he has fine-tuned his routine to incorporate what works for him and eliminate what doesn't. To create more time for his growing family, he's been forced to alter or reduce his demanding schedule. For example, he only attended a handful of the weekly dinners with his offensive linemen on Thursday nights in 2019, events he attended regularly earlier in his career. But otherwise, it's the same regimen he followed when he arrived in New Orleans in 2006.

"I have a definite routine and it takes a lot of time," Brees said. "I know where I'm going to be at a specific time. I know what I'm going to be doing; I know what needs to be accomplished for me to feel confident and go out there and play at the highest level. I understand the amount of work and effort that it's going to take to accomplish the things I want to accomplish. I've always had a goal that I want to continue to get better each and every year. That's what drives me. That's what I work so hard for."

House has worked with countless elite athletes over the years. During his second career as a performance coach, his roster of quarterback clients includes Tom Brady, Matt Ryan, Eli Manning, Cam Newton, Dak Prescott, Alex Smith, Carson Palmer, Jared Goff, Andrew Luck, Jimmy Garoppolo, Carson Wentz, and Tim Tebow. He's also worked with professional golfers and former Major League Baseball pitchers like Nolan Ryan, Randy Johnson, Kevin Brown, and Rob Nen.

"A lot of people don't understand how deep the work ethic is," House said. "Drew doesn't do stuff that is marginal in the contribution end of things. Everything he does is with a purpose. As you get more experienced, you know what you don't have to do. The attention to detail, that's what amazes me about Drew and [Nolan Ryan]. They're special."

Brees doesn't know any other way. For him, it's the only way he can properly prepare himself to play at an elite level on game days. He's been doing it this way for so long it's become second nature. He knows it's not the easy way. He knows it comes with significant sacrifice to his family and friends. But for him, the reward is worth the investment.

"It's a grind mentally," Brees said. "That's why when your season ends, you just want to escape for at least a month and just get away. But it's also part of the fun. There's a lot of satisfaction and a very rewarding feeling when you know the time and effort that you put into preparation—those long hours, long days, both physically and mentally—and you come out on game day and you watch these things happen that you visualized, that you played over and over in your mind. And you have that success and you watch young guys gain confidence and come out of their shells, become the players that you always hope they can be, too, there's something invigorating about that, too. That's what keeps you going."

DOME-INATION:
2011 Indianapolis Colts, New York Giants

Two years after dispatching the New York Giants and New England Patriots in memorable fashion, Drew Brees and the New Orleans Saints offense produced two more spectacular displays.

In Week 7 of the 2011 season, the Saints destroyed the Indianapolis Colts 62–7 on Sunday Night Football, setting franchise records for points and scoring margin. With Payton sitting in the coaches' box because of a broken leg suffered in a game the previous week in Tampa, Florida, Pete Carmichael called the plays and the Saints scored on their first nine series and recorded a then-franchise-record 36 first downs. Brees completed 31 of 35 passes for 325 yards and five touchdowns before yielding to Chase Daniel late in the third quarter. The point total tied for the most in any NFL game since the league merger in 1970. While impressive, the blowout came against a winless Colts team with Curtis Painter at quarterback in place of the injured Peyton Manning. Five weeks later, the Brees-led Saints delivered another jaw-dropping performance, this time against a 6–4 New York Giants team.

The Giants came to New Orleans on a mission. Their backs were to the wall. They'd lost two consecutive games and knew a home game with the Green Bay Packers awaited the following week. If ever a Week 12 game could be considered a "must-win," this was it.

The Saints, meanwhile, were coming off a bye, a holiday, and the emotional Gleason Gras celebration Sunday. The potential for distraction was there, but the Saints never showed signs of a holiday hangover. They were efficient and enthusiastic from the start. They gained 354 yards in the first half and recorded touchdown drives of 80, 80, and 88 yards. They took a 21–3 lead into the break, and it could have been more had they converted a fake field goal attempt on their opening possession. The Saints' first 11 drives ended this way: downs, touchdown, punt, touchdown, touchdown, touchdown, touchdown, punt, touchdown, downs, and touchdown. This against a Giants defense that would finish the season ranked third overall and first in scoring, allowing a meager 14 points a game.

The 577 yards were the most the Giants had surrendered in their modern history. The last time they allowed that many yards in a game was in 1948, when the Chicago Cardinals totaled 579 yards in a 63–35 win at the Polo Grounds.

"The statistics are alarming to me," NFL analyst Jon Gruden said during the ESPN broadcast. "I've never seen offensive numbers thrown up like Drew Brees, Sean Payton, and the New Orleans Saints. The statistics are amazing. When you get a great quarterback and a great coach and you surround them with great skills players, this kind of thing is possible."

Brees completed 24 of 38 passes for 363 yards and four touchdowns. He wasn't sacked and was hit just four times in 41 dropbacks. His eight-yard scoring run in the third quarter was part of a rushing attack that netted 205 yards and averaged 6.8 yards a carry.

"There's that confidence that players around him have, and obviously we have in him," Payton said afterward of Brees. "He made some fantastic throws tonight."

The blowout loss was a wake-up call for the Giants, who went on to win seven of their next nine games and upset the New England Patriots 21–17 in Super Bowl XLIV.

15

Fighting the Stereotype

LUKE MCCOWN REMEMBERS THE MOMENT DREW BREES convinced him he was inhuman.

To be precise, it was at the 2:55 mark of the third quarter in the Saints' Week 10 game against the San Francisco 49ers on November 9, 2014. On a third-and-6 play from the 49ers' 11, something very rare happened as Brees retreated into the shotgun formation. The 49ers fooled him. They overloaded their defensive alignment to the strong side of the Saints offensive formation, then attacked with a blitz from the weak side. Normally Brees is an expert at identifying such tactics. But this time, the Niners' subterfuge worked.

Safety Eric Reid and linebacker Michael Wilhoite both went unblocked as they converged at full speed on Brees in the Saints backfield. The pair was on him so quickly Brees barely had reached the top of his three-step drop when he was forced to react. Wilhoite had a direct bead on Brees and went in for the kill. Brees instinctively planted his right foot in the turf, juked to his left, and dipped his right shoulder as Wilhoite flew by to his right. The move took Brees directly into the path of the onrushing Reid, who never broke stride and lowered his head to deliver a knockout blow. Brees instinctively pirouetted at the 20-yard line and spun in a complete 360 to his right, causing Reid to completely whiff and take out the befuddled Wilhoite at the same time. Brees then re-gathered himself, reset his eyes downfield, and lofted an 11-yard touchdown pass to Jimmy Graham in the end zone.

"Wizardry from Drew Brees!" said play-by-play announcer Kevin Burkhardt on the Fox Sports broadcast, which panned to a shot of defensive coordinator Vic Fangio, standing hands on hips, staring incredulously down at the field from the coaches' box.

Brees had just conducted a magic trick, something straight out of a Warner Brothers cartoon.

Three stories below Fangio, McCown stood on the Saints sideline in awe.

Did he just do that?! McCown remembers thinking. "You've got to be kidding me. It was like he was Luke Skywalker and just turned invisible on them."

It would be one thing if Brees' Houdini act were an isolated incident, a one-off in his 19-year career. But he's performed these magic acts so many times the Saints offensive coaches have a phrase for it: the Brees Jedi Mind Trick.

There was the spin move he put on Robert Alford and Bryan Poole to leave the Falcons secondary tandem in his dust at the 5-yard line in Week 3 of the 2018 season. And the crafty juke he laid on Jimmy Smith four weeks later to cause the Ravens cornerback to whiff as an unblocked blitzer on a blind-side sack attempt, after which Brees found Dan Arnold for a 10-yard gain. The list goes on and on.

"I could pull up half a dozen of those plays on film," Lombardi said. "He does a shoulder twitch and guys fly by him like he's not there. It's become a joke in the quarterback room. I don't know how he does it."

Analysts and scouts have used myriad adjectives to describe Brees' brilliance over the years, among them: *cerebral, accurate, poised, driven.* But few have ever portrayed him as an athlete—a runs-fast, jumps-high, throws-hard type player. Most often, he is characterized as an overachieving, unathletic gym rat. But make no mistake, Brees is a great, great athlete.

Ask anyone in the New Orleans locker room about Brees' athletic skills, and you'll hear a litany of testimonies. He's not just the unquestioned leader of the Saints, he's also one of the best athletes on the entire team. Brees might lack elite straight-line speed—he ran a pedestrian 4.85-second 40-yard dash at the 2001 NFL Scouting Combine—but the rest of his athletic skills are way above average, even by NFL standards. He recorded a vertical leap of 32 inches at the NFL Scouting Combine, better than Derrius Guice (31.5), Tarik Cohen (31.5), Cooper Kupp (31.0), and Calvin Ridley (31.0). His time of 7.09 seconds in the three-cone drill was also very good, better than Teddy Bridgewater's 7.17.

One of the most enduring memories of the 2009 Super Bowl season was Brees, in helmet and full pads, dunking the ball over the goal post while celebrating a touchdown he scored on a quarterback sneak in the Saints' comeback win against the Miami Dolphins in Week 6.

"What is mislabeled is his athleticism," Payton says. "He's a rare athlete. When you look at his foot agility, his release, his accuracy, and the fact he has hands as big as mitts, he's got a skill set that is perfect for the position. He's an amazing athlete."

Part of Brees' problem, of course, is perception. At a touch over 6'0", he's short, at least by NFL quarterback standards. He plays a position that often values a strong arm and sound judgment more than raw athleticism. Quarterbacks made in Brees' mold tend to get stereotyped as cagey overachievers who overcome a lack of athletic skills with intelligence and unrelenting work ethic.

Brees has felt the slight since he began playing sports as a kid in Austin.

"I guess I'd just say this: As a 6-foot quarterback in this league you had better have some athletic ability, because that's really all you have going for you in a lot of ways, right?" Brees said.

Former Saints tight end Billy Miller learned the hard way about Brees' all-around athletic skills. During USO Tours overseas in 2008 and 2009, the pair would often train together. To mix things up, they would square off in basketball or racquetball. Miller, at 6'3", 252 pounds, figured he had an advantage over Brees. Each time, Brees soundly defeated the tight end, who was a good enough athlete at Westlake Village (California) High School to play running back and start for three seasons in basketball.

"Don't let him fool ya," Miller said. "He's a very good athlete, and he's not shy in telling you about it, either. He's extremely competitive."

Brees owes his precocious athletic skills to superior genetics. His mother was an all-state track, volleyball, and basketball player in high school. His father played freshman basketball at Texas A&M. His uncle was an All-American wishbone quarterback at Texas in the early 1970s. His grandfather, Ray Atkins, was one of the winningest high school football coaches in Texas history.

With a heritage like that, athletics were a part of Brees' life from the outset. He played every sport introduced to him and dreamed of becoming an Olympic athlete.

"I loved the decathlon," Brees said. "I wasn't that fast, but I could do a little bit of everything."

There was hardly a sport Brees couldn't master. As a youth and into his early teens, Brees starred in football, basketball, soccer, baseball, and tennis. At the age of 12, he was the top-ranked tennis player in Texas and defeated a younger Andy Roddick three times as a junior. That same year, Brees set an Austin city record with 14 home runs in Little League and was chosen to play on a youth soccer select team. A few years later, he starred at Westlake High School in football, basketball, and baseball, where he was a power-hitting infielder and a right-handed pitcher with an 88-mph fastball.

"Baseball was really the sport I thought I had the best opportunity of playing at the next level," said Brees, who wears No. 9 to honor his boyhood idol, Ted Williams. "I wanted to be a three-sport athlete in college: baseball, basketball, and football."

Football eventually became his meal ticket. But to this day, Brees continues to awe his friends and peers with flashes of his all-around athletic brilliance.

Before he became a father, when he had more time to golf, he was a scratch golfer, a sport he didn't start playing regularly until his junior year of college. At one time, he carried a 3 handicap. He has shot a couple of 71s, including one at New Orleans Country Club. In 2009, he hit his first hole-in-one while playing with General Manager Mickey Loomis and Greg Bensel, the team's vice president of communications. Brian Schottenheimer, the Seattle Seahawks offensive coordinator, who coached Brees in San Diego, said Brees owned an "uncanny, unbelievable" short game made possible by his delicate touch around the greens.

Over the years, Brees has wowed fans at the Saints' annual charity softball game by hammering home runs over the fences at Tulane's Turchin Stadium and Zephyr Field. Back in the Super Bowl years, Brees and former Saints backup quarterback Mark Brunell pounded several home runs off then Zephyrs manager-turned-batting-practice-pitcher Ken Oberkfell before a Triple-A baseball game at Zephyr Field. One of Brees' home run balls landed in the swimming pool over the fence in right field.

When the Saints used to play pickup basketball games on their off days, Brees was a force on the court. When the Saints went bowling on a team function, he was the team's best bowler. When they played paintball at a team function, Brees was the best paintball player.

"Everybody thinks he's just smart," former Saints center Jonathan Goodwin said. "I definitely think he's underrated as an athlete. He just doesn't get credit for it."

The Saints coaches understand this better than anyone. They incorporate Brees' athletic skills into their offense and take advantage of his mobility as often as possible. They've designed their protection schemes around his footwork and innate ability to feel the pass rush and "climb" the pocket. Bootlegs and rollouts, which take advantage of his mobility and uncanny accuracy as a passer on the run, are a staple of the system.

New Orleans offensive linemen said they routinely marvel at Brees' athletic skills during weekly video study. His extraordinary footwork and pocket presence are big reasons why the Saints annually rank among the least-sacked teams in the league. He said he employs skill sets from each sport while directing the Saints—the footwork of soccer, the hand-eye coordination of hitting a baseball, and the motion of a tennis serve in his passing mechanics.

"He really is a tremendous athlete," Lombardi says. "He's not fast, per se. He's just so coordinated and balanced. And when it's time to go, he's better. There's a lot of things to playing quarterback that are not necessarily about being fast or strong. He has a mental skill of awareness and it comes from studying and his mental energy, but there are a lot of guys that could still do everything he does in preparation and still not have that. He has a sixth sense."

Brees is not Lamar Jackson or Patrick Mahomes. He's not even Taysom Hill, who recorded a time of 4.44 in the 40-yard dash and a vertical jump of 38.5 inches at his Pro Day workout at BYU. But at what he does for a living, maneuvering in the chaotic phone booth of an NFL passing pocket, few are more adept.

"He is a tremendous foot athlete," former NFL quarterback Trent Dilfer said. "He extends plays, but he extends them in the pocket. He's not a spin out of tackles, scramble, run around type guy. He has subtle little movements, bounce around, make guys miss in the pocket, went a little bit to his left and threw an accurate ball."

Brees' movement skills in the pocket are a big reason he's taken fewer than 1.5 sacks per game during his NFL career, well below the league average.

"He's more athletic than people think," Carmichael said. "What you see with him moving in the pocket is athletic. Plus, he's very aware. He knows when he's short in protection and what he has to do, whether it's get the ball out quickly or climb the pocket. He has great awareness."

Brees uses his athleticism in many ways, but primarily to avoid sacks and buy time in the pocket to extend plays. Staying "on schedule" during an offensive possession is one of his great strengths as a quarterback. He prides himself on avoiding negative plays and has focused on that aspect of quarterback play in recent years. It goes back to Parcells' Commandments of Quarterback play. *VII: Throwing the ball away is a good play. Sacks, interceptions, and fumbles are bad plays. Protect against those.* And like so many things Brees does, it doesn't show up in box score.

"I've always had a goal that I want to continue to get better each and every year," Brees said. "Sometimes you can't always measure that. But the thing that's tough about our position is there's—if a guy breaks free, and I scramble and throw the ball away and avoid a sack, well, how does that show up on the stat sheet? It shows up 0-for-1 as an incomplete pass, so that could be deemed as a bad thing. But, in fact, that was a good thing. You avoided a negative play. You threw the ball away. You gave your friends a chance to be in a better situation, so there are certain things that stats don't always show in terms of your true production."

Because he stands only 6′0″ tall, Brees often can't see over his taller teammates on the offensive line. He has learned to adapt. He scans the field through windows between players and has learned to anticipate and gauge the speed and location of his receivers the same way you would see a car driving along the street through the windows at your office.

"I stood there behind the Saints on the field for three days at training camp asking myself, 'How does this guy do this?'" Jon Gruden said of his time visiting Saints training camp as an NFL analyst for ESPN's *Monday Night Football*. "I stand back there. I can't see two feet beyond the line of scrimmage. He can throw sidearm. He can throw off his back foot. He can reset [his feet] and throw—and when the ball comes out of his hand it is quick. He is a way better athlete than people realize. He is a phenomenal, gifted, talented athlete."

16

Trust and Confidence

IF YOU ASKED DREW BREES HOW HE HAS THE FEARLESSNESS TO throw blindly to players he can't see, his answer would be simple: trust and confidence. Brees repeats the phrase often. The trust and confidence Brees has nurtured in the system have been two of the biggest keys to the New Orleans Saints' offensive success in the Payton-Brees era.

Because the scheme relies so much on timing and Brees' historic accuracy, every detail of the passing attack—alignment, motion, formation, and personnel grouping—is evaluated, tested, and considered before being included in the game plan. This places the onus on the Saints receivers to be precise in their alignments and routes so Brees can pull the trigger with confidence when the bullets are flying. Payton calls it "painting the picture for the quarterback," and the Saints are uncompromising in the standards they set for their receivers and other skill players.

"When I drop back to pass, I have this vision according to the coverage on where everybody's supposed to be," Brees said. "In many cases, as a quarterback, you have to throw the ball with trust and anticipation to spots based upon coverage and what it looks like and anticipate the guys are going to be there."

To that end, a poster hangs in the team's wide receivers meeting room that reads: YOU MUST BE A DETAILED PLAYER AT A DETAILED POSITION. At perhaps no other position other than quarterback in the Saints offense is attention to detail as important as it is at wide receiver.

Emmanuel Butler learned the importance of attention to detail early in his Saints tenure. During a team drill at a minicamp practice in June 2019, the rookie wide receiver broke the huddle and aligned in his split to the right of the formation, inside the numbers. Except he wasn't three yards inside the numbers, as he was supposed to be. He was two and a half yards inside the numbers.

Payton immediately stopped practice, strutted to Butler's spot, pulled his visor from his head, and tossed it on to the ground.

"This is where I want you," Payton barked, pointing at his visor. "This is where you're supposed to be."

The dressing-down was an eye-opener for Butler. Details were important at Northern Arizona University, where Butler played his college ball. But players could get away with an inexact alignment or pass route here or there. He quickly learned that wouldn't fly with the Saints.

"In the NFL, it's not happening," Butler said. "If you're too short, it's a pick or it's an incomplete pass. If you're not where you're supposed to be, then something's getting thrown off, something's going bad. The details of the game are so important. Drew, Sean, and my receivers coaches have taught me that."

A meager half yard can change the outcome of the entire play, especially in the Saints offense, where spacing and timing are so critical to the success of the passing attack.

"It's a game of inches," Butler said. "If I have a deep crossing route, and I'm supposed to get across the field and settle, if I'm supposed to be at a three-yard split, and I'm at a five-yard split, it's going to take way longer for me to get over there. Now the quarterback's drop is thrown off. Now the timing of the play is thrown off."

In addition to his visor, Payton has also been known to use chalk or shaving cream to denote landmarks of a receiver's splits and/or breaks. The visual aids are one of his favorite teaching techniques. He'll also use goal posts or pylons for aiming points to help guide receivers on their routes.

"Coach [Payton] and Drew make a big to-do about that," Taysom Hill said. "When we break the huddle, if the receivers are not lined up perfectly, he will get them lined up perfectly. Every play has a specific plan and a purpose. In order for that play to have the best chance of succeeding that person has to be in the right spot. Drew realizes it. Coach realizes it. They're both that way."

Over the years, the Saints receiving corps has featured similar prototypes. Slot specialists Lance Moore, Willie Snead, and Austin Carr were smart, quick, and precise route-runners. Flankers Robert Meachem, Devery Henderson, and Ted Ginn Jr. were speed merchants who stretched field on post and corner routes. Split ends Marques Colston and Michael Thomas were do-it-all types, equally capable of working outside on hitch routes or inside on crossing routes. Tight end Jimmy Graham was a master of the seam route because of his 6'6" frame.

"Sean is very specific: What kind of receiver do we need?" Carmichael said. "Those inside routes that Lance Moore, Marques Colston, and Michael Thomas run—those inside routes aren't for everybody. The guy has to a feel for or a knack for finding the void or running a route off a certain defender."

The Saints run new receivers through a gauntlet of route workouts after they arrive to evaluate their strengths and weaknesses and identify which ones might work best for them in the system. Brees throws to each of them to get a feel for their speed and body language. His input goes a long way in determining which receivers play in certain route packages.

"One of the top five things he does as a quarterback is he throws to the receivers, gets a feel for them, and learns very quickly who he likes throwing to on what routes," Lombardi said. "Everyone runs certain routes a little bit differently. Receivers talk to the quarterback with body language, and they have a feel. It's just Drew learning the capabilities, smarts, and the feel for every receiver on the roster."

When new players are signed in the offseason, Brees often invites them to California to train with him and start the feeling-out process. During these sessions, Brees constantly tweaks the receiver splits and adjusts alignments to fine-tune the connection. Smart players quickly learn the importance of spending time with Brees when asked.

"There's a lot of time on task that takes place during the week just to absorb all of (the offensive game plan), but I'd say the concepts and the splits and the depths and a lot of the stuff that we're doing is stuff that we rep, we rep, we rep," Brees said. "From offseason until through the preseason until the regular season, there's a lot of time on task that's taken place and a lot of muscle memory and so there's a lot of trust and confidence that comes with that."

Like everything else, the emphasis on route technique and alignment has evolved over time as Brees and Payton have fine-tuned the scheme. In time, receivers are cross-trained at different positions. The Saints' best offenses have traditionally been the ones with the most experienced receivers. During the Super Bowl run, Colston, Henderson, Meachem, and Moore were interchangeable in the scheme, giving the offensive staff myriad options in the game plan. This flexibility allowed the coaching staff to move the receivers around like chess pieces in the offensive formation and target favorable matchups against defensive backs. One of the reasons Thomas has emerged as one of the NFL's most dominant receivers is because of his ability to line up anywhere in the formation on a given play.

"It's gone from very simple to much more advanced, to where maybe back in '06 it was, as a receiver you were either plus two [yards from the tackle], outside edge, or inside edge, right?," Brees said. "And now we've got all kinds of different splits, according to the route, according to the formation, according to who we're playing. If a team does a good job of reading these splits, we're going to change it up. It's why we spend so much time in what we do. It's why I have the guys come out with me in July in San Diego. It's why we spend so much time after practice, every practice."

For the receivers, mastering the nuances of the scheme can be a daunting task. The ones who earn the trust of Brees and Payton eventually receive more playing time and, in turn, more opportunities to shine. The standouts like Colston, Graham, and Thomas become so in tune with Brees they're allowed to improvise on routes.

"There's rules guys and guidelines guys," Lombardi said. "Certain guys are told, here are the rules to this route and you follow them. And then all of a sudden, he does something off script and it works and we say, all right, maybe you're a guidelines guy. You understand the guidelines of this route and maybe you can get away with fudging it a little. They have that feel, and that their feel matches Drew's feel. So once they become synchronized with Drew, then all of a sudden they're allowed to do that."

These nuances can take years to master. Receivers, tight ends, and backs in the Saints system don't necessarily need to be football geniuses, but they need to be students of the game and diligent in their study habits. It's why smart, reliable role players like Moore, Snead, Carr, and Josh Hill have carved out productive careers in New Orleans after being bypassed in the NFL Draft. Players who regularly misalign, run the wrong route, or aren't willing to put in the extra reps with Brees don't last long in New Orleans.

"The receivers in this offense are asked to learn so much," said Strief, now the play-by-play announcer for the Saints radio broadcast team. "Lance Moore used to always say it's so different than anywhere else he played. The wide receivers here have to understand that, 'Hey, in this route concept, I'm the spacing guy. I'm the guy that's here to space, so that I understand now when he changes the route for the guy outside of me, so too does my spacing. I'm spacing a different thing.' That's the kind of minutia they have to know and deal with. They have this system that they work within, and yet the combinations within it are endless."

This high standard prevents the Saints from pursuing certain receivers during the draft and free agency. Saints scouts place a heavy emphasis on intelligence, football IQ, and mental toughness at all positions, but especially at receiver. A Saints receiver has to have sure hands and the athletic ability to beat NFL defensive backs, but he also must be willing and able to handle the heavy mental workload the Saints system requires.

"Coach Payton has such a clear vision for what he's looking for in players," Joe Brady said. "He finds players that understand their roles and are accountable. If you look at the wide receivers, the tight ends, and the running backs in New Orleans, Drew wants accountable players that he knows, when I throw that ball he's going to be where he needs to be.

"When you're game-planning and you're watching Coach Payton, Pete [Carmichael], and Joe [Lombardi] put together these plays, it's fascinating how they find ways to put their players where they know this is what this guy does best, let's get him on this spot in this play. It's one of the biggest reasons why the system has been so successful for so many years. Coach Payton and the staff are going to put their players in positions to be successful."

Sean Payton, who attended high school in Naperville, Illinois, suited up for the Chicago Bears as one of the replacement players, known as the "Spare Bears," during the 1987 NFL players strike.

All Drew Brees would do in his career at Purdue was set Big Ten Conference records in passing yards (11,792), touchdown passes (90), total offensive yards (12,693), completions (1,026), and attempts (1,678).

(Joe Robbins/Getty Images)

When the New Orleans Saints hired Sean Payton to help turn their team around in early 2006, he and general manager Mickey Loomis identified quarterback Drew Brees as their top free-agent target. After a competitive battle with the Miami Dolphins, the Saints won over free agent Drew Brees and signed him to a six-year, $60 million deal on March 14, 2006.

When he took over the New Orleans Saints program, Sean Payton knew he had to do more than install a new offense and bring in difference-makers through the draft and free agency. He needed to implement a top-to-bottom culture change.

A year after Hurricane Katrina ravaged New Orleans, Sean Payton, Drew Brees, and more members of the Saints met President George W. Bush and First Lady, Laura, at the airport.

When he signed with the Saints, Drew Brees said it was about more than just business. He saw an opportunity to make a difference by working on post-Katrina community projects, including Habitat for Humanity.

After a first season in New Orleans that saw him go 10–6, win the NFC South, and go all the way to the NFC Championship Game against the Chicago Bears, Sean Payton was fittingly awarded AP NFL Coach of the Year and Motorola NFL Coach of the Year awards.

(Matthew Emmons/USA TODAY Sports)

Drew Brees celebrates winning his first playoff game with the New Orleans Saints 27–24 over the Philadelphia Eagles in the divisional round. It was New Orleans' first playoff appearance since 2000.

After his wildly successful first season with the Saints, Drew Brees was named first runner-up behind former teammate, San Diego Chargers running back LaDanian Tomlinson, for league MVP by the Associated Press. The two were also co-recipients of the Walter Payton NFL Man of the Year Award.

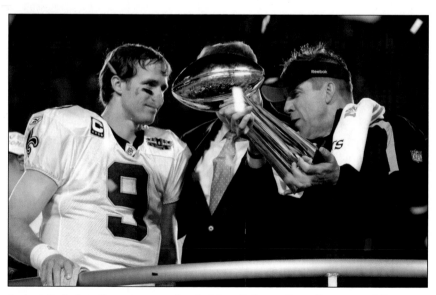

In just their fourth season together in New Orleans, Sean Payton and Drew Brees brought the franchise its first-ever Lombardi Trophy when they led the team past the Indianapolis Colts 31–17 in Super Bowl XLIV.

Drew Brees shares the pure joy of winning a Super Bowl (as well as being named the game's MVP) with his son, Baylen.

Drew Brees set multiple records in the 2011 season, including breaking Dan Marino's longstanding mark of 5,084 passing yards in a single season with a nine-yard touchdown pass to Darren Sproles (far left) in Week 16 against the Atlanta Falcons.

Drew Brees, who has finished second in voting for the NFL MVP award four times, has twice been named NFL Offensive Player of the Year, in 2008 and (pictured) 2011.

During their tenure in New Orleans, Drew Brees and Sean Payton have helped the Saints offense set countless team and league records and become the second winningest coach-quarterback duo in NFL history.

17

"Who Throws That Ball?"

OVER THE YEARS, PAYTON HAS DEVISED A PERSONAL SYSTEM TO attribute the success of offensive plays. He'll ask his staff, "Was that play or player?" Sometimes a play succeeds solely because of a player's individual effort, skill set, or talent. Payton attributes such plays to the player's ability rather than the play's design. Marshawn Lynch's famous Beast Mode run, for example, had little to do with scheme and everything to do with Lynch's strength, vision, and will. When Mike Thomas overpowers a defensive back for a competitive catch in tight coverage, technique, film study, and coverage concepts are rendered irrelevant. It's why many successful NFL play-callers say they often "think players, not plays" when faced with a clutch down-and-distance situation.

The unique part of the Payton-Brees partnership is they manage to produce both—play and player. As one of the most creative play designers in NFL history, Payton will often produce plays journeyman quarterbacks could execute successfully. Those are the ones he jokingly says his son Connor could make. Then there are other times where Brees' brilliance as a quarterback makes it happen—when player, not play, is the reason the Saints offense hums. It is this potent combination that has made the Payton-Brees combination the most prolific duo in NFL history.

As great as Brees is in the mental side of the sport, he wouldn't be one of the game's all-time great passers if he weren't blessed with extraordinary ability. Analysts and journalists focus so much on his extraordinary intelligence and preparation habits that his natural, God-given talent often gets shortchanged. Simply put, Brees is one of the best pure passers to ever play the game.

While arm strength has never been a hallmark of Brees' game, his is more than strong enough to deliver every throw necessary at the NFL level. And Brees has learned to compensate by anticipating defensive coverages and delivering his passes earlier, especially on deep routes.

"I tell young quarterbacks, 'If you want to learn how to throw deep balls, study Drew Brees,'" said former Washington Redskins quarterback Joe Theismann, who has worked for more than two decades as an NFL analyst at ESPN and NFL Network. "He puts great trajectory on the ball, and he gives the guys a chance to be able to run to it. He doesn't have a rocket arm but his anticipation, his timing, the way he delivers the ball with trajectory, the velocity, it's just amazing. I think Drew should be every guy's 6-foot-tall hero."

Since joining forces with Payton, he has established a new standard in completion percentage for quarterbacks. His 67.6 percent career completion rate is the highest in NFL history, and he owns five of the six best single-season completion percentages in league annals.

Saints coaches attribute Brees' historic accuracy to his unusually large hands and his flawless mechanics. His hand width of 10.25 inches ranked among the top 11 percent of quarterbacks at the NFL combine, while his 6'0" height ranked among the bottom 8 percent. His hand width spans nearly an inch wider than Tom Brady's (9.3), who stands four inches taller. Because of his large grip, Brees can control the ball and deliver it with maximum rotation. It's one of the reasons why he excelled in the windy, cold conditions of West Lafayette, Indiana, as a college star at Purdue University.

"He can spin that ball," former Saints linebackers coach Mike Nolan said. "For a relatively little guy, he has really big hands. Those things are difference makers."

Brees was an accurate quarterback in high school, college, and early in his pro career with the Chargers. But he's taken his accuracy rate to a different level since working with Tom House, his throwing coach and performance specialist. Thanks to years of work with House, Brees has become an expert on biomechanics and can go into great detail on the "kinetic chain" of a throwing delivery: the transfer of energy from his feet to his hips, shoulders, and ultimately the index finger in his throwing hand as he unloads the ball. House and his staff are so technical with their scientific research they can identify the mechanical flaw behind every poor throw. Their research shows that a single inch of a quarterback's head movement at the time of delivery can mean the difference of a foot of ball placement on his passes.

"Drew was always accurate," House said. "But now we can identify what goes into command for a pitcher or accuracy for a quarterback. We can tell you, when you miss right or left [on a pass], 99 percent of the time it's your front side causing the issue. And when you miss high or low, 99 percent of the time it's because of a posture change, a shoulder turn or head move. Every one inch of inappropriate head movement costs you two inches of release. Two inches at the release point can mean a foot [of ball placement] to the receiver. Each inch can mean the difference between a catch and run, a 50-50 ball or an interception. We're giving Drew the 'why' to go with the 'what.'"

In April 2009, the ESPN show *Sport Science* tried to gauge Brees' accuracy. The show's hosts had Brees throw footballs at an archery target 20 yards away and compared his accuracy to Olympic archers. Brees astounded the producers by hitting the 4-inch bullseye on 10 out of 10 throws. The secret to his accuracy was his consistent mechanics. Amazingly, Brees threw each of his passes with the same 6-degree launch angle, 600-revolutions-per-minute spin rate, and 52 mph launch speed.

It's no surprise Brees was the only quarterback to rank in the top five of all three pass depths—short, intermediate, and deep—of Pro Football Focus' advanced accuracy metrics in 2018, when its analysts introduced a new charting formula for quarterbacks. Brees ranked second on one- to nine-yard passes with an accurate ball placement of 73.8 percent. His 65.1 percent accuracy rate on intermediate throws of 10 to 19 yards led all quarterbacks. And he ranked fifth on deep throws of 20-plus yards with a 48.9 percent accuracy rate.

"Drew has an accuracy that is just uncanny," former Saints backup quarterback Luke McCown said. "You could put every quarterback in the league on the same field and tell them to throw all of the same routes, and you're just going to notice something different about the way Drew places the football, when and where. It's just different. The hand of God reached down and touched Drew and said, 'You're going to be the most accurate guy to ever throw a football.'"

McCown tells the story of a practice throw Brees made during McCown's first season in New Orleans in 2013. Brees had pressure in his face and made a throw on a seam route to Jimmy Graham while falling backward and bracing himself against the rush with his left arm.

"You couldn't have paused time and stood everybody in the same spot and walked the football downfield 22 yards and placed it any better with your hand than he did where he threw it," McCown said. "Joe Lombardi and Pete Carmichael and myself just looked at each other like, 'Did you just see that? Holy cow, did that throw really just happen?'"

It's not the first throw that became legendary around the Saints facility. In 2008, Brees made a throw that Saints coaches still talk about, and it illustrates another of his rare quarterbacking gifts: anticipation.

In a game against the San Diego Chargers at Wembley Stadium in London, England, Brees completed a 15-yard pass to tight end Billy Graham in the fourth quarter. The pass seemed routine enough at the time. It converted a late third-and-5 play and helped the Saints hold off a late rally by the Chargers, but there was nothing particularly spectacular about the pass—until the coaches watched the video from the end zone view and were able to see it from Brees' perspective.

On the play, running back Pierre Thomas ran a shallow crossing route out of the backfield, cutting from left to right. A couple yards behind him, receiver Robert Meachem ran another crossing route from right to left, creating a scissors action for the Chargers defensive coverage. Miller, aligned to the left side of the formation, ran a 12-yard in cut to the right about 10 yards behind them. From behind, the field was a maze of crisscrossing chaos. As Brees completed his three-step drop and climbed the pocket to avoid the pass rush to his right, four Chargers defenders converged downfield in man-to-man coverage, stacked one by one between the hash marks, right where Miller's route was taking him.

"It should have looked like a stop sign to the quarterback," Lombardi said. "It's just a cluster of defenders."

But as Brees cocked his right arm and uncorked a spiral downfield, something magical happened: the Chargers defense parted like the Red Sea, each defender vacating the middle of the field to follow his man in coverage. Brees' pass spiraled into the void, hitting a wide-open Miller in stride at the 30-yard line for a 15-yard gain and first down.

In the film room, the Saints coaches were stupefied. Not just that Brees completed the pass, but that he had the anticipation and audacity to attempt it in the first place.

"Who throws that ball?!" offensive coordinator Pete Carmichael asked incredulously. "There's no way you throw that ball. What QB would throw that ball?!"

Lombardi and Carmichael had worked with some elite quarterbacks over the years, guys like Doug Flutie, Michael Vick, Tim Couch, and Tim Rattay. They'd never seen anyone throw a pass like that.

"It's a great find," Lombardi said. "He's got a broad focus. He sees more. His lens is wide. He sees everything, and he processes it so quick. It's something different."

It wasn't the first time the Saints coaches had seen Brees do something extraordinary. And it certainly wouldn't be the last. But it quickly became the stuff of legend among the offensive coaches. They would routinely show it to incoming Saints quarterbacks for amusement.

"It's pretty funny when you watch it," Lombardi said. "Everyone [on defense] was right over the ball and the ball is in his hand, and then they just all disappear, and the ball is completed. The anticipation is uncanny."

Brees' passing exploits have become legendary around the Saints complex. Almost every player and coach who has played with him has a favorite pass they can cite off the top of their head.

For Taysom Hill, it was a pass Brees threw to Ted Ginn against the Green Bay Packers during Hill's rookie season in 2017. As Hill and fellow backup quarterback Chase Daniel watched the play unfold from the sideline, they were convinced Brees' vision was blocked by the wall of linemen in front of him and that he simply threw the ball blindly to an open spot in the coverage. They were right. The trust and confidence Brees had in Ginn to be exactly where he was supposed to be on the pass route paid off. Brees' blind pass hit Ginn right between the numbers, and the veteran speedster streaked through the Packers secondary for a 47-yard gain to set up a go-ahead field goal in the third quarter of a 26–17 Saints win.

"I just felt it," Brees said later. "I knew what coverage they were in and could see the flat defender to that side of the field go with Brandon Coleman so I just kind of knew where to go with the pass."

Another throw Hill still talks about is one Brees made to Ginn against the Carolina Panthers in Week 3 of the wideout's rookie season. The play occurred early in the third quarter with the Saints leading 17–7. The play was designed to go to Mike Thomas, who was being covered by linebacker Shaq Thompson in the left slot. Brees set up the play by looking right toward tight end Coby Fleener, who ran a stick route outside the numbers along the far sideline. This drew safety Mike Adams out of his position in the middle of the field. Brees then turned back to the left to look for Thomas on his wheel route. But the Panthers were ready for it. They had cleverly disguised their coverage and rolled free safety Kurt Coleman over the top of Thomas, trying to lure Brees to target the obvious mismatch. This left Ginn one-on-one on his post route down the left seam against cornerback James Bradberry, the Panthers' best cover man. Ginn beat Bradberry with an inside release and Brees, after seeing his first and second reads double-covered, uncorked a perfect bomb that led Ginn away from the fast-closing Adams. Ginn adjusted to the pass in midair and caught the ball at the goal line while falling backward in the end zone as Bradberry and Adams crashed over him.

"This ball is placed so perfectly behind the defensive back," Fox Sports color analyst Ronde Barber said during the broadcast of the game. "The placement on that ball was absolutely sublime."

As the play unfolded, Hill said he assumed Brees would go to his checkdown option when he saw the Panthers coverage technique. But Brees surprised him.

"Chase and I just looked at each other on the sideline and thought, 'How did he find him?'" Hill said. "That's Drew."

DOME-INATION:

2013 Dallas Cowboys

Before Sean Payton took the job in New Orleans, the Saints had struggled mightily against the Dallas Cowboys. In 21 meetings with America's Team, the Saints had managed just seven wins. But Payton reversed those fortunes quickly, posting wins in three of four contests against the Cowboys.

When Dallas visited New Orleans in Week 10 of the 2013 season, it was 5–4 and desperate for a marquee win. But the Cowboys' banged-up defense had allowed four quarterbacks to pass for more than 400 yards against them in the first nine weeks and entered the game ranked 31st in total defense, surrendering 419.1 yards a game. And they were no match for the Saints, who did just about whatever they wanted in a 49–17 rout on *Sunday Night Football*.

The Saints scored touchdowns on seven of their first nine series and averaged 9.1 yards per play. Six of the Saints' touchdown drives covered 75 or more yards. They gained an NFL-record 40 first downs and amassed a franchise-record 625 yards of total offense, the most ever allowed by a Cowboys defense. In fact, it was the most yards an NFL team had produced in a regulation game in more than three decades and remains the fourth most yards gained in a game since the league merger.

"There just were very few plays that we stopped," Cowboys coach Jason Garrett said. "They were able to go to a lot of different things."

The Saints rushing attack compiled 242 yards on the ground. It was the most rushing yards in a single game since Payton became coach, and the most by the Saints since they rushed for 249 against Cincinnati in 1990. Mark Ingram led the way with a career-high 145 yards on only 14 carries.

The powerful ground game set up the Saints' play-action passing attack and Brees picked apart the Cowboys' overmatched secondary. He completed 34 of 41 passes for 392 yards and four touchdowns. At one point, he strung together 19 consecutive completions, tying his personal best and franchise record. He completed passes to nine different receivers. Four Saints receivers caught touchdown passes.

"Spreading the ball around, getting everybody involved—these are the days you love to have," Brees said. "You strive for efficiency both in the run and the pass game. We had that today."

18

Two Minutes to Paradise

IF THERE'S AN AREA OF THE GAME WHERE ALL OF DREW BREES and Sean Payton's talents, abilities, and football IQ are distilled and displayed, it is the two-minute offense. It is during these hectic, high-pressure situations when the game is on the line that Brees and Payton excel, when the countless hours of practice and preparation are unbound and a virtual Big Bang of football knowledge and intuition unleashed. It is during the two-minute drill that two of the game's most beautiful minds go to work.

The two-minute drill Brees ran to beat Houston in the Saints' 2019 season opener was the 35th comeback victory of his career, the third most in NFL history behind Peyton Manning (43) and Tom Brady (36).

Later in the 2019 season, Brees successfully orchestrated a two-minute drill to set up a game-winning field goal and help the Saints escape with a 34–31 win against the Carolina Panthers at the Superdome. He drove the Saints 65 yards in 11 plays with one timeout to put the Saints in position for Wil Lutz's 33-yard game-winner against the Panthers.

Brees completed six of seven passes for 56 yards in the drive, including a 24-yarder to Mike Thomas on third-and-6 to move the Saints into Carolina territory.

The back-breaking connection was a vintage Brees play and textbook execution by Thomas. The Saints set up Panthers cornerback James Bradberry by running a double move, a slant-and-go pattern called a Sluggo route, designed to take advantage of his aggressiveness in coverage. The Saints had run several slant patterns to Thomas throughout the game and waited to spring the Sluggo route at just the right time. Bradberry bit on the slant fake, and Thomas was wide open for the easy pitch and catch to the Panthers 40.

"You're referencing everything [that transpires] throughout the course of the game," Brees said of the strategy involved on the play. "That formation, that alignment, that release pattern, what did they see, how did they react to it, what can you kind of keep in your back pocket for later on. That's the game within the game."

One play later, Brees hit Alvin Kamara on a perfectly timed and blocked 16-yard screen pass to the 24, then was able to get the Saints even closer by running Kamara off left guard for nine more yards before stopping the clock with a spike at 0:03. Brees did all of this with just one timeout at his disposal and after having been sacked for a six-yard loss on the drive's opening play.

"That two-minute drill by Drew was outstanding, the execution of it was outstanding," Payton said after watching the game film on Monday.

Brees isn't exactly sure when he started calling the two-minute drill on his own. He said he's done it throughout his Saints tenure. The Saints offensive coaches essentially become bystanders during the two-minute drill. They're watching Brees orchestrate the offense, just like the fans. Other than a suggestion or two from Payton, the two-minute offense is all Brees.

"We don't even know what's going on," Lombardi said of the coaching staff. "Sean will talk to him and tell him to think about a play here or there but for the most part, he's got it. That's very unique. The Bradys and Mannings can do it by themselves, but that's very unique. He can see it and have a plan. He's coming up with [route] combinations that aren't even in the playbook and signaling them to the receivers. It's amazing."

The Saints turn the offense over to Brees in these situations for a couple reasons. One, it saves time. Since the Saints usually don't substitute or huddle in the two-minute, Brees can call the play at the line of scrimmage using hand signals and code words and save valuable seconds. Two, they do it because they can. Brees knows the offense. He has earned the trust of the Saints coaches over the years and leans on his diligent pregame preparation to identify opposing defenses and their coverage tendencies.

"You can take those chances with Drew," Lombardi said. "You know he's not going to mess it up. There's so much trust in Drew. He's not going to make us look dumb here. He's really good at operating in those stressful situations."

Brees couldn't have operated the two-minute offense so efficiently and effectively early in his Saints tenure, because he wasn't as familiar with the offense. But after a couple of seasons, he became fluent in the system and the Saints turned the two-minute over to him. It's unclear how many other quarterbacks in the league have this autonomy. Brees said established veterans like Brady, Aaron Rodgers, and Ben Roethlisberger also run their own two-minute drills, but the situation is rare.

"It is exciting and butterflies, but it is also confidence and unity," Brees said. "We feel like everybody knows we have a challenge ahead. Everybody knows what we need to do in order to accomplish whatever we need to accomplish to go win the game. Everybody kind of just locks in and goes. It's where a lot of the things that happen and transpire over the course of the game kind of give you that information, that confidence, that assurance on how you're going to handle that drive and how you're going to accomplish the task."

Coaches and teammates marvel at his intensity during the moment. His poise relaxes them and reduces their stress. His decisiveness in calling and executing the plays breeds confidence.

"There's this look in his eye and the way that he goes about calling his plays that, I don't care if you are a coach or player, you think, 'Man, I don't want to be the guy that messes this up,'" Campbell said. "What makes Brees such a great leader is his intensity. You can tell by the look on his face that this is something serious to him, and players know they've got to do their job."

The best two-minute drive of Brees' career might have come in a losing cause. Coaches and teammates still marvel at the 11-play, 50-yard drive he executed to give the Saints a short-lived 24–23 lead in the 2017 NFC divisional playoff game against the Minnesota Vikings.

When he took the field in Minnesota that day, Brees knew exactly what needed to be done. After the touchback, the Saints took possession at their own 25-yard line with one timeout at their disposal and 1:29 on the clock. U.S. Bank Stadium, where the Vikings had won eight of their past nine games, was at peak hostility. The situation was bleak. But it was far from hopeless, especially with Brees pulling the trigger.

The Vikings opened in their usual defensive package for these situations, a Cover 3 defense with Anthony Harris playing center field and zone coverage underneath. Harrison Smith and Xavier Rhodes bracketed Thomas underneath, forcing Brees to target alternative options on the perimeter. After a first-down incompletion, Brees threaded the needle to Josh Hill on a seam route over the middle for an 18-yard gain to the 43.

On the next snap, the Vikings switched to man-to-man coverage, and Brees quickly spotted some confusion from nickel back

Mackensie Alexander on the call. He quickly snapped the ball and delivered a strike to Ted Ginn Jr., who beat Alexander for an easy 11-yard reception and got out of bounds. Just like that, the Saints were in Vikings territory at the 46-yard line with 55 seconds left. Realistically, they would need to gain about 10 more yards to get into Lutz's range for a go-ahead field goal attempt.

The Vikings switched coverages again, this time to something the Saints did not expect. They went to a coverage they had not played previously in two-minute situations, a scheme known in NFL vernacular as Two Man, which aligned two safeties on each deep half of the field and the other pass defenders in man-to-man coverage underneath. It was a curveball. The Saints had not prepared during the week for the Vikings to play Two Man in this situation. And now Brees was staring at it with the play clock ticking down and a berth in the NFC Championship Game on the line.

Brees initially tried to beat the defense by going to Thomas, but Xavier Rhodes' tight coverage forced three straight incompletions. It was now fourth-and-10, and with the Saints' season on the line, Brees called one of his favorite plays, Flutie. The play, named in honor of the former NFL and Boston College star, was an old standby in the Saints playbook. In fact, offensive coordinator Pete Carmichael believes it might be the most frequently called play in the Saints' playbook.

"Quarterbacks like plays that have answers, and Flutie has answers versus every coverage, every look, every pressure," Brees said. "That play was probably part of Day One installs back in 2006."

Flutie is one of the Saints' favorite Two Man–beaters because it features two out-breaking underneath routes, in this case by Willie Snead in the slot to the left side and running back Alvin Kamara out of the backfield to the right, which theoretically would be open against the inside leverage technique of the defense.

"We like Flutie versus Two Man, and Drew got to it," Lombardi said.

With the sellout crowd roaring, Brees dropped back and fired a perfect strike to Snead between three defenders in the left flat. The ball was perfectly placed—hitting Snead just below the chin, where Brees always tries to target his receivers—and perfectly timed, arriving just after Snead made his break and before three Vikings defenders could converge on him. Brees' pass was so perfect Connor Payton could have caught it, and the 13-yard gain silenced the crowd and got the Saints into field-goal range at the Vikings 33.

"It was an amazing read and just a great pass by Drew," said Chase Daniel, who was the Saints' backup quarterback at the time. "It was such an impressive drive to me because the Vikings had never shown Two Man before and Drew had to quickly figure that out and get to [Flutie]."

Brees added a couple more short completions to Ginn and Thomas, and Lutz drilled a 43-yard field goal to give the Saints a seemingly safe 24–23 lead with 25 seconds left.

"That was one of the best drives I've ever seen," Taysom Hill said. "My jaw hit the floor on the throw that he made to Willie Snead on fourth down."

It was Brees at his best. On the go-ahead drive, he completed passes to four different receivers against four different Vikings coverages. And he did it against the league's top-rated defense on the road in one of the loudest stadiums in the league. And he did it all while making each play call on his own.

"I was sitting up in the box, thinking, 'Wow,'" said Joe Brady, who was in his second season as an offensive assistant on the Saints staff in 2017. "Obviously, Sean was giving his thoughts but basically it was just, 'Here ya go, Drew. You got it.'

"It says a lot about both Sean and Drew, that you have so much faith in a quarterback that he is going to prepare himself and you trust him that whatever play he feels like he can get into, he's going to find a way to make it work. Essentially we were just up in the box watching one of the best quarterbacks of all time go to work."

Brees, Payton, and the Saints offensive staff go over the two-minute plan for each opponent during the dot meeting on the eve of the game. Brees and Payton formulate a plan based on the defensive tendencies of the opponent provided in the scouting report by the club's pro personnel department. Brees identifies potential weaknesses in the defense from his own film study and prep work. A menu of preferred plays is listed on Payton's call sheet. The plays are assigned one-word tags to facilitate and expedite the communication process when every second is precious.

"It all goes back to his preparation and consistency in those moments," Strief said. "On the fly, in that moment, processing that much information under all that pressure. That's when that stuff pays off. It doesn't pay off on the third play of the game when you're trying to feel everything out. It pays off in the biggest moment, when your back is against the wall and you get a curve ball. That's when all of those reps that you spent all that time on matters. Because now Drew has the mental capacity to sit there and analyze the defense and come up with an answer and a solution on his own. He doesn't think about anything else."

Jacksonville Jaguars head coach Doug Marrone has played and coached in the NFL for more than three decades. He said he's never seen a synergy like the one Brees and Payton share during the two-minute drill.

"Drew and Sean are so in tune sometimes it feels like Sean's playing quarterback through Drew, and Drew's coaching through Sean," said Marrone, who served as the Saints offensive coordinator from 2006 to 2008. "When those guys get out there, it's like they have such a great relationship and feel for each other that I'm sure if Sean went out there and played quarterback, he can go through the same reads as Drew, and Drew can coach the game the same as Sean. I mean, those guys, they're so in sync. It's just, I hate to say it because I'm a coach, I mean, I'm a man, but it's beautiful to watch."

19

Driven to Compete

MARK BRUNELL QUARTERBACKED THE WASHINGTON HUSKIES TO the 1991 National Championship. He played 19 seasons in the NFL, earned three Pro Bowl invitations, and won a Super Bowl ring with the Saints in 2009. But one of the proudest athletic achievements of his career had nothing to do with football. It occurred in the spring of 2008, when he defeated Drew Brees in an impromptu home run derby contest at Zephyr Field near the Saints training complex.

The competition between Brunell and Brees is still legendary around the Saints offices, not because of Brunell's power show but because of the defiant way Brees went down in defeat. Brunell doesn't recall exactly how many homers he hit that day off Zephrys manager Ken Oberkfell, who pitched to the group of six Saints players and coaches. All he knows is it was more than Brees, who, as a former standout baseball player in high school, surely considered himself to be the heavy favorite that day.

And Brees smashed some impressive long balls that day, including one that landed in the swimming pool beyond the right-field fence. But what stood out to Brunell and others was the effort

Brees put forth to try to overtake Brunell once he established a lead. Brees extended his session well beyond the agreed-upon 50-swing limit in an attempt to outdo Brunell.

"The poor guy throwing batting practice almost needed to switch out for a reliever," joked Pete Carmichael, who, as a former scholarship baseball player at Boston College, was part of the competition. "We got out there at 2:30 and the Zephyrs were supposed to take batting practice at 4:30, and I think they had to start BP under the stadium because we were eating into their time."

Payton, Carmichael, and Joe Lombardi were shagging balls in the outfield and began to wonder if Brees was ever going to give up. They noticed they were starting to get sunburned as Brees continued to pound away in the batter's box.

"At some point, there's a law of diminishing returns on your swings, an attrition to the repetition," Payton said. "It's like when your golf coach tells you, 'Enough.' Everything from a certain point forward is going to be bad habits and blisters."

Brees never did catch Brunell. And the short car ride back to the Saints facility was an awkwardly quiet one. "Crickets," as Payton described it.

Payton related a story about a golf outing he, Brees, Taysom Hill, and Saints communications director Doug Miller made to City Park in the spring of 2018. One hole featured a blind drive over a hilly fairway. Each member of the foursome smashed his drive on the screws. When the group arrived at their balls on the other side of the hill, they were clustered almost on top of each other in the fairway. Much to Brees' chagrin, his was the farthest from the green.

"He was pissed," Payton chortled. "He didn't realize it was a one-in-500 drive for me and a one-in-250 drive for Doug. We had each just hit the best drives of our month, but, in his mind, he was clumped in with the seniors. He told Taysom that he needed to refocus his workout in the weight room. It bothered him for two holes.

"But it's the trait that you love about him," Payton added. "You want him on your team. He's extremely competitive that way, and way more often than not, he's on the winning end of it."

The home run derby was Brunell's first encounter with what Lombardi jokingly calls "the dark side" of Brees. Brunell had signed a free-agent contract with the Saints only three months earlier and was just starting to get to know the man he'd back for the next two seasons. He knew Brees' reputation as a stellar all-around athlete. He knew he was good at many things. That day at Zephyr Field, Brunell learned that losing wasn't one of them.

"I loved every second of it," said Brunell, who was a good enough prep baseball player in Santa Maria, California, to get drafted by the Atlanta Braves in 1993. "It was one of the favorite athletic moments of my life. If I brought it back up today, I'm sure he'd come up with some excuse because Drew is the most competitive person I've been around in my whole life. He wants to win in everything. I would go so far as to say he *has* to win. And it he doesn't win, it's just going to drive him crazy."

If Brees' maniacal competitiveness wasn't evident to Brunell after the home run derby, it was hammered home a few months later on a bowfishing trip to Port Sulphur, Louisiana. The informal fishing contest between Saints players began at 8:00 PM and stretched well into the next morning. As Brunell recalled, all of the boats had reported to the dock and weighed their catches with the guides by about 2:30 AM. Yet, one boat remained on the water, more than an hour after the others had returned to the dock. Finally, sometime in the wee hours before dawn, it came in.

"We're all just sitting there waiting," Brunell said. "We're nasty, disgusting, and we just want to go home. But to a man, we all knew why his boat was the last one to come in. And sure, enough, he had the most fish. He's even competitive in bowfishing. That's Drew Brees."

Brees has ascended to the elite ranks of NFL quarterbacks for many reasons, from his underrated all-around athletic ability to his versatile skill set to his legendary work ethic. But those who know Brees best say his extraordinary competitiveness is what sets him apart, the single trait that has driven him from an under-recruited prep player to the highest level of his sport. In a league of extraordinarily competitive men, Brees' almost obsessive competitiveness stands out.

The Saints knew Brees was competitive when they signed him in 2006. They were counting on it to fuel his rehab from shoulder surgery. But no one knew just how competitive he was until they got him in the building. And it became apparent very quickly that they were dealing with a different animal.

Nearly everyone who has spent any length of time with Brees over the years has a story about his legendary competitive streak. Brees grew up in an athletic family and competed in sports at an early age alongside his brother, Reid. But Brees doesn't limit his competition to organized sports. He'll compete in just about anything, from ping-pong to darts to seed spitting to rock skipping to skeet shooting. Anything to stoke his competitive juices.

His roommate at Purdue, Jason Loerzel, still shakes his head at the sleepless nights he endured at the teammates' on-campus apartment because of Brees' marathon late-night electronic dart games. Chase Daniel said when he played for the Saints from 2009 to 2012 Brees would create games like "pencil football" in the quarterback meeting room and "football golf" on the practice field to stoke the fire. McCown remembers seeing Brees spend 20 minutes in the weight room one day trying to toss a physio ball and land it on the weight rack.

"He wouldn't leave until he did it," McCown said.

At times, Brees' competitiveness can border on obsessiveness—so much so that friends and teammates have learned that letting him win is sometimes better than beating him.

Former NFL quarterback Carson Palmer told the *Los Angeles Times* he and Brees would train together near their San Diego homes each offseason, and Brees would somehow turn the workouts into a competition.

"He was so over-the-top competitive," Palmer said. "We would jog from drill to drill, and he would have to be first. After a while it was, 'All right, dude, just go.' He couldn't turn it off. We would finish every workout with little agility games like catching cards. You'd throw playing cards in the air and catch them with one hand.... Your mind is exhausted, your body's exhausted, and Drew just can't turn it off. As a peer and a competitor, I was in awe. But his competitiveness got to the point where it can be annoying."

During bowfishing trips, Loerzel said he would surreptitiously gesture to his fishing guide to steer the boat toward fish in Brees' direction so he could shoot the most fish in their angling derbies.

"I would give a nod for him to turn the boat so Drew can shoot the fish because if we didn't we were going to be out there all night until he got the most," Loerzel said. "We joke with him about it, but it's real."

Over the years, Brees even found a way to multi-compete. During practices, while trying to move the ball against the defense, he would simultaneously compete with fellow quarterbacks. The mini-competition assigned point values to various aspects of quarterback play. Players received points for throwing a touchdown pass, completing a pass after a scramble, checking down to the proper receiver, or making the right read. Points were deducted for interceptions, inaccurate reads, etc. As the senior member of the group, Brees reigned as judge, jury, and arbiter of the daily tally. He was even known to tweak the scorekeeping criteria when necessary.

One day during organized team activities in the spring, McCown said Brees introduced a bonus score: one point for a completion on a throw in the flat. The other quarterbacks readily agreed. Later, McCown noticed the script for that practice. Brees' series featured numerous plays in which the primary receiver ran a flat route.

"He's a manipulator," McCown said with a smirk.

Brees' competitive drive fits like a glove with Payton. Saints scouts grade personnel for their competitiveness in the evaluation process. Payton also fosters a culture of competition in daily workouts, even joining the players in the informal post-practice contests.

"There is a high value on [competitiveness] I think, just as there is on intelligence," Payton said. "I think it is extremely important. And it is also on us to create those environments. It is okay to have winners and losers."

Brees, as you would imagine, rarely loses. Payton kidded that the few times he's managed to defeat his quarterback involved competitions "like throwing a ping-pong ball in a fish bowl."

Loerzel recalled Brees missing a short putt on the golf course and replaying the putt over and over until he finally made it, much to the dismay of the foursome behind them. Jamie Martin said Brees once missed a single pass in a two-hour practice and then spent 15 minutes after practice re-running the same route with receivers until he perfected the throw.

"That stuff just eats him up," Martin said. "It's a little thing that may or may not matter, but he's never satisfied with shrugging things off. It's that little edge that drives him."

Michael Jordan was so ruthlessly competitive he reportedly belittled teammates and even made then-teenager Kwame Brown cry during practice. He rarely showed mercy when vanquishing fellow competitors. Brees always manages to keep the competitions light-hearted. He never takes it too far.

Of course, that doesn't mean he takes losing well. At the home run derby competition before the 2013 Ben Grubbs celebrity softball game at Zephyr Field, a group of reporters approached Brees for interviews. Brees said he planned to talk after the home run contest. When McCown upset Brees in the derby after three tiebreaker rounds, everything changed. One of the most accessible and media-friendly superstars in sports was nowhere to be found by reporters afterward.

"He was definitely upset about it, no question," McCown said.

A year later, to no one's surprise, Brees reclaimed the home run derby title. The trophies for each derby were displayed on top of the quarterbacks' lockers at the Saints facility. Brees' trophy was notably—and not accidentally—one inch taller than McCown's.

"He wants to be the best at whatever he does," McCown said. "That's what makes him great. That's what makes him Drew."

McCown was confident he finally had Brees where he wanted him during Saints training camp in 2014, when the quarterback group visited the skeet shooting range at The Greenbrier resort in Sulphur Springs, West Virginia. An avid outdoorsman who grew up duck and deer hunting in east Texas, McCown owned a set of shotguns, and he showed off his deadeye, hitting 33 of 50 sporting clays, well ahead of fellow Saints quarterbacks Logan Kilgore and Ryan Griffin. But it still wasn't enough to beat Brees, who hit 41 of 50 targets.

"There's nothing that Drew Brees could do that would surprise me," said LSU offensive coordinator Cam Cameron, who served in the same capacity with the San Diego Chargers for four of Brees' five seasons.

Cameron recalled a meeting he had with Brees after the Chargers' grim 2003 season in which the quarterback and coach discussed plans for the approaching offseason. The Chargers had just finished 4–12—tied for the worst in the league—and Brees had lost his starting job to 41-year-old Doug Flutie. Brees told Cameron that he and Brittany were making plans to celebrate their first wedding anniversary in the second week of February.

"I said, 'How did you pick that [wedding] day?" Cameron said. "And he said, 'Well, the Super Bowl is this date and the Pro Bowl is this date, and I knew I couldn't do it those dates."

Cameron chuckled privately at Brees' ambition. The Chargers hadn't had a Pro Bowl quarterback in 18 years. They'd made the playoffs only seven times since the league merger in 1970.

The next year, the Chargers went 12–4, won the AFC West Division title, and advanced to the playoffs for the first time in eight years. And a few weeks later, on February 8, 2005, Brees played in his first Pro Bowl.

"That kind of tells you about Drew Brees," Cameron said.

20

The Fire and Fury of Sunday Sean

IF THERE'S A SINGLE TRAIT THAT SEAN PAYTON AND DREW BREES share more than others, it is their maniacal competitiveness. Above everything else, their shared drive to win creates a foundation for their relationship, a commonality that harbors deep mutual respect. This competitive drive fuels their long work weeks during the season and burns throughout the offseason as they prepare for another season.

Yet they display this competitiveness in vastly different ways, especially during games. Brees is focused but calm on game days. As the on-field leader of the team, he consciously maintains a poker face and positive body language during games. By Brees' demeanor and expression, it's difficult to tell whether the Saints are leading or trailing by three touchdowns against an opponent. The idea is to not give the opponent any mental edge and instill confidence in the Saints sideline.

"The greatest players in all sports make everyone around them better players," Strief said. "What you notice about Drew when you're in the huddle with him in the biggest moment of the game, he is the exact same in that moment as he is in the walk-through in the afternoon before a game in the indoor practice facility. That breeds confidence in the situation. His consistency puts everybody at ease in the biggest moments in games."

Brees compares playing quarterback to captaining a ship. The captain must communicate the plan and instill confidence in his staff. To do that, he must check his emotions and remain poised and calm.

"I find that I'm best when I can be calm, composed, and then I can think very clearly," he said. "There's a difference between being on the sideline versus being in the huddle. In the huddle, you're driving a ship. You've got to be able to communicate with everybody. You've got to get everybody on the same page. You've got to get everybody up to the ball. You've got to get it all orchestrated. And then make that quick split-second decision. So I find that there's probably a little bit more calm and poise that has to take place there than on the sideline."

Payton, on the other hand, is often a cauldron of emotions during games. He prowls the sideline with a noticeable intensity. And if things aren't going well, his wrath spares no one. Players. Coaches. Opponents. Officials. Over the years, TV cameras have caught Payton giving an earful to various Saints players and assistant coaches, most notably running back Mark Ingram and former defensive coordinator Rob Ryan. Even innocent bystanders simply trying to do their jobs aren't immune. Members of the chain gang have felt Payton's icy stare if they infringe on his sideline coaching turf. Saints media relations executives have manned the sidelines for years to monitor members of the network broadcast crew and proactively prevent run-ins.

"It's just who I am on game day," Payton said unapologetically. "It's what's natural and comfortable for me. That's me. Pick a player or coach and they've heard it from me. That's just me being fired up. Yeah, I get upset when there are 12 guys on the field. That doesn't mean I'm looking for another defensive coach. I'm going to be more upset again. There's going to be more [video] clips of it."

Payton's game-day behavior is strikingly different from his demeanor anywhere else. During the week of a game, he employs a professorial demeanor at practice and during meetings. Payton has long compared coaching to teaching. In his mind, great coaches are inherently great communicators and instructors. With that in mind, he rarely raises his voice at practice and spends much of his time calmly instructing players on individual techniques and responsibilities. But on game days a transformation occurs: Professor Payton becomes Sunday Sean, a gum-chomping, sideline-pacing, hell-raising, football-coaching firebrand. Payton's animated sideline antics have become infamous around the league and legendary among his own players and coaches. They refer to Payton's game-day alter ego as Sunday Sean and Game-Day Sean. In fact, his sideline demeanor is so notorious it has become part of the informal orientation that veteran players give to newcomers and rookies when they join the club.

"Sean's definitely a different guy on Sundays," defensive tackle Sheldon Rankins said. "On Sunday, he's got his Juicy Fruit, and he's locked in."

Payton's sideline attacks are nondiscriminatory. Errors of omission and errors of commission from his players are equally egregious in his mind. Drop a ball. Jump offside. Fail to account for the opponent's best player in pass protection. Whatever. A failure to execute mentally or physically is going to earn a sideline rebuke from Payton. When the game is on the line, any person in his way will face his fire. Players say they see his pursed-lipped, steely-eyed glare in their sleep.

"If things don't go right on the field, you're going to hear about it, you're going to feel his eyeballs piercing through you," former Saints offensive lineman Jermon Bushrod said. "You can feel him coming after you."

Like Pavlov's dogs, Saints players have been conditioned over the years to avoid Payton on the sideline after committing a mental error or mistake during a game. They'll take serpentine paths to the sideline to skirt him and almost always avoid eye contact with him when they reach the bench.

"I've seen [former star receiver Marques] Colston run almost around to the visitor's bench to get back to our sideline to avoid Sean," Saints wide receivers coach Curtis Johnson said of the former star receiver.

But Payton has wisened to these tactics. He might have to wait until after completing a series as the offensive play-caller, but he eventually finds time to get his point across and air his grievance. And, players say, he never forgets a transgression.

"Oh, he's coming," veteran receiver Ted Ginn Jr. said. "You might dodge him that first time, but he's going to catch you again. It's not like you're not going to hear it."

Former tackle Jon Stinchcomb remembers being assessed a holding penalty during a game against Tampa Bay and feeling Payton's wrath from the sideline.

"You could see the glare on his face from midfield," Stinchcomb said. "He chewed me and up down when I got to the sideline. You just have to go and eat it. There's no getting around it."

Strief recalled Payton stomping up to him after he gave up a particularly bad hit against an opponent one year.

"He came to the sideline and asked me, 'Is this too big for you? As in, is playing in the NFL [too big for you]?" Strief said. "If you've been here long enough, it's happened to all of us."

Terron Armstead remembered a mistake he made during his rookie season, just months removed from a stellar career at Arkansas–Pine Bluff. Payton tore into Armstead before he could reach the sideline.

"I'd never had anyone talk to me like that before in my life," Armstead said. "I was wondering what I got myself into."

Taysom Hill said Payton once jumped him during a game for failing to make the proper decision on a read-option run. He kept the ball instead of handing it off to Kamara, and Payton let him know about it on the sideline. Later in the game, Payton sent in another read-option run to Hill and reminded him in the headset "to just give it" to Kamara. But when Hill took the snap, the correct read was to keep the ball and he did, scoring a touchdown on the run.

"He told the coaches in the headset, 'Taysom's got guts,'" Hill said. "Or something a little more colorful than that."

Payton's theatrics aren't limited to his own team. He used to regularly exchange trash talk with former Carolina Panthers receiver Steve Smith during the team's biannual NFC South battles. In the 2017 season, Payton yelled demonstratively across the field at Tampa Bay Buccaneers coach Dirk Koetter during a game at the Superdome after Bucs quarterback Jameis Winston instigated a fight between Mike Evans and Marshon Lattimore. A few weeks later, Payton brandished the choke sign at Devonta Freeman after a carry by the Falcons running back, a gesture that earned Payton a $10,000 fine from the league. Payton also prematurely trolled Vikings fans by performing the Skol clap on the sidelines during the final minutes of the Saints' 2018 NFC divisional playoff game at U.S. Bank Stadium.

This fiery behavior is a distinguishing characteristic of Payton's coaching. Many of the NFL's great offensive minds have been stoic, cerebral men, and they coached that way. Tom Landry. Joe Gibbs. Mike Holmgren. Andy Reid. You'd never see one of them going after a player or coach on the sidelines.

"It's kind of a running joke as to the 'Game-Day Sean' demeanor," Brees said. "He can be so calm, cool, composed at practice, in the meeting room, that kind of thing. And then game day rolls around....

Do not get on his bad side. He's intense. He's fiery, ultra-, ultra-competitive."

Over the years, various Saints coaches have been assigned get-back duty during games. The unenviable task in recent years fell on the shoulders of coaching assistant Kevin Petry and strength and conditioning coaches Dan Dalrymple, Charles Byrd, and Rob Wenning. In the early days, Saints wide receiver coach Curtis "C.J." Johnson drew the short straw. He was assigned get-back coach duty in the 2006 NFC Championship against the Bears in Chicago.

"[General manager] Mickey [Loomis] said if Sean runs down to the end zone one more time, C.J., you know him the best, you've got to go get him," Johnson said. "Lo and behold, Reggie Bush makes a long run and the refs call it back and there goes Sean on the field. We're in Chicago, it's minus-75 degrees, I'm trying to pull Sean back and getting my butt chewed, 'You get away from me! Don't you touch me!'

"With Sean you know what you're getting. As coaches, I think we've all been fired a couple of times in our minds, and that was one of mine. It goes with the territory."

Lombardi has felt the wrath, as well. As the replay liaison for Payton on game days, he has the unenviable task of advising the head coach on review challenges with the officials. Payton isn't the most patient soul while awaiting word from Lombardi, who is positioned in the coaches' box high above the playing field. Lombardi has learned to err on the side of caution in most situations.

"I always say, 'Sean is the greatest coach to work for—for 349 days a year," Lombardi quipped.

As wired as Payton is during games, he unwinds pretty quickly afterward and returns to his normal self shortly after the game ends. By the time he addresses the team in the locker room and meets the media for his post-game press conference, he's usually calmed down. If he's lashed into someone particularly hard during a game, he often will seek them out and smooth things over.

"He's so good after the game," Taysom Hill said. "I think everybody that knows him well enough knows to not take any of his stuff personally. He just gets into the moment. He's just a fiery, competitive guy."

Payton's sideline antics have made him Public Enemy No. 1 for opposing fans. He's regularly heckled on the road, a tactic he embraces. At the Saints game at CenturyLink Field in 2019, fans brandished signs mocking his role in Bountygate or time as a replacement player during the 1987 labor strike. When Payton jogged off the field after the Saints' 33–27 win that day, he mockingly applauded the group above the exit tunnel to the locker room and exchanged taunts with them as he left the field.

But in New Orleans, a city that celebrates passion and eccentricity, Payton's fiery game-day persona is beloved. He's become a cult hero, especially among the team's diehard fans, who, after years of suffering ignominious defeats and having proverbial sand kicked in their faces by the 49ers and Falcons, view Payton as their bully savior. Images of his pursed-lipped, icy-eyed glare are popular on T-shirts and Internet avatars across the Crescent City.

Payton, meanwhile, makes no apologies for his behavior. Football is an emotional game, and he wants his players to have an edge on game days. His sideline intensity has set the tone for the Saints throughout his tenure.

"Every one of us has been in a basketball game where you're on a court and the winners stay and if you lose, you're done and it's four deep on who's waiting," Payton said. "There's a good chance if you lose that, unless you want to stick around for an hour and a half, you're not going to play anymore. And it's 10–9 and you're going to 11 and you think about at that moment how you compete because you don't want to be that guy that gives up the shot [that loses the game]. That last bucket in that pickup game, you had to earn that last bucket. When you get guys caring like that, then you've got something there."

DOME-INATION:
2015 New York Giants

November 1, 2015, marked the 49th anniversary of the founding of the New Orleans Saints, and Brees christened All Saints Day with one of the most memorable performances of his career.

Against most teams and most quarterbacks, Eli Manning's six-touchdown, 350-yard passing day would have been more than enough for victory. It was a career day, one of the best of his storied tenure in New York. In the long, proud history of New York Giants football, only Y.A. Tittle had thrown for as many touchdowns in a single game. And still it wasn't enough. Because Brees was better.

Brees outdueled Manning and became only the third quarterback in the modern era of the NFL to pass for seven touchdowns as the Saints outlasted the Giants 52–49 in one of the wildest shootouts in NFL history.

How wild?

The teams combined for 101 points, 1,030 yards, and an NFL-record 14 touchdowns. And on the final snap of the back-and-forth shootout, Kai Forbath's 50-yard goal was the game winner. It was the third-highest-scoring game in NFL history.

The Saints gained 608 yards, the most ever allowed by the Giants in modern NFL history.

Brees (seven) and Manning (six) combined to throw 13 touchdown passes, the most in a single game in NFL history.

For the Saints, it was the second-most points and third-most yards they'd amassed in club history. And they needed every one of them to secure the win.

The Saints had six touchdown drives of 80 or more yards and scored 10 points in the final 41 seconds.

"I've never been a part of something like that," said Brees, who completed a team-record 40 of 50 passes for a career-high and Saints-record 511 yards.

The Saints and Giants combined to average 7.3 yards per play. Of the 141 combined offensive snaps, only seven resulted in lost yardage. Thirty-six of the combined plays gained at least 10 yards. Eight of the touchdowns covered 20 or more yards. There were five scores in the fourth quarter alone.

The penultimate play of the game featured a 24-yard punt return by Marcus Murphy; a fumble, which the Saints recovered; and a 15-yard face-mask penalty on Giants punter Brad Wing, which set up the Saints at the Giants 32-yard line for Forbath's game-winning kick.

"This was certainly one of the craziest games that I have ever been a part of," Brees said. "It was punch for punch. We knew we couldn't slip up. There were a lot of things about today that were kind of mind-boggling."

Brees completed passes to nine different receivers and hit five different players for touchdowns. Late in the fourth quarter, Brees had completed 18 consecutive passes and had as many touchdown passes (six) as incompletions (six). It marked the 10th five-plus-touchdown game of his career, a new NFL high.

For the Giants, it was just the latest nightmarish experience in the Superdome. The Brees-led Saints routed them 48–27 and 49–24 on their previous two visits to New Orleans in 2009 and 2011, respectively.

"I've played here before and when Drew plays like Drew plays at home, he's almost unstoppable," said Giants linebacker Jonathan Casillas, who won a Super Bowl ring with the Saints in 2009.

21

Don't Eat the Cheese

THE NFL REGULAR SEASON COVERS FIVE LONG MONTHS. IT begins in the humid heat of September and ends in the frigid frost of January. Along the way minds can wander, focus can falter, motivation can wane. Coaches like Sean Payton know complacency can be enemy of focus and execution.

During the season, motivation is a weekly challenge for Payton. In addition to compiling a game plan for the upcoming opponent, he spends time each week preparing a mission statement to mold the minds of his players and hone their focus. He delivers it in a PowerPoint presentation at the team meeting on Wednesday morning to set the tone for the week ahead. The message typically highlights a few simple statistical metrics Payton believes are keys to success in the upcoming game. An opponent's record in games after the bye week. Or their success in home games on *Monday Night Football*.

But strategic plans often aren't enough. Players sometimes need a little extra motivation to get ready for an upcoming game. And few coaches in the NFL are better motivators than Payton.

Payton learned most of his tactics from Bill Parcells, a master motivator who knew exactly which buttons to push and when to push them for each of his players. Payton has employed a similar M.O. over the years, and many of his ploys have become legendary among his players and coaches.

One of the most famous tactics came during the week of the 2019 NFC divisional playoff game against the Philadelphia Eagles. When the team reconvened after the bye week that Monday morning, Payton wanted to make a statement to the players. He enlisted his assistant, Kevin Petry, and do-it-all executive, Jay Romig, to carry out his plan. The idea was to seize the players' attention and motivate them for the playoff run. To pull it off, he asked Romig to order $201,000 in cash from a local bank. The booty represented the bonus money at stake for each player if they won the Super Bowl.

The cash arrived in a Brinks truck, and Romig housed it in the cylindrical glass case used to display the Lombardi Trophy in the lobby of the club's Metairie offices. Not only was the case big enough to corral the 210 bricks of 1,000 $1 bills, but it also would provide the proper showcase for unveiling.

At the start of the team meeting, Payton began the session in usual fashion by addressing the team with his points of emphasis for the Eagles game. At the end of his speech, he gave the cue for Romig and Petry to enter the room from a side door, where they wheeled in the covered case on a cart. For effect, two armed guards accompanied the pair.

Then Payton read off the playoff bonus amounts for each round of the postseason: $29,000 for winning the divisional round, $54,000 for winning the NFC championship, and another $118,000 for winning the Super Bowl.

Payton then signaled for Romig to remove the cover of the display, and the players saw the glass case full of cash, along with the Lombardi Trophy. He then told his players if they wanted it, go win three more games. The room erupted. Players excitedly swarmed the display for selfies.

"It's just Sean trying to give everybody a vision, especially the young guys, obviously as to what we're after and the opportunity that we have, especially as the [No.] 1 seed," Brees said.

Payton's ploy was a reprise of a stunt he pulled during the Saints' Super Bowl run in 2009. But the bonus money has doubled in the decade since. And because Brees and punter Thomas Morstead were the only players on the roster left from the Super Bowl team, the scheme hit home.

"It was surreal because I've never seen that much money in person, so when he brought that out...I was like, 'Oh wow, this is for real? This is what we're playing for?'" rookie defensive tackle Taylor Stallworth said.

In previous years, Payton littered the locker room and meeting rooms with mouse traps to warn players not to "eat the cheese" during a winning streak, a Parcellsian ploy to ward off complacency and overconfidence. Translation: don't get too full of the good things people are saying about you.

Another time, he left empty gas cans in players' lockers to remind them to keep fuel in the tank for the long season. He also brought baseball bats to the facility before a game to encourage players "to bring the wood" on Sunday.

At other times, he dropped leaflets with motivational messages into players' lockers. One year it was a photo of the Superdome beneath shots of Panthers quarterback Jake Delhomme and coach John Fox and a message: WHOSE HOUSE IS IT: THEIRS OR OURS? The reference was to Carolina's then six-game winning streak against the Saints in the Superdome at that time. (The Saints snapped it with a 30–20 victory.)

Another year it was a motivational cartoon depicting two men in dress shirts and ties carrying pickaxes in separate tunnels. The one on the bottom was slouched over with a glum expression on his face, holding his pickax over his right shoulder, and walking away from a thin barrier of mud separating him from a trove of diamonds. The man at the top was wielding his pickax over his head and digging frantically toward the diamonds, which he'd reach as long as he kept moving in that direction. The message: don't give up.

"It's one of Sean's great strengths," Brees said. "How do you find a way—and it's one of the biggest challenges in the NFL—to make sure your team is ready to play 16 weeks? It's a long season. It's a marathon. How do you make it to where your team is always concentrated and never having a mental lapse? And you have to continue to find a chip to put on your shoulder, a motivational tactic of some kind that will get guys to play each week."

Payton will also push individual players' buttons if he feels they need a motivational kick. One year he gigged Jon Stinchcomb about his pre-snap penalties. He would regularly prod Jammal Brown and Larry Warford about their weight. Scott Shanle recalled Payton getting on him about his ability—or lack thereof—to cover the tight end.

"He's always finding ways to give us an edge," Shanle said.

The motivational ploys are one of Payton's ways to "tend the garden." He knows it's human nature for players to let up or look ahead during a long season. So he relentlessly lives in the precious present. He works the locker room, the meeting rooms, the cafeteria, giving everybody something to think about.

"If it were every week it might come across as gimmicky," Stinchcomb said. "But he knows when to pick his spots."

In recent years, Payton has employed various visual aids to liven up team meetings. He would recruit mascots from Saints players' respective colleges to make appearances at the meeting. Alabama's Big Al elephant mascot (Mark Ingram), LSU's Mike the Tiger (Will Clapp, Travin Dural), and Michigan State's Sparty (a gig at Brees after Michigan State beat Purdue) were all flown to New Orleans and put up in hotel rooms.

When Georgia State upset Tennessee 38–30 in Week 1 of the 2019 season, Payton had the school's Panther mascot outfit flown to New Orleans, and assistant equipment manager Blake Romig donned the outfit and handled the appearance duties.

"Sean always has something up his sleeve to get you excited and motivated and focused and locked in," Ingram said.

The travel and hotel expenses for flying a mascot and his assistant to New Orleans and putting them up for a night at a local hotel would often cost thousands of dollars. What's more, it required staff members to arrange the trips and escort the visitors to and from the airport, etc.—all for a five-minute appearance at the team meeting.

"It helps lighten the mood for the team during the season," kicker Wil Lutz said. "It also shows shows how committed the team is to winning, that they would make that kind of investment for something like that."

After the Saints defeated the Seattle Seahawks in Week 3 of the 2019 season, Payton had another surprise up his sleeve. After presenting the game balls to Teddy Bridgewater and other recipients, he cut the lights in the squad room and the video staff played a 40-second historical video of Pike Place Market in Seattle. When the video ended, Romig wheeled in a cart with a cooler filled with four large gutted salmon and a dozen of bags of salmon filets on the bottom. Payton then began calling out players by name and tossing the slimy fish across the squad room. Anyone with even the remotest ties to the Pacific Northwest got a fish: Taysom Hill, a Pocatello, Idaho, native; Loomis, an Oregon native; reserve quarterback J.T. Barrett, who spent time on the Seahawks practice squad for two weeks earlier in the season. As Payton hurled the slimy fish around the room, mayhem ensued as players and coaches scurried out of the line of fire.

"That was crazy," said Joe Lombardi, who was born and raised in Seattle. "I ducked out of the way of mine, but I had blood and slime on my game plan that entire week."

The shrapnel of scales and slime on the floor was so bad the club had to have the squad room sanitized by professional cleaners that night.

"The meeting room stunk like fish for the rest of the week," said Payton, with a mischievous grin.

The extent Payton undergoes to pull off the stunts is just another example of his attention to detail. Early in his tenure, Payton would use speeches and guest speakers to enliven team meetings. But his approach has evolved with the times. In recent years, he's used audiovisual aids and props to connect with his players, most of whom are of the Millennial generation.

"He's always looking for that little nudge to get some extra energy into the team," Lombardi said. "It's a long season. It's a grind. He's looking for ways to wake guys up and get the team mentally on the same page and get them ready to play this game. You can't get up the same way for all 16 games. There are going to be some special teams throughout the the year that you can really crank the team up. That's one of his secrets. He knows how to get the team cranked up."

After wins in the 2018 seasons, Payton installed temporary light and sound systems in the locker room, effectively transforming the post-game into a disco. Fred McAfee, the team's director of player engagement, served as the DJ. Payton took it to another level in 2019 by ordering the purchase of a smoke machine and bigger speakers. And when the Saints win, Payton isn't shy about joining the post-game dance-offs with the players.

"Guys love coming to work, and we know how to have fun," Brees said. "We had lights and smoke and everything else in the locker room after the game, having a great time, and turning it into Studio

54 or something. We know how to have fun, but the level of work matches the level of fun. The culture we have created here is special."

Added Strief: "Do I think it's the reason the Saints beat teams on Sunday, absolutely not. But it's just his way of planting a seed in your head and keeping you focused."

Brees also believes in the power of motivation. His methods differ from Payton's, but they are equally effective. Whether it's buying motivational books or distributing T-shirts with motivational messages like SMELL GREATNESS or BE SPECIAL, Brees tries to have something new for his teammates every year when training camp begins.

"It's a visual way to convey the message and importance of finishing everything that you do," tackle Zach Strief said. "It's easy to tell somebody to do one more rep [in the weight room] or watch five more minutes of video. It's a lot harder to visualize what the effect of that will be."

Strief said it's also just another example of Brees' extraordinary leadership skills. Other players preach the same gospel to their teammates, but Brees takes motivation to another level.

In addition to the Finish Strong books and bracelets, he also provided copies of the motivational book *212: The Extra Degree* and T-shirts with the mission statements of the speeches guest speakers Avery Johnson, Ronnie Lott, and Jon Gruden delivered to the team during training camp.

"It's part of him being a good leader," Strief said. "He understands the psyche of a player. You hear a lot of coaching-isms as a player. It's a way to transcend all the talk and create something that might hit home with someone."

Brees also famously leads the pregame rally chant for the team during pregame warm-ups on the field. Brees has led the chant for every game since his second season in New Orleans. Horn and Bush handled the duties in 2006 and 2007. While Brees was rehabbing his thumb injury in 2019, linebacker DeMario Davis assumed the responsibility.

The first chant Brees performed in 2008 centered on the scene from the movie *300*. Instead of Sparta, Brees riffed, "This is New Orleans!" He changed the chant in the Super Bowl season to one inspired by a cadence he picked up during an offseason U.S. Tour visit to the U.S. Marine base in Guatanamo Bay.

> *When I say 1, you say 2. When I say win, you say for you....*
> *1! 2! Win! For you!*

> *When I say 3, you say 4. When I say win, you say some more.... 3! 4! Win! Some more!*

> *When I say 5, you say 6. When I say win, you say for kicks.... 5! 6! Win! For kicks!*

> *When I say 7, you say 8. When I say win, you say it's great.... 7! 8! Win! It's great!*

> *When I say 9, you say 10. When I say win, you say again.... 9! 10! Win! Again!*

> *Win! Again! Win! Again! Win! Again! Win! Again!*

In recent years, Brees has changed the message from game to game. It could be something derived from a movie or a song or a poem. During the 2017 playoffs, he based his chant on the sayings from his grandfather, who died earlier that year. Regardless, he always keeps them short, no more than 30 seconds. And he always delivers them with enthusiasm and emotion, at precisely 45 minutes before kickoff.

"It's not usually something I would do, not really even my personality," Brees said. "Typically I'm pretty calm, composed, and chilled. I have an edge on game day, but I'm not the rah-rah type. But I had mentor [Tom House] tell me once, 'You have to learn to be comfortable being uncomfortable.' So, it was one of these like, all right, if nobody else will do it, I need to be the guy who does it. So

I had to step out of my comfort zone a little bit because I thought it was something that was needed. I'm for whatever gets our team ready to play, play at a high level, gets us fired up."

The videos of Brees' pregame chants regularly rank among the most viewed posts on the Saints website and often go viral on social media. And they're just as popular with his teammates.

"I get as far into the huddle as I can because it's motivating," wide receiver Keith Kirkwood said. "Just to finally be in that huddle with somebody who is going to go down as one of the greatest quarterbacks of all time is special. He's the leader of the pack. It's amazing to hear his energy and his passion. Everybody feels it."

22

The Near Divorce

THE WALL OUTSIDE THE SQUAD ROOM IN THE NEW ORLEANS Saints training complex features several mounted placards displaying motivational quotes from famous people about teamwork, motivation, and bonding. One of them is a quote from automobile magnate Henry Ford: COMING TOGETHER IS THE BEGINNING. KEEPING TOGETHER IS PROGRESS. WORKING TOGETHER IS SUCCESS.

The Payton-Brees marriage is a textbook example of Ford's motto. Their partnership has been one of the most enduring in NFL history, representing one of the longest-tenured and most successful coach-quarterback tandems in the sport. Entering the 2020 season, their 200 regular season starts together were the second most ever, trailing only Bill Belichick and Tom Brady (281). In a league where the average coaching tenure lasts four years and the average playing career spans three years, what Payton and Brees have done in New Orleans is extraordinarily rare.

And by and large, there's been nary a hiccup between them. Unlike the sometimes-distant relationship Belichick and Brady shared in New England, the Payton-Brees partnership has remained remarkably harmonious. Payton purposely never involved himself in Brees' contract talks with the team, yielding to Loomis on such matters when Brees signed contract extensions in 2012, 2016, and 2018. This has kept their relationship problem-free throughout the entire tenure.

"One thing that's served us well over all these years is the line of communication," Payton said. "There's a level of trust and respect there."

Still, there were a couple instances during the Payton-Brees run that almost led to a breakup of the prolific coach-quarterback partnership, two occasions that played out behind closed doors, unbeknownst to the public. While the Payton-Brees partnership continued to hum along in the mid-2010s, other dynamics in the Saints organization were taking place that could have led to a split of the dynamic pairing and changed the course of sports history in New Orleans and the NFL.

It all started in 2012, when Payton was suspended for a year by the NFL for his role in the bounty scandal. Not only did the suspension cost Payton millions of dollars in salary, it also tarnished his public image. That same year, Saints owner Tom Benson purchased the New Orleans Hornets, the NBA team now known as the Pelicans. Benson hired Dell Demps as a general manager but assigned Loomis to a supervisory role as director of basketball operations. Loomis' duties were essentially to serve as a liaison between basketball ops and ownership, but the optics of putting a "football man" atop the basketball organizational chart raised eyebrows in some NFL circles.

The move especially did not sit well with the hyper-competitive, football-obsessed Payton. He believed Loomis' basketball responsibilities, however minimal, put the Saints at a competitive disadvantage with their rivals in the dog-eat-dog world of the NFL. In his mind, sustained success could only be attained if everyone in the organization was committed full-time to the mission. He believed everyone in the boat needed to be rowing in the same direction, with the same intensity.

The situation ate at Payton and became a source of friction in his relationship with Loomis. It was one of the first cracks in the once-strong foundation between the two leaders of the Saints organization. Publicly, everything seemed normal. But privately, discord brewed between the two. An incident in the spring of 2013 illustrated the dissension.

When Loomis was forced to miss the first few days of the Saints' organized team activities to accompany Benson and other Hornets executives on a trip to New York for the NBA Draft Lottery, Payton seethed. The practices were the first major on-field event Payton would oversee in the offseason program since his suspension. And it chafed him that his general manager would be a no-show, especially for something as inconsequential as the NBA Draft Lottery. Never one to hide his feelings even with superiors, Payton plotted a way to display his displeasure, this time in classic *Dennis the Menace* fashion.

In the week before the draft lottery, Payton recruited a couple co-conspirators to execute his scheme. Coaching assistant Jason Mitchell and assistant equipment manager John Baumgartner were tasked with an odd duty: Payton wanted them to buy as many ping-pong balls as they could find in the New Orleans area. After practice, a couple members of the Saints' equipment staff fanned out in cars and bought every ping-pong ball available from every sporting goods store in the New Orleans metropolitan area, an estimated 200 total.

While Loomis attended the lottery festivities in New York, Payton sent his operatives to Loomis' office and had them inundate it with ping-pong balls. They poured balls on the floor and atop his desk. They hid them in his desk drawers and filled his trash basket. There was hardly a square foot of Loomis' second-floor corner office that didn't have a small plastic ball in it.

If Loomis wasn't aware of how Payton felt about his basketball role before he left for New York, he was fully cognizant when he returned to New Orleans and opened his office door.

"The Pelicans took very little of my time and didn't affect my role with the football team," Loomis said. "I get the perspective. It just wasn't the reality of the situation."

Nevertheless, Payton's message was sent.

"I bet I could find a ping-pong ball somewhere in his office today if looked," Payton quipped.

Payton and Loomis had experienced run-ins before, most notably a heated confrontation in front of staffers and team members after the Saints' humiliating 41–36 upset loss to the Seahawks in the 2010 playoffs in Seattle. The incidents were rare but sometimes inevitable with the fiery Payton and his relentless quest for excellence. Payton's energy was one of the main reasons Loomis hired him in 2006. Loomis knew he would need someone with Payton's drive to overcome the unique challenges the Saints faced in post-Katrina New Orleans. But he also knew Payton's ambition needed to be constantly managed.

In this way, Loomis, with his steady, even-keeled personality, was the perfect yin to the high-strung Payton's yang. Loomis didn't know much about Payton when he hired him in 2006. A shrewd judge of people, Loomis didn't need long to realize Payton owned natural leadership skills, a strong work ethic, and an extraordinary offensive mind. Loomis learned to skillfully balance his role as counsel, booster, and boss to his talented head coach. He astutely knew the right time to give Payton a wide berth and when to rein him in. Payton could be a handful, but Loomis knew he was worth the hassle.

Payton was notorious around the Saints facility for obsessing over every detail of the operation. The same attention to detail that made his game plans so effective on Sundays was also directed at various aspects of the Saints' day-to-day business operations. Payton stressed over everything from the size and color of the rally towels issued on game days at the Superdome to the size of the Christmas tree in the lobby foyer. When the Saints were winning, Payton's obsessive-compulsive micromanagement was tolerable, a harmless quirk that caused staffers to privately roll their eyes. But as the team slogged through back-to-back losing seasons in 2014 and 2015, it could wear thin.

"Sean has remarkable attention to detail, that obsession with the little things," Loomis said. "He's just concerned about every little thing that he sees. That's part of what makes him a great coach. So if sometimes I have to put up with a screaming match from him about something that's bothering him, then that's okay."

In a league filled with big egos and publicity hounds, Loomis' modest comportment is rare. Rather than hog the spotlight, he shuns it. A protégé of former Seattle Seahawks and Carolina Panthers president Mike McCormick, Loomis joined the Saints in 2000 as the team's salary cap negotiator under general manager Randy Mueller. Loomis made a positive impression with the frugal Benson as a tough negotiator, not only with player agents but also with hotel managers over the team's travel expenses. When Benson abruptly fired Mueller in 2002, it took him only a few days to promote Loomis to general manager.

Loomis' management style mirrored that of McCormick, who believed that the head coach and players were the faces of the franchise. The general manager's job, in Loomis' mind, was to support the players and coaches and take the heat when times grew tough. Loomis preferred to operate in the shadows. And his quiet, steady demeanor proved to be the perfect counterbalance to the brash, volatile Payton. While they owned decidedly different personalities, both men were self-aware enough to know they needed the other to be successful. When they had their run-ins, they usually managed to quickly find common ground and smooth things over.

"I think we have complementary personalities and skill sets," Loomis said of Payton. "It doesn't mean we always agree. But we appreciate each other's perspective and try to accommodate what the other person wants."

After the ugly 2014 season, both Payton and Loomis knew they needed to make major changes, starting with the defense, which had fallen to historic levels of incompetence. Several core players from the team's successful Super Bowl era—Will Smith, Jon Vilma, Malcolm Jenkins, Roman Harper, Jabari Greer—either retired or left via free agency. The vacuum was filled with talented but unreliable players like Brandon Browner, Junior Galette, Keenan Lewis, and Kenny Vaccaro. Discipline became an issue—on and off the field.

Payton also played a part in the defensive downfall. When he moved on from defensive coordinator Gregg Williams in the wake of the bounty scandal in 2012, he hired Steve Spagnuolo and abruptly fired him a year later without ever actually coaching a game with him. Payton then hired Rob Ryan in 2013 in a move that many longtime observers questioned from the start. Ryan, the brother of former Buffalo Bills and New York Jets head coach Rex Ryan, was respected for his defensive knowledge, but his defenses had a reputation for being undisciplined, mistake-prone units, the exact opposite of Payton's highly synchronized offenses. Many thought the pairing of the exacting Payton and the laissez-faire Ryan was doomed from the start. Ryan installed the 3-4 defense that he and his brother had run so successfully in Baltimore and other stops around the NFL. But a year later, Payton changed plans and instructed Ryan to switch to a Seattle Seahawks–style defense built around safety Jairus Byrd, the team's prized free agent signing in 2014, and big cornerbacks like Lewis, Brandon Browner, and Stanley Jean-Baptiste. A good soldier,

Ryan did as he was told, even though he privately questioned the decision.

Things were starting to slip elsewhere, too. While Payton remained as dedicated as ever to film study and game-planning, his attention to detail in other matters started to wane. Team meetings sometimes began late. Walk-through practices were sloppy.

Things got so bad late in the 2014 season, veteran offensive tackle Zach Strief felt the need to meet with Payton and address some of the issues he saw undermining the team, most of which pointed directly at Payton himself. It took two weeks and multiple phone calls with his father for Strief to muster the courage to handle the face-to-face sit-down.

"As one of the leaders of the team, I felt like I had to do it," Strief said. "Drew is the unquestioned leader of our team, but he was so focused on what he was doing and was so close to the situation I don't think he was aware of what was going on. There were things that used to be important to Sean that suddenly didn't seem to matter anymore, things that he used to be concerned about that he no longer was. I told him, there were problems. We're doing stuff that we don't do. We don't start meetings eight minutes late. We just don't. We never have. It sets a bad precedent."

As Strief continued, Payton pulled out a notebook from his desk drawer and jotted down each item from Strief's list. By the time they were finished 40 minutes later, the entire notepad was filled.

"That was a difficult meeting," Strief said. "There was one thing on the list that he said was bullshit, but everything else he agreed with. I don't think it was anything intentional on his part, but things had just started to slip. It's just human nature. It happens to people. But it takes a very special mentality and self-awareness for someone to sit there and accept criticism from, quite frankly, a very average player and not get upset. He didn't reinvent himself after that meeting, but he just sort of refocused. I gained the ultimate respect for him for the way he handled it."

To his credit, Payton accepted responsibility for the fall-off and didn't make excuses, even though he had plenty. At the time, he was navigating the fallout from his 2012 divorce from his wife of 20 years, Beth. As the marriage fell apart in late 2011, the family relocated to Westlake, Texas, a tony suburb in the Dallas-Fort Worth metroplex. The news made headlines across New Orleans and did not sit well with many residents of the proud, parochial city. Payton was forced to commute on weekends to visit his children, Meghan and Conner. Payton had the full support of Loomis and ownership, but the situation was less than ideal and eventually took its toll on him.

"Coaching is like gardening: you've got to do it every day," Payton said. "It needs that constant attention to detail. If you're not careful things can go south quickly. Coaching can grind on you and one of the first things that goes is the attention to detail. It happens with players and coaches. At some point, they're retired and haven't announced it yet. It's human nature. We all lost track of what it was that had given us a chance to be successful. I don't know that there was a specific day that it happened, but it was ignored, starting with me."

The first step Payton and Loomis took to address their locker room issues was to hire Jeff Ireland as director of college scouting. Ireland was a Parcells acolyte who had been the general manager of the Miami Dolphins from 2008 to 2013. When the Chicago Bears hired Saints director of player personnel Ryan Pace, Payton pushed for Loomis to hire Ireland and replace Rick Reiprish as the head of the team's personnel department. Ireland had a golden reputation around the league as a shrewd talent evaluator. Ireland would oversee the Saints' drafts and was charged with finding players that fit the Saints' profile. Payton and Loomis wanted smart, high-character, mentally tough players who were passionate about football, the kind of players who were the foundation of the club's famed 2006 draft class and formed the core of the 2009 Super Bowl team.

By the time Ireland was hired, most of the work had been done for the 2015 draft. But as soon as the 2015 draft ended, he immediately went to work overhauling the scouting department. He dismissed three scouts and hired four new ones. Over the next few seasons he would essentially remake the entire department, and the results showed in his draft selections. During Ireland's first four years of overseeing the NFL Draft, the Saints selected Michael Thomas, Sheldon Rankins, Vonn Bell, David Onyemata, Marshon Lattimore, Ryan Ramczyk, Alvin Kamara, Marcus Williams, Marcus Davenport, Erik McCoy, and C.J. Gardner-Johnson, a group that would form the core of the roster in subsequent years.

"Our goal was to find guys that were unselfish and put the team first," Payton said. "There's an accountability that comes with that. The turnaround had to start with the players we were bringing into the building. If we're not signing or drafting the right player, then it becomes more challenging. Getting the right leadership and creating the right atmosphere in the locker room was critical."

Payton and Loomis didn't stop there. They made another difficult move in Week 11 of the 2015 season, when they fired Ryan as defensive coordinator and promoted Dennis Allen to the role. The move to the Seahawks-style defense had been an unmitigated disaster and the Saints defense nosedived to the bottom of the league rankings. In 2015, they allowed an NFL-record 45 touchdown passes and an opposing passer rating of 116.1. They finished 31st in the league in total defense (413.4 yards per game allowed) for a second consecutive season and were dead last in scoring defense (29.8 points per game allowed).

And while Payton believed hiring Ireland and promoting Allen were steps in the right direction, his relationship with Loomis had continued to devolve behind the scenes. The back-to-back losing seasons in 2014 and 2015 strained the entire organization and exacerbated the issues between the two leaders. By the end of the 2015 season, things were growing worse instead of getting better.

"There's nothing in that building that goes on that Sean doesn't know about, and he would get mad about the dumbest things," said Mike Ornstein, a longtime marketing executive and friend and business associate of Payton and Loomis. "Sean was treating people so poorly, and Mickey would have to deal with it. It had gotten so ugly between Sean and Mickey that either Sean was going to get fired or he was going to quit."

Payton had become so frustrated he began to seriously explore an exit strategy. He leaned on his mentor, Bill Parcells, who was a proponent of change. During his Hall of Fame career as a coach and general manager, Parcells famously moved from job to job, rarely staying with one club longer than four seasons. Payton had always believed he would coach in New Orleans for his entire career. But the situation had become so frustrating to him, he now was seriously considering a move for the first time.

Payton, through intermediaries including Ornstein himself, held back-channel talks with the San Francisco 49ers and Indianapolis Colts after the 2015 season. The 49ers and Colts were attractive for different reasons. The Colts were rebuilding around quarterback Andrew Luck, whom Payton viewed as a Brees-like franchise talent. The 49ers were run by general manager Trent Baalke, a Parcells protégé, and owned a bevy of draft picks and salary cap space to facilitate their rebuilding plan. Each was a potential quick fix, certainly less challenging than the job he inherited in New Orleans. But neither the Colts nor 49ers situation ever grew serious enough to merit a formal interview. Instead, Payton and Loomis conducted a series of in-depth meetings after the season and mended fences, and Payton signed a five-year contract extension that paid him $9.5

million annually, compensation that made him the second-highest-paid coach in the NFL behind only Bill Belichick.

During an emotional press conference on January 6, 2016, Payton pledged his commitment to the organization and city. NFL head coaches typically conduct postseason press briefings to wrap up the year, but this get-together was different. Payton spoke for 61 minutes. The session was conducted in the Saints media room rather than on the practice field and was attended by Loomis, Saints president Dennis Lauscha, and owners Tom and Gayle Benson in a show of support and solidarity.

"I knew in my heart of hearts, [leaving the Saints] was not going to be something that came to fruition, and that was something I knew in my heart that I didn't want to come to fruition," Payton said that day. "And yet, there's a part of what we do that we can't control. There will be a time where they don't want you back anymore, and that's okay. One by one that train stops for all of us."

But the positive vibes didn't last long.

After another disappointing 7–9 season in 2016, reports surfaced that Payton was putting out similar feelers with the Los Angeles Rams, who had fired head coach Jeff Fisher that December. By this time, Loomis and Saints ownership had grown weary of Payton's dalliances with other teams. After three consecutive losing seasons, there was a feeling by some inside that organization that a change might be best for both sides. The Saints were prepared to lose Payton and start a new chapter. The Rams asked to interview Payton the week after the Saints' season-ending 38–32 loss to the Atlanta Falcons, but once Loomis informed them any "trade" for Payton would involve compensation in the form of high draft picks, the Rams backed off and turned their sights toward Washington Redskins offensive coordinator Sean McVay, whom they eventually hired a week later. With encouragement from Ornstein, who was playing the role of consigliere, Payton and Loomis once again met behind closed doors and reconciled their differences.

Loomis knew smart, talented leaders like Payton were hard to find. But he also knew that these things happened sometimes in the NFL. Great coaches can lose their way. Environments can go stale on them if they stay too long in one place. It happened to Andy Reid in Philadelphia and to Mike McCarthy in Green Bay. Sometimes a change can be the best thing for both sides. Loomis didn't want to lose his head coach. He was loyal to Payton. But his first loyalty was to the organization, and he believed the Saints needed and deserved a coach who was "all in." Loomis knew the landscape of the NFL. He knew the Saints, with their respected, hands-off owner Gayle Benson, fawning small-market media corps, and favorable lease arrangement with the state of Louisiana, were a unique franchise with several built-in advantages Payton wouldn't experience elsewhere.

"Those three years had been rough, and I had some pretty frank and hard discussions with him about it," Loomis said. "And I think he eventually arrived at the decision that this is where he wanted to coach for the rest of his career. And that was a change from previous years."

Added Payton: "Mickey and I talked that offseason about the direction we were going. It was not renewing our vows but reconsidering what we created [in 2006] and how fragile that can be. Mrs. Benson has been great to work for. Mickey and Dennis [Lauscha] have done a lot of tremendous things for the organization. This is where I plan on coaching the rest of my career. I'll be here as long as they'll have me. I read something a few weeks back...'Leave early a hero, stay late and become a villain.' And if I have to someday become that villain, I plan on staying until everyone says we're burning your wagon out of town. And I'm comfortable with that. I am."

After three consecutive losing seasons, something had to change, though. Payton and Loomis agreed to overhaul the defensive and special teams coaching staff. Payton fired five assistants, including longtime loyal lieutenants Joe Vitt, Greg McMahon, and Bill Johnson.

"One of the biggest mistakes executives make in professional sports is they make decisions based on the record instead of making decisions on whether you believe you have a great coach," Loomis said. "If the record didn't reflect that there's other reasons for it. It's not just the head coach. I knew we had a great head coach."

Loomis' steady hand throughout the tumultuous 2014–16 seasons was critical in maintaining organizational stability. Another general manager almost certainly would have moved on from Payton, given his transgressions. Someone with a bigger ego would have jettisoned the head coach and found a more malleable replacement. Loomis, after all, was the one who plucked Payton from anonymous assistant coaching ranks in 2006 and willingly allowed him to become the face of the organizational makeover after Hurricane Katrina. But Loomis knew the Saints were better with Payton leading the way. At times, Payton was a handful to manage, but his talent more than compensated for the hassles he sometimes created.

"Sean needs Mickey, and Mickey needs Sean," Strief said. "They make each other better. There's no question Sean works best when he has people around him to rein him in. And Mickey is the perfect guy for that."

Added Brunell, the former backup quarterback who played in five different organizations during his 17-year playing career: "Mickey is a key guy in this whole thing. He realized what they had was special. He knew how to navigate the situation and keep Sean around and that was very impressive."

DOME-INATION:
2018 Philadelphia Eagles

When the Philadelphia Eagles visited the Superdome in Week 11 of the 2018 season, they were only 10 months removed from the franchise's first Super Bowl title. Coach Doug Pederson was still the talk of the town and quarterback Carson Wentz was still being hailed as the city's next conquering hero. A spate of injuries and the inherent challenge of defending their title had conspired to wreck the first half of their season. The Eagles arrived in New Orleans at 4–5, having lost all five games by a touchdown or less.

"If you want to be one of the best teams in the league, you have to beat the best, and I know teams are saying that about us," Pederson said during a conference call with New Orleans–area reporters the week of the game. "We just haven't lived up to how we're capable of playing in a couple of situations this year. The team understands it, listen you got to be ready each week."

After suffering a close 27–20 loss to the longtime-rival Dallas Cowboys the previous week, the Eagles undoubtedly were ready for the challenge of facing the Saints in the Superdome.

But were they able?

They entered the game with a makeshift secondary. Their two starting cornerbacks (Ronald Darby, Jalen Mills) and one of their starting safeties (Rodney McLeod) were sidelined with injuries. Corner Sidney Jones was in the lineup after missing three games with a hamstring injury but was not 100 percent.

The Saints wasted no time in attacking Jones, who limped into the game with a balky hamstring. Sean Payton targeted him all week in the game plan, and the Saints went after him on their first snap from scrimmage. Drew Brees put Alvin Kamara in motion to the left and slid the offensive line in that direction. The Eagles defense bit on the motion, leaving the right side wide open for Mark Ingram, who rambled past a weak arm tackle by Jones for a 38-yard gain.

It didn't get any better from there for Philly. Jones was injured early and played just 22 snaps. Safety/nickel corner Avonte Maddox suffered an injured knee in the second quarter and didn't return. That left defensive coordinator Jim Schwartz with a defensive backfield manned by seldom-used 2017 third-round draft pick Rasul Douglas and three players who weren't even on the roster two weeks earlier: Chandon Sullivan, Cre'Von LeBlanc, and De'Vante Bausby.

Brees and Payton mercilessly attacked the Eagles' overmatched secondary with an array of motions, formations, and play-action fakes. The Saints kicked a field goal on their opening drive, then scored touchdowns on their next two possessions. A little more than a quarter into the game, they led 17–0 and had outgained the Eagles 232 to 15 in total yards.

By the time it was over, the Saints had scored on 8 of 10 possessions and embarrassed the Eagles with a 48–7 demolition, the most lopsided defeat ever for a defending Super Bowl champion. It was also the worst loss in Eagles history and by far the worst in Doug Pederson's coaching career.

"I haven't gotten my butt kicked like that in a long time," Philadelphia defensive end Chris Long said.

Brees completed 22 of 30 passes for 363 yards and four touchdowns. His passer efficiency rating of 153.2 was the fourth highest ever recorded against the Eagles. He wasn't sacked and was moved off his mark just twice the entire game.

In all, the Saints piled up 546 yards of offense, the third-highest total against the Eagles in the modern era. And it could have been worse had Payton not called off the dogs and subbed Teddy Bridgewater for Brees with 5:28 left in the game.

Brees' fourth touchdown exemplified Payton's take-no-prisoners approach to the game. He hit Kamara in stride down the right sideline for 37 yards on a fourth-and-7 play that gave the Saints a 45–7 lead early in the fourth quarter. Eagles safety Malcolm Jenkins, a 2009 first-round Saints draft pick, defiantly flipped the bird at Payton after being beaten on the play.

The Eagles tried to throw a curveball at the Saints by consistently double-teaming their top two playmakers—Michael Thomas and Kamara—and playing man-to-man on everyone else. It was a look the Saints had not seen from the Philadelphia defense during film study. But Brees and Payton simply called on other options. Tre'Quan Smith caught 10 passes for 157 yards and Ingram added 103 rushing yards.

Afterward, Brees gave a classic answer when asked about the Saints' offensive efficiency and production.

"There's still a process," he said. "Each and every week, the game plan that the coaches work so hard to put together, the time that we need in practice to make sure that we are executing that plan to perfection. The time that I need with the receivers and the running backs and the tight ends. There's just so much that goes into that. We don't take that for granted. You don't just snap your fingers and come out and play like that. A lot of time on task, and great effort, and great focus and attention to detail. We do come out with a lot of confidence because we know the amount of preparation that has gone into that."

23

The Saint Patrick's Day That Almost Was

THE PAYTON-LOOMIS SPAT WASN'T THE ONLY POTENTIAL THREAT to the Payton-Brees partnership.

A few months after Sean Payton recommitted to New Orleans, a different dilemma nearly presented itself to the head coach, one that also might have led to a premature split in the marriage.

The Saints didn't enter the 2017 NFL Draft looking for a quarterback. Drew Brees was still playing at an elite level, and the club had not invested a high draft pick in a quarterback in decades. Since Brees joined the Saints in 2006, the club had largely avoided quarterbacks in the NFL Draft. With Brees around, they had the luxury of concentrating on other positions in the draft. While Payton would say the Saints were "always in the quarterback business," the position was a low draft priority. Garrett Grayson, who was selected in the third round of the 2015 draft, and Sean Canfield, who was picked in the seventh round of the 2010 draft, were the only quarterbacks drafted by the Saints in the Payton-Brees era.

Besides, the Saints had more pressing needs that year. New Orleans was still fortifying its defense from the grim 2014–15 days, and cornerback was viewed as the team's top priority.

But as the first round transpired on Thursday, April 27, the prospect of using the No. 11 overall pick on a quarterback gradually inched closer to reality for Payton and the Saints, because the highest-rated quarterback on their draft board, Patrick Mahomes, was falling their way.

Slowly but surely, the picks improbably ticked off the board.

Wide receiver Corey Davis to the Titans at No. 5.

Safety Jamal Adams to the Jets at No. 6.

Wide receiver Mike Williams to the Chargers at No. 7.

Running back Christian McCaffrey to the Panthers at No. 8.

Then, at precisely 9:12 PM, things got real.

The Cincinnati Bengals surprisingly selected Washington receiver John Ross at No. 9, a curveball few draft analysts or NFL scouts expected. Suddenly, as Payton sat at the large conference table in the Saints war room deep inside team headquarters, the reality of the situation started to sink in. With the Buffalo Bills on the clock at No. 10, the Saints were one pick, maybe 10 or 15 minutes away, from making their selection. And the top two prospects on their draft board were still available: cornerback Marshon Lattimore and Mahomes, in that order.

Mahomes wasn't just any quarterback. The Saints graded him higher than any quarterback they'd evaluated in recent drafts. They had worked him out privately a month earlier in Lubbock, Texas, where Mahomes played collegiately at Texas Tech University. They spent the entire day with him, sending him through a battery of interviews, tests, and on-field workouts before ending the night over dinner.

"He was exceptional in the meeting that we had," Payton said. "The one thing that stood out, this player could climb, escape, throw from all the positions. And we play in an imperfect game where there's protection issues. And we just saw him make throws going left, going right, through the pocket, up in the pocket, I mean, really unique throws. And look, man, in a conference and on a team where they had to go into a game feeling like scoring 45 was gonna give 'em a chance. He was very impressive and certainly a targeted player for us in that draft."

It was the first time the Saints had seriously considering taking a quarterback so high in the draft during Payton's coaching tenure.

With Buffalo on the clock at No. 10, and the Bills expected to select a defensive player under first-year coach Sean McDermott, Payton suddenly realized there was a very real possibility Lattimore could be picked and the Saints would have no choice but to select Mahomes, the best player available by far on their board.

Further complicating the situation, Brees, by sheer serendipity, just happened to be in the building. He and a couple of his college buddies, Jason Loerzel and Ben Smith, had just completed a wild boar hunting trip in south Louisiana and were back at the Saints training facility, their chosen meeting spot. After dining in the team cafeteria, they received an invitation from Payton to visit the war room just as the first round was getting underway. They weren't the only VIPs there that day. Payton had also invited PGA golfers Jordan Spieth and Ryan Palmer, who were in town for the Zurich Classic of New Orleans and had played with Brees and Payton at the event's pro-am tournament the previous day.

When the Bengals selected Ross at No. 9, Payton knew he needed to have a conversation with Brees and apprise him of where things stood. This, after all, was a potentially unprecedented situation. Taking Mahomes with the No. 11 overall pick would create shock waves across the NFL and throughout the Saints fan base. You don't use such a valuable commodity without a plan. And the Saints, particularly Payton, were high on Mahomes' potential.

"He was a target at No. 11," Payton said. "The only thing that happened that we weren't expecting, although you kind of aren't surprised anytime when you're selecting that early, when it got down to [Marshon] Lattimore, you keep this bubble right on the board in front of you, and you're on pick 8 and you might have four in this bubble, and then one goes and another goes. Here it was—pick 10— and we have two players in the bubble, Lattimore and Mahomes."

Payton knew taking Mahomes would be a potentially franchise-altering decision. And with his franchise quarterback sitting in the room, he knew he couldn't blindside Brees by selecting his potential replacement. So he met with him outside the war room and gave him a heads-up of the situation.

"Drew was great," Payton said. "It didn't faze him a bit. He always thinks of the team first."

Brees had been in this spot before. In 2004, just three years after taking Brees in the second round of the 2001 draft, the San Diego Chargers used their first-round pick, the No. 4 overall selection in the 2004 draft, to select Philip Rivers.

Then-Chargers offensive coordinator Brian Schottenheimer remembered running into Brees in the weight room on the eve of the draft that year and informing him of the Chargers' plans to select a quarterback.

"We were chatting and he's like, 'Hey, who are we gonna draft?'" Schottenheimer told *Sports Illustrated* in 2019. "I said, 'Hey, bro, listen, you need to prepare yourself, we're probably taking a quarterback.'...It went from a real fun, jovial conversation [to] his eyes kind of just locked in. And he looked at me and said, 'That would be the worst f——ing mistake this organization could ever make.' And I'm like, 'Hey, man, don't shoot the messenger.' He goes, 'Worst mistake ever.' And he walked off."

Two years later, the Chargers went all-in with Rivers and allowed Brees to walk in free agency. Now the scenario was potentially playing out again, this time in New Orleans, 11 years later.

"I understood," Brees said. "I knew our guys loved Lattimore but didn't think he would be there. So, man, if Mahomes is there at 11 it would be hard not to take him, talent-wise. Hey, a really talented player, a guy that could be your guy in the future."

Alas, fate intervened.

The Kansas City Chiefs, fully aware of the Saints' interest in Mahomes, traded a package of three draft picks to the Bills for the right to move up from No. 27 to No. 10 and snag Mahomes. At No. 11, the Saints happily pounced on Lattimore, who would go on to win the 2017 Defensive Rookie of the Year award and earn a Pro Bowl invitation as a rookie.

Mahomes, meanwhile, assumed the starting spot in Kansas City in 2018 and quickly developed into one of the elite players in the league. He won the Most Valuable Player Award in 2018 after passing for 5,097 yards and a league-high 50 touchdowns. A year later, he led the Chiefs to their second Super Bowl championship in franchise history. Along the way, he has drawn comparisons to Hall of Famers Brett Favre and Steve Young.

If the Bills had stayed put and selected another player other than Lattimore and Mahomes, Payton said the Saints would have picked Lattimore.

"I don't know if we would have changed because Lattimore's grade was so good," he said. "The challenge is, Lattimore helps your team immediately with Brees. The other player [Mahomes] is a potential franchise quarterback that helps your team long-term. We deal with that [question] a lot."

If the Bills had stayed put and selected Lattimore instead of trading with the Chiefs, Payton said the plan was definitely to take

Mahomes, barring some over-the-top offer from a rival team. And taking Mahomes likely would have changed everything for the Saints.

A slew of questions would have presented themselves over the ensuing years.

Would the Saints have seen the same eye-popping potential in Mahomes that the Chiefs did during practices in 2017?

If so, would they have signed Brees to the two-year, $50 million contract they gave him in 2018?

Or would they have wanted to start earning a return on their investment in Mahomes?

And given his past, would Brees have even wanted to play in New Orleans in that situation?

Would the Saints have gone 11–5 and won the NFC South without Lattimore locking down opposing receivers last season?

If not, would Brees have been more willing to consider other options?

Would Brees have moved on and—gasp—broken the NFL career passing yardage and touchdown records somewhere other than New Orleans?

Thanks to the Chiefs' daring draft-day deal, Payton and the Saints never had to answer those questions. But it's fascinating to think about the players who finished first and second in voting for the 2018 NFL MVP Award sharing the same quarterback room. And it's scary to think what Mahomes could have done in the Saints' high-flying offense with Payton calling the plays.

"He was a fantastic prospect," Payton said of Mahomes. "We saw a lot of traits that we saw with Brett [Favre]. He was such a likable player. You watched him on film, and you saw a high ceiling.

"But it all worked out. I think Kansas City and Andy [Reid] and those guys got a heck of a player. It all worked out real good."

When a reporter asked Brees in 2018 if he would have been okay with the selection of Mahomes, he was completely unruffled by the prospect. "Yeah," he said, while shrugging his shoulders, "as long as he's okay to sit for a few years."

24

In NOLA to Stay

THERE WAS A TIME NOT LONG AGO WHEN FOLKS AROUND THE
New Orleans Saints training facility thought Bill Parcells haunted
the building.

Bill this.

Bill that.

This is how Bill does it in Dallas.

Sean Payton seemingly couldn't make a decision without
referencing his mentor. The initial approach was understandable.
Payton arrived in New Orleans fresh off, as he would call it, a three-
year graduate term in the Big Tuna School of Coaching. Learning at
the side of one of the most accomplished and respected coaches in
NFL history left an indelible impression on Payton, both as a man
and coach. When he left Dallas for New Orleans, he was a walking
encyclopedia of Parcells-isms.

Over time, though, Payton has gradually emerged from Parcells'
shadow. Entering his 15th season in New Orleans, Payton has grown
comfortable and confident in his own coaching skin. He has learned
that not everything Parcells said or did is the gospel, similar to how

a son one day learns that his father doesn't hold the monopoly on worldly wisdom. Payton still talks to Parcells frequently and considers him his mentor. He always will. But he's no longer Parcells' acolyte. He's become his own coach. In fact, his .630 winning percentage (131–77) is well ahead of Parcells' career mark of .569 (172–130–1).

"We're different in some ways, and that's okay," Payton said of Parcells. "I'm very clear, I'm very happy and focused and excited about what's to come, with no script."

Loomis has played a key role in Payton's evolution. Under his patient guidance, he has allowed Payton to stretch his wings, to maintain his coaching persona while learning from mistakes along the way.

Payton has matured and evolved. He is inarguably a better coach now than he was five years ago. He's certainly more malleable and open-minded, two qualities for which Parcells was never known. While Parcells' irascible style might be perfectly suited for franchise overhaul, it doesn't have a long shelf life. Consequently, he tended to bounce from job to job. And his final two tenures in Dallas and Miami weren't exactly success stories.

Payton arrived in New Orleans with the same scorched-earth attitude. In the beginning, it was necessary. The challenge of overhauling the football operation and transforming the culture of the Saints organization required a no-nonsense, take-no-prisoners approach. Payton's obsessive drive spurred the Saints to a Super Bowl title in 2009 and an unprecedented run of success. But along the way, he developed a reputation as a rebel, someone who could be difficult to deal with professionally.

Ornstein recalled a meeting with an NFL Network executive at the 2018 Pro Bowl that opened Payton's eyes when he and the Saints staff coached the NFC team in Orlando, Florida.

"She told Sean, 'I'm going to go back and tell everybody what a good guy you really are,'" Ornstein said. "Sean said, 'What do you mean?'

And she said, 'Well, everybody at NFL Films thinks you're an asshole.' And he said, 'What are you talking about? Really?' And after she left, I told him, 'Sean, I told you this. You have treated people so poorly over the years. You were an asshole. You need to change.'"

A classic story from 2011 illustrates the old Payton. That year, Payton coached a handful of games from the coaches' booth while mending the broken leg he suffered from a sideline incident against the Tampa Bay Buccaneers. During the broadcast of the Saints' 62–7 rout of the Colts, NBC Sports cameras accidentally caught Payton eating a hot dog at halftime. Payton was unhappy about the perception it gave fans and colleagues, especially since he had to be cajoled into allowing NBC to post the camera in the booth in the first place.

First, Payton got mad. He delivered a tongue-lashing to NBC executives. Then he got even. When NBC's *Sunday Night Football* crew arrived in town a few weeks later to set up for the broadcast of the Saints' home game against the Detroit Lions, a Lucky Dog stand and vendor greeted them at the airport. Another was strategically posted next to the NBC production truck outside the Superdome on game day. Everyone had a big laugh. Ambush II was a rousing success.

Early in his Saints tenure, Payton might have stewed about the perceived slight for a full season. In 2011, he had mellowed to the point of using humor to send his message. Today, a more mature Payton probably wouldn't even waste time with the situation.

"Doing this long enough, you learn to focus on the things you can control," Payton said. "It took a while. It certainly wasn't a strength of mine in '06, '07, or '08. Over time, you begin to really focus your energy, your battery life, for instance. And that's come from experience."

During a press briefing with reporters before the Saints' wild-card playoff game against the Minnesota Vikings in January 2020,

Payton reflected on this evolution. He joked about the wasted energy he spent obsessing over trivial details like the size of the Christmas tree in the team cafeteria.

"Sometimes I can be a little bit obsessive that way," Payton said. "I guarantee you in '09 I spent wasted time on stuff like that. You just begin to understand, hey, there are certain things that you are not going to be able to control.

"But I think the small things are important things and all of it. As soon as those begin to erode, I think then that's not good. I don't know that that's wasting time. But there are certain things, though."

Payton still has his moments. He blew up on Saints executives behind closed doors about the amenities—or lack thereof—at the team hotel in suburban Minneapolis during the 2018 season. But he's learned to pick his battles rather than jousting at every windmill he encounters.

Unlike early in his tenure, he rarely spars with media members. He buried the hatchet with many reporters he once blackballed because of various perceived transgressions. He even sends members of the local media corps a holiday pack of Jeni's ice cream each Christmas.

And to the surprise of everyone, he mended fences with NFL Commissioner Roger Goodell and worked closely with him to implement a new replay rule on pass interference during the 2019 NFL owners meeting in Phoenix, Arizona. The two had experienced a rocky relationship for years and were essentially on non-speaking terms after Goodell suspended Payton for his role in the Bountygate scandal. Today, Payton is an active and involved member on the league's competition committee.

Even his mentor, Parcells, has noticed a maturation in Payton, both on and off the field.

"Sean has grown as a coach because he's experienced so much over the years," Parcells said. "He's gone through a couple of cycles of players in New Orleans now, and until a coach has been through a couple of those cycles you haven't really been through the whole gamut. Only experience...only trial and error—owning and being accountable for your mistakes—will allow you to grow and improve. Sean has done that in New Orleans. I'm very proud of what he's accomplished, because it's not easy."

Many NFL officials and observers thought Payton would follow his mentor's lead and bolt for a job in a big market as soon as Brees' tenure with the Saints ended. A year seemingly didn't go by that he wasn't rumored to be headed to Dallas to coach for his longtime friend and former boss, Cowboys owner Jerry Jones.

In the fall of 2019, he attempted to quell the speculation once and for all. He signed a five-year contract extension that paid him approximately $15 million a year, a deal that made him the second-highest-paid coach in the league behind Belichick. It also sent a message to the rest of the NFL.

"This is home," Payton said. "I have a house here. I'm here full-time. Every year, we do more."

In 2018 and 2019, Payton oversaw the renovations of the Saints training facility, including a state-of-the-art locker room, training room, and $3 million squad room replete with a $600,000 video board. He was intimately involved in plans for a new dining hall adjacent to the team's indoor practice facility.

"The level that he is doing things right now is totally off the charts," Zach Strief said. "It's everything. He cares about and is involved in every detail of the facility."

Case in point: the cold trailer the Saints use to regulate core body temperatures during training camp. The climate-controlled long trailer is a lifesaver during camp. Parked in the end zone of the team's practice fields, it allows 20 or so players at a time to cool off in the 32-degree chill and escape the unrelenting triple-digit heat indices of the Louisiana summer. Payton updated the plain, nondescript trailer they used in Year One. The new model was custom-painted in Saints black and gold colors and furnished with benches and windows. He had inspirational messages painted on the inside in gold lettering.

"That's Sean," Strief said. "He doesn't just want a cold trailer that looks like a shipping container. He wants something the players can be proud of, something first-class. And he's like that across the board. It's the food. It's the weight room equipment. It's the new technology. He's relentless in his detail for every aspect of that building. And I think that's really coincided with this kind of refocusing on the job. But he's even more effective now, because there's less big-ticket items that he has to worry about. The culture is there. It's embedded."

Off the field, Payton put down roots, as well. In November 2019, he became engaged to longtime girlfriend Skylene Montgomery and the couple moved into a new house, a classic antebellum home in the heart of New Orleans' Uptown neighborhood. They regularly go for walks to nearby Audubon Park and take bike rides around the neighborhood.

"He's come to love New Orleans," Loomis said. "And I think it means something that he's done it for as long as has in one place, like a Tom Landry or a Don Shula. There's a little pride in that."

Only three years ago, Payton had wandering eyes. He seriously flirted with leaving. Now says he says he doesn't want to coach anywhere else and plans to end his coaching career in New Orleans.

"I've got fleur-de-lis tattoos that can't be erased!" Payton cracked in a 2019 interview with WWL-AM radio in New Orleans.

At some point, he knows the run will end. But for now, he's happy and committed to trying to win another Super Bowl for the city he's called home for the past decade and a half.

25

40 Is the New 30

DREW BREES TURNED 41 ON JANUARY 15, 2020. ONE MONTH AND three days later, he announced his plans to return for the 2020 season, which would be his 20th in the NFL. In eschewing a potential eight-figure annual salary to work as a network television analyst, Brees joined an exclusive fraternity. Earl Morrall (21 seasons), Vinny Testaverde (21), Tom Brady (21), and Brett Favre (20) are the only NFL quarterbacks to play the position for two decades.

But Brees' decision to return did not come without serious contemplation. Once Brees reached his mid-thirties, he said he began taking his career year to year. But this was the first time he seriously considered retirement. Just a year earlier he was convinced he would play into his mid-forties. But things changed during the 2019 season. He suffered the first serious injury of his Saints career in a Week 3 loss to the Rams in Los Angeles. TV network executives began courting his services. And his family and business obligations grew larger than ever.

During his exit interview after the Saints' disappointing 26–20 playoff loss to the Minnesota Vikings, Brees told Payton he needed some time to contemplate his future. Emotions were high. Tears were shed. Hugs exchanged. With his contract set to expire that March, it was a good time to take a step back and consider his options.

During Brees' month-long period of contemplation, Payton turned into a recruiter. He texted Brees daily. Some of the messages were of support and encouragement. Some lobbied for his return. One of Payton's texts read, "You know, there's 500,000 people that are as talented as you in the business world. There might be 10 people as talented as you if you want to get into TV. And then probably two or three if you want to play quarterback in the world."

If it were up to Brees' competitive side, the decision would have been simple. But it was much more complicated than that. Things change when you reach 40, especially with a growing family in tow. Priorities recalibrate. Life views alter.

At this stage of his life, Brees had myriad considerations to ponder—first and foremost, his family. How much longer could he ask them to sacrifice for his career? How much longer could he and Brittany divide the kids between schools in New Orleans and Del Mar? Then there was the question of his health. He missed only six games because of injury in 14 years with the Saints. But how long would this game of Russian roulette last in a league where the defenders grow bigger, stronger, and faster each year?

"In the beginning of your career, you don't know what you don't know," Brees said, explaining his thought process at the time. "So the more that you have a chance to be around great coaches and other great players, you begin to learn how to become a pro. And you know what? At some point, you kind of formulate that routine of, all right, now I've got it down. Now I've got the preparation down, right?

"Well, what people don't realize is that preparation, as you get older, it's not like that goes away. It's not like each week I sit there and go, 'Oh, man. I've started like 300 NFL games. I've seen it; I've done it. I don't need to prepare the way I used to.' No. You're going through the same process that you always have, the same number of hours watching the film and going through the checklist of things. So, the grind remains mentally, psychologically, the stress of, 'What if they do this?' and 'I've got to have a plan for this.' So you're still investing that time. Well, oh, by the way, you're getting older, so you've got to spend even more time on your body. And, oh, by the way, your kids are getting older. They're involved in more things that you want to be a part of—more time. So at some point, there is a breaking point, right? Where there's just not enough hours in the day to do all the things that you need to do, and want to do, that fulfills you and balances you out to be able to go and play the game—and play it at the highest level."

In his 19th NFL season, Brees started to sense his career mortality for the first time. When he returned from his thumb injury, he quipped about playing on borrowed time. When he set the passing touchdowns record in October, he spoke wistfully about his career passing in front of his eyes. A historian of the game, Brees was fully aware that 2001 NFL Draft classmate LaDainian Tomlinson had already been fitted for his gold jacket in the Pro Football Hall of Fame.

So it wasn't a shock to Payton when Brees told him he needed time to think about his future. While Payton was bullish on Taysom Hill's potential and truly believed in his ability to be a bona fide starting quarterback, he knew that Brees, even at 41, still gave his team the best shot to win a championship in 2020. Brees wasn't limping to the finish line the way Favre and Peyton Manning did. In 2019, he led the NFL in completion percentage (74.3) for a third consecutive season and ranked second with a passer efficiency rating of 116.3. Like many of his teammates, he didn't play his best in the season-ending loss to the Vikings, but he finished the regular season on a roll, posting sterling performances against the 49ers, Colts, and Titans.

There was no question Brees could still play. The question was: Did he still want to play?

For the first time in his Saints tenure, Payton had to seriously think about life without Brees in his huddle. When Brees announced his plans to return, Payton was ecstatic.

"I'm excited because I know exactly how he played last year," Payton said. "He's playing at an elite level still. He's done a fantastic job taking care of [himself] both mentally and physically, and it is really a credit to him."

When Payton and the Saints offensive staff graded Brees' performance in 2019, they didn't see any decline in his physical skill or ability to execute. There weren't any throws he couldn't make. No plays were eliminated from the offense to compensate for Brees' age.

"There hasn't been that moment where we've looked at the film and thought, 'Man, back in the day we used to complete those passes,'" Payton said. "We haven't seen that [decline]."

Every offseason, Brees evaluates his routine, starting with two questions: *Why do I do what I do? And how can I get better?*

He evaluates his performance from the previous season, then considers ways he can improve his offseason routine. That might be trying something new in regard to his preparation. It might be a different recovery technique. No stone is left unturned in his quest for improvement.

"I feel like I'm pretty aware of what you lose with the aging process, so everything I do from a training perspective, from a recovery perspective, is to combat that," Brees said. "You just try to stay ahead of that curve. And so far, I feel like I'm beating it."

In recent years, Brees shifted his offseason workout regimen toward extending his playing career. He placed an emphasis on listening to what his body told him. He likened his routine to that of

Major League Baseball starting pitchers, who follow a regimented plan to peak their physical condition every fifth day of the week.

Brees refers to this process as prolonging the prime. He and Tom House have focused his offseason workouts on certain areas of his body in an attempt to ward off the aging process and extend his shelf life as an effective NFL quarterback.

"In the beginning of your career, you have these unbelievable physical skills, and we're able to recover so quickly," Brees said. "But your mental understanding of the game is lacking. Well, the more experience you gain, the more wisdom you gain. And your mental, emotional, psychological ability grows. But the unfortunate thing is the aging process, right? The physical skills begin to diminish. When your physical and mental ability both reach the same level, that's your prime, but at some point the physical starts to drop off. Mentally, emotionally, you've got it. You see it. But your body won't allow you to do it anymore, right?"

Brees and House have tried to fight off Father Time by practicing the latest techniques in recovery, diet, and sleep. Brees met House in the early 2000s through former Chargers offensive coordinator Cam Cameron and began working regularly with him in 2004. He's continued to work with him and his assistant Adam Dedeaux at 3DQB, their training facility in Huntington Beach, California. Brees regularly flies House in for training sessions and evaluation work during training camp and the season.

House, 72, a former college and major-league pitching coach, started as a pitching tutor before turning his attention to football. House and his staff teach players the biomechanics of throwing a football. They work on balance, posture, and stride momentum. They focus on mechanics, footwork, and weight shift to build arm strength and increase throwing accuracy.

These days, House works as much on Brees' mental approach as he does his physical work. House connected Brees with Major

League Baseball Hall of Fame pitcher Nolan Ryan, who pitched into his mid-forties and was one of Brees' favorite players while growing up in Austin, Texas, to serve as a resource.

"Our research says there's no reason you can't do at 45 what you did at 25—if you can pay the price," House said. "Nobody knows how hard Drew actually works. He's the hardest-working quarterback I've been around. He's special. There are all kinds of guys who can throw a football. They know what to do, but they don't know why. Drew is a what and a why guy, and his goal literally is to identify problems and come up with solutions."

House is convinced Brees can continue to play at an elite level into his mid-forties because of his work ethic, discipline, and open-mindedness.

"What happens with a lot of elite athletes, they get to a certain level of expertise and they stop learning," House said. "Drew and Nolan, the two superstars in my eyes, are trying to learn something new every day and you can throw that in front of people, not all of them input like they should. Drew does. He might be the best quarterback ever, and he's still getting better. He's better this year than he's ever been for me. For all his checkpoints, he's a better quarterback this year than he was last year."

Brees is still wired to compete. The drive that fueled his ascension from an overlooked high school prospect and NFL Draft afterthought to the top of his profession still burns hot in his belly. The competitor in Brees wants to make another Super Bowl run. Legacy matters to him. Winning titles has always motivated him more than breaking records. He won a state championship in high school, a Big Ten championship in college, and a Super Bowl title with the Saints. And he knows the Saints roster is loaded with several Pro Bowl talents in their primes. He also knows he's still playing well enough to lead the team back to the Promised Land.

"Once you get to your late thirties, that's when everybody starts telling you the end is near," Brees said. "And I'm like, "No, it's not. We're just going to push this thing back as long as we want.' The longer you play, I feel like experience and wisdom can take you a long way, especially at the quarterback position. There's not much that we see on a weekly basis that we haven't seen before. You kind of know the type of game it's going to be, and as long as you can keep your physical traits at a level where you're able to play at a high level, [and] combine that with where you are mentally with the game, with all the experience and wisdom. I think that just allows you to maintain your prime for longer and longer."

Through his army of consultants and specialists, Brees stays on the cutting edge of advances in nutrition, conditioning, and training. He practices the latest recovery techniques to keep his body in top form during the season.

"We're so much more knowledgeable now than we ever have been in regard to recovery and how to take care of your body and diet and all of those things," he said. "I feel like each and every week should be better than the last week and each and every year should be better than before. It's not just maintaining. It's improving, constantly improving."

Brees and longtime trainer Todd Durkin have tweaked his workout regimen in recent years to address potential problem spots. He's focused heavily on his core strength and added fascial stretch therapy to his routine.

Physically, Brees is as fit and strong as ever, Durkin and House said. That's why Durkin believes when Brees eventually hangs up his cleats it will be because he hits a wall mentally rather than physically. No one invests more into a Saints season than Brees. To play at an elite level at his age requires an extraordinary mental and physical expense. Teammates nearly half his age still marvel at his drive and mental stamina. His aging body requires more recovery work than ever. His free time during game weeks is limited to the times he flies to a road trip or coaches one of his kids' flag football games. The football nerd in Brees loves the process, but the father, husband, and family man in him is conflicted by it.

Brees has steadfastly maintained that he will continue to take his career one year at a time. He believes he can still compete at a high level. And while he thinks he can keep going, he also knows there will come a time when he simply wants to walk away.

"There's definitely a process that takes place when you think about this," Brees said. "It's not like you just wake up one day and decide you want to retire.... When I walk away, I don't want it to be because I can't play the game anymore because there's 32 teams saying, 'All right, see ya later.' I want it to be on my own terms first. And I want it to be because I just want to spend more time with my family. I'm ready for that next chapter. When that time comes, I'll know."

And when that time does arrive, Brees believes his relationship with Payton will change, as well. As close as Brees and Payton are on the field, they don't get to see each other as often as they would like outside the Saints facility. But that has more to do with circumstance than preference.

As the crow flies, they live only a mile apart from each other in the historic Uptown neighborhood of New Orleans. Yet, despite their close living proximity, Brees and Payton rarely see each other outside the Saints offices. Once they leave the training facility in suburban Metairie, their lives often go separate ways.

The rare times Brees and Payton do socialize, it's usually to squeeze in dinner or a concert or a round of golf. Brees and his family have visited Payton at his beach house in Florida. They also watched the College Football Playoff National Championship Game with Payton in his suite at the Superdome.

But those times are fewer and farther between these days because of Brees' growing family and myriad business interests. Plus, he spends his offseasons in Del Mar, California, where he has maintained a residence since his playing days with the Chargers.

Payton also is on the go a lot, relaxing at his second home in the Florida panhandle or visiting his son, Connor, in Texas, or daughter, Meghan, in California.

"It's hard," Brees said. "There's not a lot of time. During the season, he lives here [at the office], and when I'm not here I'm with my family.

"Once I'm done playing, there'll be a different type of relationship between us. I think there'll be even more of a friendship than there is now. Because right now there is that line of player/coach and I get that. Certainly, he's a guy who changed my life by bringing me here, and there's a genuine appreciation certainly that I have for him for believing in me and giving me this opportunity."

DOME-INATION:
2019 Indianapolis Colts

During his three decades as an NFL player and coach, Frank Reich has been around some elite quarterbacks, among them Hall of Famer Jim Kelly and future Hall of Famer Peyton Manning. But the performance he witnessed from Drew Brees on December 16, 2019, was something he'd never seen before and likely will never see again.

The Indianapolis Colts came to New Orleans in a tailspin after losing five of their previous six games. They were still reeling from the stunning retirement of Andrew Luck in the preseason. What's more, the Saints were coming off a tough loss to the San Francisco 49ers the previous week and would be honoring the 2009 Super Bowl team. So Reich knew his Colts (6–7) would need to play well to upset the Saints (10–3) in the Superdome on *Monday Night Football*. But he fully expected them to be competitive. After all, six of their seven losses had come by seven points or less.

Brees opened the game by completing his first seven passes and staking the Saints to a 3–0 lead. He threw his first incomplete pass on the second play of the second quarter, when he rushed a throw in the right flat to avoid pressure and missed Latavius Murray on a checkdown. He wouldn't throw another incompletion the rest of the game.

With Brees dissecting the Colts defense with pinpoint accuracy, the Saints scored on their first six drives and took a shocking 34–0 lead into the fourth quarter. By then, the only suspense involved Brees' pursuit of history. When the Saints took the field early in the fourth quarter, he needed one more completion to surpass Philip Rivers' record for completion percentage in a game. A quick pass to Michael Thomas in the left flat secured the milestone, and Brees yielded to Teddy Bridgewater the rest of the way.

Brees' final numbers were staggering: 29-of-30, 307 yards, four touchdowns. One of those scoring passes—a five-yarder to Josh Hill in the third quarter—gave Brees 541 in his career, surpassing Peyton Manning in the NFL record books.

"He was outstanding tonight," Sean Payton said. "He was efficient, and it was impressive. As a play-caller, you begin to gain confidence and your [call] sheet looks a lot bigger when he's playing like that."

It was a vintage Brees performance. He spread the ball to nine different receivers. Four different Saints caught touchdown passes. He wasn't sacked and was hit just twice in 30 drop backs.

"He has done that to a lot of defenses," Reich said. "I didn't realize it, but I looked up there at one time and he was 27-of-28 or something. When he gets like that, I don't know anybody that can stop him. I mean 29-of-30, he has proven it year in and year out for a very long time. Even when you have a guy covered, he really isn't covered. He always finds a hole. He can do that as well as anybody who has ever played the game."

For Brees, it was another epic performance on *Monday Night Football*. A year earlier, he broke Peyton Manning's record for career passing yards against the Washington Redskins on Monday night. Now, a year later, he set the mark for all-time touchdown passes, while improving his record to 11–5 in Monday night home games at the Superdome.

"It was special, everything about the night," Brees said. "I'm not sure how we got here. It just, kind of, makes your whole life and career flash before your eyes. I never thought that I would have had a chance to be a part of something like this; and, just looking at the entire journey, 19 years, 5 years in San Diego and 14 years here, all of the incredible teammates and coaches that I have had the chance to play with and for, [and] this team right here is very special. Of course, our fan base, the Who Dat Nation, everybody in the dome tonight, everybody watching tonight, loved ones, my family, my kids here, both of my college roommates, who are my best friends in the world, they were here with their kids. It was just an incredible night, incredible experience, (and an) incredible moment to be able to share that with so many people, because all of them are a big part of it."

26

A Tree Grows in Baton Rouge

Drew Brees, Sean Payton, and Mickey Loomis watched LSU's 47–25 rout of Clemson in the College Football Playoff National Championship Game on January 13, 2020, from Payton's luxury suite at the Superdome. At one point, Payton asked Loomis for his binoculars and trained them on the LSU coaches' box.

"I just want to make sure we're looking at the same Joe Brady," Payton quipped about the Saints' former offensive quality control coach, who in one season became the hottest assistant coach in college football after transforming the LSU offense into a juggernaut.

Brady wasn't the only thing that looked familiar to Payton that night. The offense the LSU Tigers used to run roughshod over the Clemson Tigers and the rest of college football in 2019 was essentially Payton's scheme, give or take a tweak here or there. The passing concepts were directly from Payton's playbook, as was the offensive philosophy of utilizing quick timing throws by the quarterback and spreading the ball to all five skill-position players. There were some minor differences. Brady employed a read-option running game that he learned from Joe Moorhead when they worked together on the Penn State coaching staff. LSU also operated out of an empty backfield set 85 percent of the time, considerably more than the Saints did with Brees. But otherwise the offense was heavily influenced by Brady's two years in New Orleans.

"The plays that we're running here, the system that we're running here, the vision, the type of players that we're trying to recruit here, it's all things that I took from New Orleans," Brady said before the 2019 season.

That's why Brady had LSU quarterback Jow Burrow watch film of Brees and the Saints offense throughout the 2019 offseason to become better acquainted with the game plan. And when he worked with running back Clyde Edwards-Helaire, he showed him tape of Alvin Kamara. The LSU receivers watched cut-ups of Lance Moore and Devery Henderson.

"I hear myself out on the practice field with all the coaching points that I heard instilled in me in those two years there, the ways to try to motivate the guys, or trying to paint the picture to the guys that I learned from Coach [Payton]," Brady said. "The system isn't broke, and it's been working for so long at the NFL level that it's exciting to me to be able to take Coach Payton's system and bring it to the college level."

When veteran passing game coordinator Jerry Sullivan retired from the LSU staff in 2019, LSU head coach Ed Orgeron targeted Brady, who had impressed the Tigers staff during a presentation he made with Carmichael the previous summer. It was essentially a one-man search. Orgeron served as the defensive line coach on Payton's staff in 2008 and had always wanted to adopt his offensive scheme as a head coach. He hired Brady to install the Saints' state-of-the-art passing attack and overhaul LSU's antiquated offensive approach.

Almost overnight, LSU's offense transformed from jugger-not to juggernaut. The Tigers vaulted from 69th nationally in total offense to first; from 65th in pass efficiency to second; from 67th in passing offense to second; and from 38th in scoring offense to first. And with Brady's guidance, Burrow went from a preseason third-team All-SEC selection to the Heisman Trophy winner.

Brady's astonishing work during his one season as LSU's passing game coordinator might be the best greatest validation yet of Payton's offensive system.

"He was in our meetings every day," Brees said of Brady. "We had a great rapport, and he did a great job for us. I felt like he had a great understanding of the Xs and Os of what we were doing but also just his background with a lot of the RPOs, the stuff that you see in LSU's offense. That's a real prevalent part of what a lot of teams do. You've got to have a smart, athletic quarterback that can execute those things and know when to give, know when to keep, know when to find open receivers, and obviously Joe Burrow [did] an excellent job of executing that offense."

Payton called LSU's season "historic" and said he "absolutely" could see the Saints' offensive influence when he watched the Tigers operate. Sometimes, he joked that he would see Saints plays appear in the LSU offense "a week or two after one of our games."

Payton's fingerprints were all over the LSU offense. The Tigers operated almost exclusively out of three- and four-receiver sets, and Brady empowered Burrow to make pre-snap reads and checks at the line of scrimmage. In addition to his No. 9 jersey number, Burrow was Brees-like in his execution. He completed 76.3 percent of his passes and threw touchdown passes to eight different receivers. Running backs combined to catch 80 passes. Tight end Thaddeus Moss caught more passes (47) than his predecessor, Foster Moreau, did the previous two seasons combined.

"When I watch the LSU offense, it is a heavily schemed pro-style route tree that resembles the New Orleans Saints—in terms of how they put defensive coverages and defensive players in conflict," former NFL safety Matt Bowen told ESPN when asked to compare the LSU and Saints offenses. "And what that requires is for an elite-level quarterback to go through pro progressions, to find the voids in zone coverage and to find the matchups that are created within this offense.

"You can watch those route concepts, there's a bunch of high-lows, there's a bunch of flood, there's a bunch of three-level stuff. It is leveled reads for the quarterback that require him to process information quickly, to throw on time and to anticipate where the windows are gonna be. You don't see that a lot in college."

With the heady Burrow at the controls, LSU rewrote the program, Southeastern Conference, and NCAA record books. Burrow was the first quarterback in SEC history to throw for 5,000 yards and 50 touchdowns in a season. His 5,671 passing yards and 60 touchdown passes shattered the league's single-season records. LSU also became the first school since 2010 to have a 5,000-yard passer, a 1,000-yard rusher, and two 1,000-yard receivers on the same team. All this at a school that failed to rank in the top 100 nationally in passing offense from 2014 to 2016 and had had only one quarterback (JaMarcus Russell, 2007) taken in the first three rounds of the previous 29 NFL Drafts.

"That's basically what we do," Burrow said of the Saints offense. "We do a lot of the same stuff with Coach Joe coming from [New Orleans]. It's getting five guys on a route every play and making them defend every single person. Anybody can get the ball on any play. We're not designing plays to go to this one guy. We have progression reads that everyone can get the ball on, so you have to be on your toes as a defense and really understand who has each individual player, otherwise we'll beat you, or I'll find a guy, and that's what makes it so difficult to defend. You've got to find your guy, and we make it difficult to do it and change up people's eyes with motions and moving different guys around from the slot to the backfield to outside. We do a really good job of finding matchups that are favorable for us."

After LSU's historic season, Brady cashed in. He won the Broyles Award, given annually to the top assistant coach in college football, and was hired by Matt Rhule to be the offensive coordinator of the Carolina Panthers, making him, at 30, the youngest offensive coordinator in the NFL.

LSU isn't the only school enjoying success with the Saints offense. The Ball State Cardinals, coached by former Saints scout and quarterback coach Mike Neu, led the Mid-American Conference and ranked among the national leaders in total and scoring offense in 2019. Ball State's average of 463.0 yards and 34.8 points per game were the second highest in school history and ranked 15th and 18th among NCAA FBS teams. Like the Saints and LSU, the Cardinals also boast a healthy balance between the run and pass. Ball State averaged 243.6 passing yards and 219.4 rushing yards a game.

"It's the Saints system," Neu said. "Everything we do is based on what I brought with me from New Orleans. We don't see as many exotic coverages and pressure packages as you do in the NFL. And we have reduced the terminology because we're a no-huddle operation so we have to signal our plays. So there's not as many tags. But the passing concepts would be exactly the same [as the Saints]."

Neu said he studies the film from every Saints game each season. Every Monday during the 2019 season, he and the offensive staff would watch cut-up tape of specific passing concepts from the Saints, LSU, and his own team, then compare how each team executed the same play.

"LSU didn't have any snaps under center, but the passing game concepts were the same ones I teach my offense here," Neu said. "It was awesome to see how they used their weapons, how they sprinkled the infield, as I like to say. It's the same stuff we do. The Saints have been on top offensively throughout Drew and Sean's time in New Orleans, and LSU just had the best season in college football history. I made time every week to study those two offenses. It's another way to solidify how awesome the offense is to our players."

The infield sprinkling required more time to take hold at Ball State than it did at LSU. Neu's first three seasons were marred by injuries and the growing pains of rebuilding a program that has not won a bowl game in its 45-year history. But things started to come together offensively for the Cardinals in Neu's fourth season. Quarterback Drew Plitt passed for nearly 3,000 yards and backs Caleb Huntley and Walter Fletcher combined to rush for 2,001 yards. Five receivers had multiple touchdown receptions and produced between 300 and 700 receiving yards. Offensive lineman Danny Pinter was selected by the Indianapolis Colts in the fifth round of the 2020 NFL Draft, and Plitt received an invitation to the prestigious Manning Passing Academy, which was canceled in June because of the COVID-19 pandemic.

"I'm proud that we ranked No. 1 [in the MAC] in scoring offense and total offense," said Neu, who quarterbacked Ball State for three seasons and was the 1993 MAC Offensive Player of the Year. "I wish we would have done better record-wise up to this point, but I'm excited about this being our window of opportunity."

Neu's ties to New Orleans run deep. Loomis hired him to coach the New Orleans VooDoo of the Arena Football League from 2004 to 2008. He then took a job on the Saints scouting staff for the next three seasons before moving across town to Tulane University as the quarterbacks coach on former Saints receivers coach Curtis Johnson's staff. He returned to the Saints as the quarterbacks coach in 2014 and 2015 when Joe Lombardi left the staff to become the offensive coordinator for the Detroit Lions.

Neu uses his ties to Brees, Payton, and the Saints offense as a recruiting pitch when meeting with prospects. He shows game film of Brees' footwork and fundamentals to quarterback recruits and will use highlights of the Saints passing attack to illustrate to receivers how they'll project to the Ball State attack. Neu even signed his own version of Taysom Hill to the Ball State roster in 2020. Ryan Lezon was a three-sport star at Indianapolis Southport High School but will play tight end and H-back in college. Neu envisions a Hill-like, Swiss Army knife role for the 6'2", 210-pound Lezon at Ball State.

"My work with the Saints is the best selling point ever," Neu said of his two-year experience as the Saints quarterbacks coach. "I always want to make Mickey [Loomis] and Sean [Payton] proud that I have taken an offensive page from the Saints. What's unbelievable about the offense is that every player on the field has a chance to make a play on every single play. It's lasted so long because of the thought, preparation, and detail that goes into it. I just have a strong conviction that this is the best offense there is."

It would be hard to argue with Neu's proclamation after seeing the impact the Saints offense had on college football in 2019. The Saints' influence is unmistakable and indelible. Thanks to the successful work of Brady and Neu, Payton's offensive system has taken root and blossomed outside of New Orleans. And for the first time, Payton's coaching tree has branches in Charlotte, North Carolina, and Muncie, Indiana.

27

The Payton-Brees Legacy

In December 2019, the NFL unveiled its NFL 100 All-Time Team, a roster of 100 all-star players and 10 coaches to commemorate the league's 100th season. The blue-ribbon committee of 26 coaches, executives, former players, and media members selected 10 quarterbacks for the squad: Sammy Baugh, John Elway, Brett Favre, Otto Graham, Peyton Manning, Dan Marino, Joe Montana, Roger Staubach, and Johnny Unitas.

There were plenty of snubs from the list, but none bigger than Brees. The league's all-time leading rusher (Emmitt Smith), receiver (Jerry Rice), and scorer (Adam Vinatieri) made the team. But the NFL's all-time leading passer did not. It was the latest snub for the Saints quarterback, who, despite all of his wins, accolades, and accomplishments, might go down in history as the NFL's most underrated superstar.

Brees is widely considered the best player to never win the NFL's Most Valuable Player Award, having finished second a mind-boggling four times. Each time he was victimized by poor timing, beaten out by a peer who produced a historic season.

In 2006, LaDainian Tomlinson won the award after leading the league in yards from scrimmage with 2,323 yards and setting NFL season records for rushing touchdowns (28) and points scored (186), the latter of which had stood for 46 years. Both of those marks are still NFL records.

In 2009, Brees led the Saints to a 13–0 start, making them just the seventh team in NFL history to go unbeaten in their first 13 games, but was one-upped by Peyton Manning, who led the Indianapolis Colts to a 14–0 start, just the third team in league annals to enjoy just a spectacular start.

In 2011, Brees had the best statistical season of his career, passing for an NFL-record 5,476 passing yards, 46 touchdowns, and a then NFL-record 71.2 completion percentage. But Aaron Rodgers won MVP after producing the greatest passing season in NFL history, throwing 45 touchdowns and only six interceptions while posting a league-record 122.5 passer rating.

In 2018, Brees led the league in completion percentage (74.4), passer efficiency rating (115.7), game-winning drives (seven), and fourth-quarter comebacks (six) but was beaten out by Mahomes, who became the second quarterback in NFL history to throw for 5,000 yards and 50 touchdowns in a season.

The MVP award remains the lone missing honor in Brees' otherwise illustrious résumé. He has won nearly every other major individual honor in his distinguished career: 13 Pro Bowl invitations, two NFL Offensive Player of the Year awards, and the Super Bowl XLIV MVP award. He was the NFL's Comeback Player of the Year in 2004, the Walter Payton Man of the Year in 2006, the Bert Bell Award winner in 2009, and *Sports Illustrated*'s Sportsman of the Year in 2010.

"As crazy as it sounds, I think Drew is one of the most underrated quarterbacks ever," said Taysom Hill, who spent time with Rodgers in Green Bay before joining the Saints in 2017. "What he has done week in, week out, year in, year out, is really, really special. I don't think he gets as much credit as he deserves."

Statistically, Brees is peerless. He has more passing yards, touchdowns, and completions than any quarterback in NFL history, the first and only quarterback to simultaneously hold those three milestones since Baugh (1937–52). Brees was the fastest quarterback ever to reach the 50,000-, 60,000-, and 70,000-yard thresholds. He's the all-time leader in completion percentage, and he has the most consecutive seasons of both 4,000 and 5,000 passing yards and most consecutive seasons with both at least 20 and 30 touchdown passes. In the history of the NFL, there have been 12 seasons where a quarterback has topped 5,000 passing yards. Brees owns five of them.

"Yes, Super Bowls and wins matter, but when you break down the quarterback position, the No. 1 job is to throw the football to a receiver in the right spot at the right time that gives the receiver the best chance to advance the ball for the offense," Luke McCown said. "And nobody's done that single thing better than Drew Brees in all of football."

Before joining Payton's staff as linebackers coach from 2017 to 2019, Mike Nolan spent most of his first three decades in the NFL as a defensive coordinator, preparing game plans to try to slow down the league's top quarterbacks. In Nolan's mind, two quarterbacks stand above the rest: Brady and Brees.

"Drew has got to be listed with the all-time greats, if not *the* guy," said Nolan, who coached on the Denver Broncos staff in 1987 and 1988 when future Hall of Famer John Elway was the quarterback and is now the defensive coordinator with the Dallas Cowboys. "And I'm not just saying it because I [was] a Saint. I think he would compete with Tom Brady in the discussion as the best ever. I love [Peyton] Manning to death, but Manning never really was the problem that Tom and Drew have been from a [defensive] coordinator's standpoint. He was great. He was a 9 on the problem scale of 10. Drew and Tom, those guys were 10s."

Optics are part of the problem for Brees. His teammates and coaches say he executes so efficiently, he makes the job of playing NFL quarterback look easy. His greatness is more nuanced than that of big-armed peers like Favre, Marino, or Patrick Mahomes. In that way, Brees is like the NFL's version of Greg Maddux. He's a superstar without superpowers, a 6'0" Everyman, who succeeds by "painting the black" in his passes rather than blowing away opponents with his overpowering fastball. To fully appreciate Brees' genius requires a sophisticated football mind.

"When you watch Aaron Rodgers run around the backfield for 25 seconds and throw a 70-yard pass across his body on the money for a touchdown, that play is easy for the casual fan to appreciate," Zach Strief said. "There's a wow factor. That kind of play has more impact on your opinion of that player than any amount of flawlessly executed passes in an offense in rhythm over the course of four quarters. Drew throws 35 passes in a game and all 35 of them are within two feet of where they were intended to be. You will walk away from that game going, 'Man, that guy is efficient.' But you don't necessarily walk away going, 'That guy is a freak of nature.' Now in reality, he is absolutely a freak of nature. But the flash is not there for him."

Consequently, Brees' game doesn't make great creative currency for social media. GIFs and memes of his highlights rarely go viral. In a day and age where sizzle often trumps substance, the subtlety of Brees' talent can be grossly underappreciated. But among quarterbacks, Brees is not just respected. He is revered.

"He's clearly the best quarterback I've been around," said Brunell, who played behind Favre in Green Bay to start his career. "He's the most professional guy I've been around, too. He does everything very, very well. It's not just one aspect of being a quarterback. He's good at everything: the locker room, off-the-field, his study habits, his work ethic, his family, the media. I've never seen anything like it."

In a way, Brees' partnership with Payton might have hurt his case in some corners. Because of Payton's play-calling aptitude, Brees often is labeled as a "system quarterback" by detractors. It's a tag that's hounded him throughout his playing career, from Westlake High School to Purdue to the NFL. The fact that the Saints went 5–0 without Brees during the 2019 season was not lost on his skeptics. Of course, the same could be said of the New England Patriots, who went 11–5 in 2008 without Tom Brady.

And while Brady (Rob Gronkowski, Randy Moss) and Manning (Marshall Faulk, Marvin Harrison) each benefited from Hall of Fame–worthy teammates, Brees might be the only Saint in the Payton era to earn that distinction. Before Mike Thomas and Alvin Kamara joined the team, the Saints managed to rank among the league leaders annually in total offense and scoring offense with just one Pro Bowl player in the perimeter corps (Jimmy Graham in 2011).

"People can say and think whatever they want," Strief said. "Put that guy [Brees] in any system in the NFL, and he's going to excel... Brady is the same way. They're the same person. To claim that he is a product of the system because we throw the ball a lot and he gets a lot of yards is preposterous. He *is* the system. The stuff that we are running is the same stuff that other teams are running. We are not running magical plays. We have a quarterback that on the last step of his drop already knows where the ball needs to go and when, and can put it in a window twice the size of a football. *That* is the system."

Quarterback coach Trent Dilfer went so far as to call Brees a "transformational" player at the quarterback position. While Fran Tarkenton and Doug Flutie enjoyed successful careers before him, Brees' spectacular career has changed the way coaches and front office executives view quarterbacks. He paved the way for a generation of 6'0"-and-under passers to become franchise quarterbacks. Without Brees' success, Russell Wilson and Kyler Murray might have suffered the same fate as Charlie Ward, who was forced to pursue a professional basketball career in the NBA because of the NFL's skepticism of a quarterback with his size and playing style when he came out of Florida State in 1994.

"Drew changed the narrative from quarterbacking is about being big to quarterbacking is about making everyone around you better, completing the ball," Dilfer said on the MMQB podcast with Albert Breer in 2019.

Before Brees, Dilfer said, many NFL coaches, scouts, and personnel executives subscribed to the theory that size mattered for quarterbacks. To succeed at the game's most important position, quarterbacks had to be big and strong, with a great arm and able to throw the deep out pattern.

"Drew changed that," said Dilfer, who won a Super Bowl ring as the starting quarterback for the Baltimore Ravens and now trains elite quarterback prospects at Nike's prestigious Elite 11 camps. "He showed that you could throw it earlier, you didn't have to throw it harder. It wasn't about seeing over everyone, it was about seeing through passing lanes. It was about being a surgeon not a butcher. He literally looks at every little detail, every minuscule aspect of quarterbacking and perfects it."

Dilfer uses highlights of Brees' work as a teaching tape at his camps. Brees' mastery of the position's fundamentals makes him the perfect model for young players.

"Drew is really the first 6-foot surgeon, the first guy that meticulously took you apart with how he played the position and made you bleed out by a thousand cuts," Dilfer said. "He made your offense more robust because you do more things than just turn your back to the line of scrimmage and rip heaters down the field.... I think Drew will forever be in that conversation as one of the greatest quarterbacks that's ever played the game when you look at quarterbacking holistically. Quarterbacking is making your team better, production, the leadership, impact on your franchise, the legacy on players that came after him that tried to be just like him."

Tom House works with half the starting quarterbacks in the NFL and has coached scores of others over the years. Brees, he said, competes and learns on a different level than any quarterback he's ever trained, including Brady. Brees routinely grades in the top percentile on the testing House and his staff perform during offseason training workouts at the 3DQB facility in Huntington Beach, California.

"What Drew does, he makes it look easy, but it's not," House said. "The window is that big and he hits it. Drew will have a spectacular play or two, but he's not a spectacular quarterback. He's just the best fucker who's ever thrown a football."

Pro Football Reference's approximate value metric might be the best argument for how grossly underrated Brees has been in his career. The statistic attempts to rank NFL players' overall value across positions and eras by measuring their production, tenure, and honors in each season that they played. Entering the 2020 season, Brees ranked as the third-best player in NFL history, trailing only Manning and Brady. He is the only offensive player in the Top 15 who has not won MVP honors.

"It's so frustrating to me," said Mike Neu, the former Saints quarterbacks coach and now head coach at Ball State University. "For whatever reason, he never gets enough respect. There's no question that he has had an impact on all of sports, not just football and not just the quarterback position. He's just a machine."

The same could be said for the Saints offense. They've rewritten the club and NFL record books and, by any statistical measure, deserve to be mentioned with the greatest offensive juggernauts in league lore, alongside the Rams' Greatest Show on Turf, the Air

Coryell Chargers, the Brady-Belichick Patriots, and the Walsh-Montana 49ers.

Since Brees and Payton joined forces, the Saints have gained more yards (89,642) than any offense in the NFL. In fact, no other team in NFL history has gained as many yards during a 14-year span, according to Elias Sports Bureau. In that time, they've allowed the fewest sacks (339), converted the highest percentage of third downs (46.3), and passed for the most yards (290.8 average per game), while ranking second only to the Patriots in points scored (27.9 ppg) and first downs gained (5,083). From 2006 to 2019, the Saints finished among the top 10 in Football Outsiders' offensive efficiency ratings an astonishing 13 times.

Along the way, they have authored some of the most dominant offensive performances in league history. The Payton-Brees Saints have handed NFL bluebloods like the New York Giants, New England Patriots, and Philadelphia Eagles some of the worst defeats in the history of their respective franchises.

What's more, the tandem has brought unprecedented stability and success to the once-moribund Saints organization. In the 39 seasons before Brees and Payton arrived, 28 men started at quarterback for the Saints under 13 head coaches. Those quarterbacks combined to post a 237–352–5 record, a winning percentage of 40.3. In that span, the Saints made 43 appearances on national television and won two division titles and one playoff game. In the first 14 years of the Payton-Brees tenure, the Saints have gone 138–84, a 62.1 winning percentage. Their winning percentage together is a robust 63 percent. In that span, the Saints have made 50 prime-time television appearances, won six division titles, and gone 8–7 in the playoffs.

The freewheeling, high-flying offensive attack has made Saints football the hottest ticket in New Orleans. Every home game at the Superdome has been sold out since their arrival in 2006, and the city of New Orleans annually leads all U.S. markets in television ratings for Saints and NFL games, according to Nielsen Company and the NFL.

"It's been the perfect marriage," McCown said. "You have one of the greatest offensive coaching minds and one of the greatest quarterbacks together, and yet they're not so egotistical that they have to have it their way. There's an understanding between the two that is unique. They know that there's nobody else out there for them. I don't see Drew ever playing in a different uniform because he knows there's no other marriage of quarterback to play-caller that will ever be the same for him. And I think Sean's the same way. We may not ever see that type of connection and productivity between two pieces of the puzzle ever again in this game."

At 15 years and counting, the Payton-Brees partnership has outlasted some of the greatest coach-quarterback duos in NFL history, making it a unique tandem. Peyton Manning played 14 years with offensive coordinator Tom Moore, but he never had one head coach for more than seven seasons. While Belichick and Brady were together for 19 years and the Pittsburgh Steelers' Mike Tomlin and Ben Roethlisberger have been together for 13 years, neither head coach in those partnerships has an offensive background, making the Payton-Brees duo the most enduring and successful marriage between offensive guru and quarterback in NFL history.

None of the 11 Hall of Fame quarterbacks who have played since the AFL-NFL merger in 1970 has enjoyed a run with the same coach to match the 15-year partnership Brees has had with Payton. Chuck Noll and Terry Bradshaw spent 14 years together in Pittsburgh. Don Shula and Dan Marino teamed for 13 seasons in Miami. Bill Walsh and Joe Montana had a 10-year run in San Francisco.

"They've changed football," said Joe Brady, the precocious passing game coordinator who led the LSU Tigers to the 2019 national championship before taking the offensive coordinator job for the Carolina Panthers. "Sean has changed the way teams play offense, and Drew has changed the way we look at quarterbacks. They're special."

And yet as great as Payton and Brees have been during their long tenure in New Orleans, for all of the games they've won, all the records they've broken and milestones they've surpassed, they still have just one Super Bowl victory on their résumé. And that inconvenient truth alone has prevented many longtime league observers and experts from ranking them alongside Belichick-Brady and Walsh-Montana among the greatest coach-quarterback combinations in NFL history.

That's why heartbreaking losses like the Minnesota Miracle and NOLA No-Call game were so painful for Payton and Brees. More than anyone, they understand how difficult it is to get to that point in an NFL season. And to have the rug pulled out from under them in such unique fashion made the losses all the more difficult to digest. The Payton-Brees narrative might read differently if Marcus Williams hadn't inexplicably whiffed on Stefon Diggs to produce the Minneapolis Miracle. Their legacy might be viewed in a different light had the referees not committed the biggest gaffe in officiating history against the Rams in the 2019 NFC Championship Game. Or if the defense could have made a late stop in the 2012 NFC divisional playoff shootout against the San Francisco 49ers. Those setbacks prevented Payton and Brees from potentially returning to the Super Bowl and bringing a second Lombardi Trophy back to New Orleans. The Payton-Brees legacy might look entirely different had those games gone the other way.

Winning another Super Bowl was the main reason Brees cited when he announced his plans to return for the 2020 season. And if Payton and Brees can make it back to the big game in 2021 or beyond, they would achieve yet another milestone: it would represent the longest duration between Super Bowl appearances for any coach-quarterback combination in history.

"There's a level of consistency with that offense that really hasn't happened before [in NFL history]," Marrone said. "When you look at the number of players and coaches who have filtered through the offense over the years, the amount of production is what's amazing to me. The one constant has been Sean and Drew. Sometimes when you have such strong personalities in those areas that sometimes conflict can arise. But with them it's just a connection and a drive for excellence. It's special, and these types of relationships don't come around very often. A lot of people are trying to get those types of relationships in this league, but those guys have it. The relationship between them will be a legacy that will last forever and rank among the best of all time."

The 2020 season went a long way toward enhancing Payton's coaching credentials. For the first time in his coaching career, he won games without Brees under center. He was winless in three games without Brees in his first 13 seasons as a head coach, losing once when Brees was injured in 2015 and twice when the Saints rested their starters in Week 17 of the 2009 and 2018 seasons. The way Payton led and strategized the Saints to a 5–0 mark while Brees was sidelined with a thumb injury in 2019 made him a leading candidate for the 2019 NFL Coach of the Year award, an honor he won in 2006. It also validated the lucrative five-year contract extension he signed in 2019.

"Drew's been the heart and soul of this team since he's been here, but Coach Payton is the leader of this team," said Taysom Hill, who has been groomed to be the eventual successor to Brees when he retires. "Everyone sees the amount of time that Coach puts into a game plan. So now you have this unique combination of Drew's preparation, along with Coach Payton's preparation, and as their teammate and as someone that's playing for Coach, the last thing you want to do is let one of those guys down. So it just elevates everybody's game. Drew and Coach make everybody around them better. It has been the best thing for my career to be there with Drew and Coach Payton."

Back in 2006, few could have seen this coming. Brees was rehabbing an injury to his throwing shoulder so severe that only two NFL teams pursued him in free agency. And Payton's reputation was still tarnished in some circles by his stint with the New York Giants, where head coach Jim Fassell relieved him of his play-calling duties in mid-season. But in each other, Brees and Payton found providence. Payton and his beautiful offensive mind could help resurrect Brees' career after it was derailed in San Diego. And in Brees, Payton had the pilot to not only land the plane safely, but also to take him to places he couldn't go in his own playing career.

Given the number of years they've spent together and the extensive work schedule they've maintained throughout their tenure, Payton and Brees very well might have worked more hours together in the same room than any head coach–quarterback tandem in NFL history.

"It's been outstanding," Payton said. "It doesn't feel that long to me. It feels like the time has flown by. We both probably look at each other and see a hairline that has receded."

The journey was an improbable one. Brees and Payton had no previous connections before 2006. They had never met before joining forces in New Orleans. But after all this time, it almost seems like it was destined for them to align in New Orleans. Together, they revived a dormant franchise and helped restore hope to a region trying to recover from one of the greatest tragedies in American history. Brees and Payton will be revered long after they leave New Orleans. Statues will be built. Brees' No. 9 jersey will be retired. And after a decade and a half together, their names have become inseparable, their legacies inextricably intertwined.

"Drew is one of these players that's got that gift to improve those around him through his work ethic, leadership, skill set, and playing ability," Payton said. "There is a mental toughness to how he plays and prepares, that will to win, that work ethic, that attention to detail, that is impressive. A player new to our team comes and sees his preparation habits, that becomes contagious. As coaches, you feel that same sense of obligation to provide the best plan possible. You want him to come in the next day to say, 'Wow. I love it.' His approach to business, to every aspect of his life, it's been amazing to watch. I don't ever take it for granted."

The serendipity of their union is not lost on either Payton or Brees. Payton could have landed the Green Bay Packers job he wanted back in 2006. Or Nick Saban could have ignored the advice of the Dolphins medical staff and made a Brees an offer he couldn't refuse in free agency. They know things easily could have worked out differently and their careers could have veered down a completely different path.

"There's no way I could have fathomed it would be anything like it is now to be able to work with a guy like Coach Payton," Brees said. "I never thought that I would have had a chance to be a part of something like this."

No one knows what the future holds or how much longer the Payton-Brees partnership will last. It's already carried on longer than anyone expected, which might explain why Brees was prone to bouts of nostalgia during the 2019 season.

Brees was in a particularly reflective mood on the night of his record-setting performance against the Indianapolis Colts in Week 15. His epic 29-of-30 passing performance thrilled a sellout crowd at the Superdome and enthralled a national television audience on *Monday Night Football*.

Brees' record-breaking touchdown pass came with 7:13 left in the third quarter of an eventual 34–7 Saints win. With his Super Bowl XLIV teammates, close friends, and family in attendance, Brees tossed touchdown pass No. 540 of his career to tight end Josh Hill to eclipse Manning in the NFL record book.

As the crowd rose from their seats and delivered a rousing standing ovation, Brees took the game ball from Hill, removed his helmet, and trotted the length of the field with his right index finger raised in a No. 1 sign to acknowledge the fans. He then blew five kisses in the direction of his wife and four children, who were watching from a luxury suite on the second level of the stadium. Brees then jogged back to the sideline and found Payton, who extended his right arm for a congratulatory handshake. Instead, the quarterback wrapped his arms around his coach in an emotional bear hug.

"First of all, I'm a hugger," Brees said with a laugh afterward to a packed crowd of reporters at his post-game press conference at the Superdome. "I'm a hugger more than a handshaker. But I wouldn't be here without Sean."

Brees then paused, his eyes turned glassy, his voice choked with emotion.

"I appreciate it a lot," Brees said. "We've had a lot of time together. Just looking at the entire journey, 19 years, 5 years in San Diego and 14 years here, playing for the same head coach and in the same offense, all of the incredible teammates and coaches that I have had the chance to play with and for, the foundation, the culture of winning and being successful. I just consider myself very fortunate and very grateful to have had this opportunity to play for such a great coach and for such a great organization. It is very special. I'm not sure how we got here."

Acknowledgments

THIS BOOK WOULD NOT HAVE BEEN POSSIBLE IF NOT FOR THE help and support of so many friends, colleagues and associates.

First and foremost, I want to thank my editors at The Athletic, Jennifer Armstrong and Paul Fichtenbaum, along with founders Adam Hansmann and Alex Mather, for allowing me to pursue the project. Without their support, the book never would have been realized.

My literary agent Doug Grad was a loyal supporter and trusted advisor throughout the 18-month project. It was his idea to tell the Payton-Brees story, and his diligent efforts throughout the process made it happen.

Triumph editor Michelle Bruton was extraordinarily patient as I wallowed in the throes of editorial dissonance during the early stages of the project. Her enthusiastic guidance, astute editorial judgment, and keen attention to detail were invaluable and greatly appreciated.

Triumph publisher Noah Amstadter believed in the book, understood its potential, and provided support throughout the process.

Colleagues Brett Anderson, Greg Bishop, Les Carpenter, Sam Farmer, Bradley Handwerger, Larry Holder, Brett Martel, Katherine Terrell, and Pete Thamel suffered through my tormented, self-absorbed struggles and lent shrewd advice and counsel. Thanks for listening.

Greg Bensel, Doug Miller, Justin Macione, Evan Meyers, and Davis Friend in the Saints media relations office were instrumental in helping to arrange interviews and assisting in historical information, as were Jaguars media relations director Tad Dickman, Bears media relations director Adam Widman, and ESPN public relations Bill Hofheimer. Macione, the Pete Carmichael of the Saints media relations staff, was particularly helpful.

I want to thank Saints general manager Mickey Loomis for participating in the book project and informing its content. I also want to thank the following current and former players, coaches, and executives for their time and insight: Players: Terron Armstead, Teddy Bridgewater, Mark Brunell, Emmanuel Butler, Austin Carr, Marques Colston, Chase Daniel, Ted Ginn Jr., Jon Goodwin, Taysom Hill, Luke McCown, Billy Miller, Lance Moore, Tre'Quan Smith, Jon Stinchcomb, Zach Strief, and Michael Thomas. Coaches: Dennis Allen, Joe Brady, Dan Campbell, Pete Carmichael, John Fox, Curtis Johnson, Joe Lombardi, Doug Marrone, Mike Neu, Mike Nolan, Bill Parcells, Dan Roushar, and Joel Thomas. Executives and staff: John Baumgartner, Mike Ornstein, Blake Romig, and Jay Romig. Carmichael and Lombardi were particularly gracious with their time and patiently helped educate me on the intricacies of the Saints offense.

Finally, I want to thank Drew Brees and Sean Payton for trusting me to tell their story. This book could not have happened without their time, insight, and interest.